THRU

MY

EYES
BOOK II

MALINDA GUERRERO CASTORENO

*All rights reserved ©2014 by Malinda's Publishing
And the Author, Malinda Guerrero Castoreno*

No part of this book may be reproduced or transmitted in any form or by any means whether it be mechanical, electronic, including photo copying, recording or by any information and storage retrieval system without the written consent of the author or the publishing company.

This book is fiction, based on events that are true. This book is a vision of the author. Names have been changed for obvious reasons. Some purely coincidental events are just that, purely coincidental. No two people see things the same way, hence the title.

Cover created by: Sarina Castoreno

*For information:
Malindaspublishing@live.com
Or
Malinda's Publishing
2012 Market Ave.
Fort Worth, Tx. 76164
817-655-3038
Printed in the United States of America*

SPECIAL DEDICATION

TO MY MOM:

IF IT WEREN'T FOR YOU,
    THERE WOULD BE NO ME.

To My Family: For encouraging me to use my imagination.

To you, the reader: For being a part of this spectacular journey.

" Much Luv" to you all!

ACKNOWLEDGEMENTS
AS IN "THRU MY EYES" BOOK I

To my husband Louis Castoreno: You stood by my side through Book I, as you do with "Thru My Eyes Book II."

To my ten kids, Louis Jr., Paul, Monica, Eric, Tony, Stanley, Vanessa, Stefany, Sabrina, Sarina, thank you. This is my legacy I leave to you all.
And, thank you to your spouses.

To my sister Sheril Rodgers, where would I be without your encouragement.

To my brother Johnny Guerrero (Gilbert to me), your laughter and comments have kept me smiling daily.

To LLCOOLJ, for your very first word when you read Chapter 1. "Powerful." That single word from you lit the fire in me that started this journey. I would not be here today if it weren't for you. Thank you Mr. Smith, you made this all possible.

To the ones that have cheered me on, and believed I could do this. "Rah, rah, rah!"

To the readers, thank you for taking the time out of your busy lives to read a story I wrote from my heart.

I wrote this story with love; I hope you each accept it with love.

I love you all,
Malinda

OTHER BOOKS BY
MALINDA GUERRERO CASTORENO

1. THRU MY EYES BOOK I

COMING 2015

1. THRU MY EYES BOOK III

INTRODUCTION:

Follow the Guetarro children as they attempt to cope with their mom's death, being separated from one another, and always, the fear of their father, Johnny Guetarro, just about the most ruthless gangster to rule the streets of Fort Worth, Texas.

There would be only one way to get the Guetarro children away from their father, whom had beat 11 year old Becky severely. Malina's aunts would step in, but not to report him for abuse, rather turn a blind eye to their brothers abuse and insist the children needed to move in with them and go home everyday after school to a warm home, and home cooked meals. But would it be enough to keep the children safe? Not likely....

"Thru My Eyes"
Book II
Prologue

"Thru My Eyes" Book I is the chilling story about life, love, hate, abuse, fear; just about every emotion 12 year old Malina could possibly feel, could possibly describe.
   It is the story of the pain six children had to endure after the unexpected death of their beautiful mother Shirley. It is a story of an abusive gangster father that cared for no one, other than the gangster life he loved. It is a story of Sher, 14 year old teenager now forced to be mother and father to her five brothers and sister.

Follow the Guetarro children as they attempt to cope with their mom's death, being separated from one another, and always, the fear of their father Johnny Guetarro, just about the most ruthless gangster to rule the streets of Fort Worth, Texas.

There would be only one way to get the Guetarro children away from their father, whom had beat 11 year old Becky severely. Malina's aunts would step in, but not to report him for abuse, rather turn a blind eye to their brothers abuse and insist the children needed to move in with them and go home everyday after school to a warm home, and home cooked meals.

Now, please join "Thru My Eyes" Book II as Malina's aunts have come to take the children away from the only home they ever knew, their mom's home.

Three aunts, their dad's sisters, would take two children each to live with them, because it would be impossible for one aunt to take all six kids.

As Book II begins, four of the children have already left the house, leaving only Sher and Malina behind to say good-bye to an old run down house and a lifetime of memories.

When you read this story, ask yourself.. Could you have survived?...

"Thru My Eyes"
Book II

1

Life was going to be different now. For better? Of course. It goes without saying. It definitely could never get worse.

Mom would never have wanted her kids split up, such a responsibility for anyone, raising another woman's children.

We weren't just any ones kids though, we were Johnny Guetarro's kids.

You really gotta love my aunts and uncles for stepping up. They were about to inherit a few more mouths to feed, yet they didn't seem to mind at all.

Our lives were definitely gonna change, we would now be allowed to be kids, not have to worry so much, perhaps breathe again.

For me, life would never ever be the same, though poor, I was rich with the love of a wonderful mother. What I would give to have my mommy, but I knew all the pleading in the world would not have my prayers answered.

Dad wasn't there when we left. He believed his sisters story about his kids going home to an empty house. It was probably the only excuse he would've ever believed.

Him not being there when we left was easier for him, us also.

He had stayed away for the past four months, coming home only when it suited him. There was no reason for him to be there now.

Fear of him and his capabilities had kept his family loyal to him. Isn't that the concept of a man like that?

Once Sher put all our stuff in the car, she came in one last time to look around. She looked sad, but didn't cry.

Her responsibilities for five kids was now lifted, she could be a normal teenager, if that were possible. Sher walked out of the house and got in the car just as Matty did.

I was left alone, in the house. No one there just me.

First I walked through the kitchen, there I actually saw my mom cooking, and making her famous Kool-aid saying, "Come on kids, time to eat."

Then I walked past the restroom, where I saw dad beating Becky, my eyes filled with tears.

I walked to our room, there it seemed in my mind were all us kids, confined to that one room most of our lives.

Walking from our room towards mom's room, I saw my mom lying on the floor-begging dad to stop beating her, just as I had seen the night he beat her. I saw dad on top of her, hitting her with the butt of his pistol over and over

Now, from where I was standing, I could have almost pushed him off of her.

Just my imagination.

I was in mom's room now. I looked around one last time. In my mind, I saw her laying on her bed, sleeping peacefully, as she had the morning I found her. She was asleep; there was no more pain for her, no ass whoopins, no cussing, and no crying.

I wanted to wake her, to hug her, to tell her one last time how much I loved her.

I walked past her bed to the living room, and there I could see her dancing and laughing with all of us, as she did so many times before. That beautiful smile, her happy laugh, all the kids laughing with her, her ponytail bouncing around as she danced. I could even hear the music she was dancing to.

She was so happy. So full of life, so full of love.

I got to the front door, turned around, and said,

"Goodbye mommy. I miss you so much; I just don't know how to go on without you. I'm sorry I didn't help you get away. I will never forget you and I will never ever stop loving you."

I was one hundred percent crying now, almost hysterical again. "Mommmmmmy" I screamed.

I did not know what to do. I turned and walked out of that old house, shutting the door behind me.

All the bad memories, I thought, would stay behind me when I closed the door. I took my mom's love with me in my heart. All the sorrow and pain was left behind.

I could hardly see where I was going with so many tears flowing from my eyes. A pain in my heart I couldn't describe even if I tried.

I walked to Matty's car, opened the door, and got in the backseat. I looked toward the house.

From the corner of my eye, I saw the little city. I looked, and there we all were, sitting on the ground- helping mom create a city for my little brothers, mom laughing, having fun and loving every second of her kids. So much laughter, so much fun, so much love with her as she created that wonderful "Little City," and my beautiful loving mom spending every second she possibly could making her children happy.

I was crying even more now, the thought of never seeing my mom that I loved so much. I was hurting so badly, wanting to scream at the top of my lungs.

I want my mom so bad I can't stand it; I just can't stand this empty feeling.

I shut the car door, and just before we drove off, I looked toward the house and there stood my mom, in the doorway, as she had almost everyday of my life.

Standing there in the doorway, that beautiful pose of hers, as she did everyday watching her kids play outside, smiling that beautiful, beautiful smile.

Now, she was watching all of us leave, saying goodbye to all of us, and saying goodbye to her pain.

Her beautiful green eyes looked directly into mine.

Her kids were safe now. She could rest.

I looked down to wipe my tears away, when I looked up again, she was gone.

2

I froze. I could not move.

I looked toward the front door.

"Mama Mama"... I tried to call out her name, but the words wouldn't come out of my mouth.

I extended my arms as I tried to reach for her, to hug her, to touch her, but she was gone..

Without thinking, without knowing what else to do, I opened the car door, jumped out, and ran.

I ran as fast as I possibly could.

Instantly Sher got out of the car and ran after me, calling my name.

"Malina... Malina."

For once in my fucked up little life I out ran my sister Sher. From behind me, I could hear her yelling my name, I could hear my aunt Matty calling my name also, but I ran anyway. I didn't look back, I didn't stop, I just ran.

I was running toward the vision I had seen of my mom.

I stumbled and fell on those fucked up raggedy stairs, but picked myself up and ran to the door.

"Mama, mama, mama!" I was yelling.

No, it was more like I was screaming at the top of my lungs for my mama.

As I got to the door, I banged my fist on the glass with all my might, shattering it, glass falling everywhere. Pieces of broken glass in my hand? I had no idea. I didn't care.

"Mama! Mama," all I could yell.

Sher now caught up with me, so did Matty.

Sher grabbed me, I swung to hit her. Matty also grabbed me, I pushed away from both of them. I wanted everyone to leave me alone. I wanted my mom.

"Malina..." Matty tried to say.

"Nooooo!" I screamed trying desperately to get past both Matty and Sher to go back into my mom's house.

I looked around as if I were lost.

Where was my mom?

Where did she go?

"Mama please!" I screamed again.

"Malina mom isn't here." Sher said.

"Shut up Sher, don't say that, yes she is Sher, I just saw her. She was here, she was just now standing at the door. She wanted me to come back to get her."

My words were now scrambled, even I couldn't understand what I was trying to say...nor could I catch my breath as I spoke.

Matty looked at Sher, Sher at Matty.

"Malina, your mama is"... Matty attempted an explanation, but I gave her no time to say what she wanted.

"Noooooooo." I screamed. "I want my mom, I want my mom." I covered my ears to drown out anything Sher or Matty attempted to say to me.

They had no idea what to do, because I was hysterical.

If only I hadn't looked down when I saw her, if only I hadn't looked away, maybe my mom would still be there.....

I was at the front door crying, banging on it, yelling for my mama, but she did not come.

Sher was there, Matty was there, but my mama was not.

My knees buckled under me, I fell to the porch, buried my face in my hands and I cried and screamed my mom's name.

Sher and Matty stood there, not really knowing what do. I didn't look up at them, but I knew they were there, because for a brief second I saw their shoes.

I wanted them both to leave, just leave me there, leave me alone. I wanted to stay there at our house, live there with my mom, if I had to, I'd live there with her spirit.

Matty knelt down beside me.

"Please Malina, you can't stay here, we have to leave." She sounded so terrified.

"Matty, mom was here, she was at the door, I saw her, I saw her." Cries from a frightened child, wanting desperately for someone to believe what she was saying. .

"I don't want to leave her. I can't leave my mom here alone. I want to be with her." My face still buried in my hands.

"But you can't stay honey, I can't leave you here with your dad after what he did to Becky."

"No, I can't leave my mommy Matty, I just can't."

"I know you miss her Malina we all do, but she's gone."

"No," I screamed. "I don't want to hear that."

Again, I covered my ears so I didn't have to hear the words Matty was saying. .

"Why did she leave? Why did mom have to leave us?" I was asking Matty questions I knew very well she had no answers for.

Now Sher knelt down beside me and said, "Malina we have to go, you don't want to be here when dad gets here do you? Don't you remember..." She couldn't even finish her sentence. So much pain in her voice from the memory of what dad had done.

I instantly recalled only yesterday, watching my dad beat the shit out of Becky with his belt, using the belt buckle to smash into her face, her body, her head over and over. Becky, curled in a fetal position in the bathtub, no way to protect herself from his forceful blows.

Sher's words echoed through my brain. At that second I had a vision of my low life father driving up, and beating my ass because I didn't want to leave. I had a vision of him beating me as he had Becky. My body shook with fear, my body shook with hate for the man that was my father.

Matty kinda tugged at me to help me up off the porch.

Sher rarely cried, she was crying now.

I was sick with pain.

We were standing right in front of the door. I could see the curtains blowing in the wind from the window I had just busted. I wanted to fight Matty and Sher to get back inside my mom's house, but I knew they could over power me.

I just wanted to see my mommy, or her image, just one last time..

God this hurts so bad.

Why did he take my mom from us?

Why didn't he take my dad?

Why didn't God take all of us so we could be together with our mom?

God?

At that very moment I didn't believe there was a God. He had taken our mom, leaving us all alone.

Why would God do that?

Now I was having to deal with all the emotions again.

I was still crying as Matty and Sher walked me back to the car. Sher locked my car door and got in the front with Matty.

Matty started the ignition. Again I looked toward the little city, this time my mom would not be there.

I looked toward the front door, she was no longer there either.

Matty hesitated to drive off, perhaps fearful I may jump out of the car and concerned she may run over me. The stop sign would be my last opportunity to jump out, instead I turned around and stared at our house.

"One last time mama, one last time." In my tired mind, I begged for her to reappear knowing I'd probably have to bust out Matty's back window with my fist to get out of her car.

I looked back, I cried, I wiped my tears, but my beautiful mommy did not appear.

3

I had only one opportunity to see my beautiful mother, and it slipped away because I looked down. That is something I would regret everyday for the rest of my life.

I was defeated.

I cried, then actually gripped the car door handle in anticipation of jumping out of Matty's car, hoping, if I did, she would run over me and I'd die, or be hurt so bad I'd remain hospitalized forever. Anything, so I would not have to go on without my mom.

I believe Matty and Sher were talking I could see their lips moving but I heard nothing they said. All I could do was think of my mom.

Then like a bomb exploding in my head, the memories came back to me. Slow at first then the memories sped up, almost in fast motion. A brain full of memories, good, bad, happy, sad.

Now, as if it were happening all over again:

Dad pistol whipping mom, my mom crying and throwing up blood. Mom hugging me. Bee talking to mom, dad threatening mom if she left him, mom's smile as she tried to eat. J.J. and the comb, the mansion, dad's garage, the jump rope skit. Ray, Helena, mom dancing in the living room with us kids. Sher wanting to go to school, my five brothers and sisters, dad's smile, mom and the little city. Finding mom dead, dad's face when he turned her over, me pounding on the coffin, all the kids crying, all of us being left alone, me wanting my mom more than I ever wanted anything in my life. Becky being whipped, mom standing at the front door telling me good bye.

A second of bad memories, then a second of good memories, as my brain was doing flip flops in my head. I was just so overwhelmed with emotion. It was all too much. My heart hurt so much.

No one told me how badly losing my mother would hurt. No one told me the pain would be there forever. No one told me I would wake in the morning with an emptiness in my heart, in the pit of my stomach, and go to bed at night with the same pain.
Why didn't anyone explain any of this to me?
WHY?
I was beside myself with grief.
It cut my gut like a sharpened knife.
Everything was bottled so tightly inside me, my heart, my mind, my body, about to explode.

As Matty drove, I tried to unscramble my brain. There was just so much in my head. So many wonderful memories, so many horrible memories. So much love, yet so much damn pain.
My heart was saying, "Go back, go back to your mom." My mind was saying, "No Malina stay in the car."

Less than a second away from opening the car door and jumping to what I prayed would be my death, the car stopped.

At that very second it would not matter what I would attempt to do to kill myself, because Matty pulled into her driveway. Though my body was physically in Matty's car, my mind, my heart was back at our house with my mom.

All those years I spent wanting to get out of that damn beat down piece of shit house, now I didn't want to be anywhere but there.

I didn't want to live with Matty, Mary or any other relative for that matter.

I wanted so badly to go back, back in time. Back to a life before I knew what pain was, before I was a witness to all the abuse and horror.

But How? How could I go back? It would be impossible.

There is no re-living your life... turn back the hands of time and relive the moments.

No, it's impossible, it just doesn't happen for anyone, no matter how badly you want it.

You can only go forward...

Pick up the pieces and start all over again.

But I didn't want to go forward, I didn't want a new life. I wanted the only life I new. I wanted my old horrible life back. I only wanted my mom.

4

We reached our destination, the place Sher and I would call home. Now, I couldn't even bring myself to open the damn car door.

Matty, Sher and even Lori, whom I had not realized was sitting in the back seat with me, opened their car doors and began to unload our things.

I sat frozen, like a marble statue, my hand still on the door handle, now lost of color because I was gripping the handle so tightly.

At one point Matty tried to coerce me out of the car, a complete look of fear on her face.

"Come on Lori, you can help the girls with their things." I could hear Matty instructing Lori.

"Ok, but this is heavy." Lori said as she attempted to pick up Sher's heaviest bag from the trunk of Matty's car.

"I got that one." Sher said as she handed Lori a much smaller bag. I saw what each of them were doing, but I had no desire to get out of the car.

Sitting in the back seat staring at my hands, remembering my mom holding my hand the day after dad beat her. Remembering her tear falling into our hands as she comforted me.

It was all still so fresh in my mind.

I was afraid to get out of the car, I was afraid to be alone in the car. My mind a million miles away, my heart so badly broken.

There would be no way for me to just sit there all day; it was already after six, that I knew because I was wearing the watch my mom had given me for Christmas, the last Christmas we would spend with her. It seemed so long ago, it seemed like only yesterday.

Sher walked past the car, she didn't say anything, just opened the door and continued doing what ever she was doing. There I sat, car door open, and crying, I could do nothing else..

I watched the three of them moving about. Lori walked by, smiling that innocent child smile. So much excitement for her, such innocence.

After what seemed an eternity, reluctantly, slowly, I got out of the car.

I stood there a few moments, looking around, observing what was to be mine and Sher's new home.

Thick green grass in the front yard, not a bunch of rocks, dirt and mud. There was plenty of shade in the front yard, just like our house.

There were no holes in the outside walls. There were no rotted stairs to walk zigzag up; there were no falling shingles from the roof. It was clean, it was tidy, it was nice, however; it was not home.

My eyes looked as Sher and Matty; even little Lori, scurrying around as if we had hundreds of suitcases. I looked, I watched them, but I saw nothing, only the image of mom, looking into my eyes.

Again I cried, again my entire being ached for my mom.

Finally, I'm not sure if it was Sher being Sher, or Sher trying to be kind, but she handed me a bag and said "Come on."

She was either tired of me standing there, or she knew she needed to think of a very clever way to get me into Matty's duplex, or be a bully and throw me over her shoulder cave man style...

Like a robot, I took the bag from Sher, and followed her into the duplex not paying attention to anything at all. I was doing all the motions of being alive, walking, moving, breathing, and it was a fact I was alive, because I could feel the millions of pieces my heart was in.

Sher and I did not speak to one another as we unloaded our things and carried them into Matty and our new home. Matty explained things to us as we went from room to room. I walked, I listened as Matty told us where things were... But I said nothing.

Because of all the issues with Becky, dad, and our need to be rescued from the abuse, aunt Matty hadn't moved in with her boyfriend to the one bedroom apartment she had talked about only yesterday.

Instead she moved into a two-bedroom duplex that was directly across the street from Aunt Mary.

Not quite sure what had happened with her plans of moving in with her boyfriend. Matty didn't say anything to me or Sher, only that he wouldn't be moving in with us, or at least that's what I thought she said.

Possibly our need for a home put her own plans with her boyfriend on the back burner. I really didn't care, and I sure didn't have it in me to ask a bunch of nonsense question that I actually cared nothing about.

5

Walking into Matty's home was different....mostly to me, it all seemed so clouded.

"Come on in girls." Matty said as Lori interrupted her. "Mommy, can I go to Aunt Mary's, huh can I?"

Matty's concern at that second was not Lori wanting to go to Mary's, she was concerned about making me and Sher feel welcome.

"Mommy, mommy, I want to go play with the kids."

Poor Lori, she was just so excited.

"Lori stop." Matty was firm with her.

"I will take you in a little while."

Matty looked proud as she said. "Ok girls, this is it."

Matty did do a walk through with me and Sher upon entering her home, she did show us where everything was and I did see the rooms and their contents. Yet, I paid no attention to the visual aspect of Matty's home or Matty's audio of her home, at least not right away. I couldn't focus.

Seems I had no attention span at all. Everything that was told or shown to me pretty much went right past me. All I remember of that first walk through, was a living room, a dining area, a kitchen, a restroom, but I don't really remember what they looked like or their contents. Before I knew it, Matty was showing us our bedroom.

"You girls decide who gets which bed." Matty said as she turned on the lamp that was on a night stand, dab smack in between the two twin sized beds.

I would now have a bed for myself, something I had my hopes on having only when dad had taken us to the mansion and insisted I would have my very own room. That day seemed so damn long ago, yet the memories of that night were perfectly installed in my mind.

I thought of my mom again, remembering her beautiful face smiling when we had gone with our dad to tour the mansion, the mansion we never knew who the hell it belonged to, or how the hell dad had a key to the front door.

Though I couldn't see a lot that night, after all, we were attempting to tour such a magnificent home with a mere flashlight, but I sure do remember my mom's smile.

Periodically dad would shine the light toward mom face and she would be smiling, loving the thought that one day, someday, she might actually get to live in such a grand home.

Hope in her eyes, that she could possibly move away from our beat down garbage heap of a home and move into a spectacular mansion.

My poor poor mom, high hopes for a better life for her kids, a better life for herself. I wondered did she ever believe it was possible, or had she known from the very beginning there was no way out, and instead lived in a fantasy world.

Shattered dreams it seemed.

Matty smiled as Sher flopped her stuff down on the bed nearest the window.

I would be getting my own twin sized bed, though I was so accustomed to getting smacked in the face a couple of times a night by my sisters; this would be a different experience for me all together, not getting smacked at all.

"Here's the closet." Matty said as she opened the closet and pulled a string hanging from the closet ceiling to turn on the light. It was a large walk in closet, with space enough for all of our things and then some.

This all seemed to me like the "rich house" game we created in our old house.

Aunt Matty's room was right next to ours, a large room with lots of windows, one that she and Lori would be sharing.

"I get the top two drawers, you get the bottom two." Sher said, as she began to put her things in a large chest of drawers. The first words either of us actually spoke to one another since leaving our house.

Once we put our things away there really wasn't much to do. Our beds had already been made, our room tidy. New or almost new bed coverings on the beds made the room appear very nice and clean. Everything was just so different. Not in a bad way, just so different from the horrible conditions we were accustomed to living.

A vision of our house, remembering the raggedy linoleum floors, the leaky restroom sink, the shabby kitchen cabinets.

As Matty talked, my mind remained focusing on our old house, how we had lived, conditions unsuitable for children, it seemed, yet we had lived there, we had survived there.

"Unbelievable!" I would think, over and over.

6

Lori could be heard in the living room, talking to herself, I suppose. I wondered if she were mad because Matty hadn't taken her to Mary's to play with the kids.

Sher scurried around putting her things on her side of the room just as she wanted them. Everything in it's proper place, so typical of Sher.

I could see directly into Matty's room as I sat on my bed. A large bed for her and Lori with a beautiful dark brown head board. A light brown bed cover and lots of throw pillows made the bed look comfortable.

A single mom with one child, Matty seemed to do very well for herself. Her gangster brother with free rent from his mother unable to afford food to feed his kids.

What a shame, what a fuckin shame.

I stopped crying because my head hurt so badly. One thing was a fact, each time I cried, the headaches got worse, yet it was impossible to hold back the tears..

I had done all I could do in our new room.

My personal things were all put away, which was a task that took very little time because; after all, I had very few things to put away.

Once finished, I went to the kitchen where Matty had begun supper...but I didn't say anything.

"Are you ok?" Matty asked.

I didn't answer, I suppose she already knew the answer to that, instead, she handed me plates and forks to set the table.

There was nothing to talk about as I set the table, I really didn't care to talk even though Matty attempted to initiate a conversation.

After setting the table, I looked around, feeling so terribly lost in a new place without my mom.

Matty's duplex could never compare to living with mom. Matty was very kind, and I gave her credit, she was doing everything she could, and from what I could see, Matty's place had one big advantage over our house, it was clean.

Not quite sure how Matty had pulled this all together in less than twenty-four hours, but however she did it, seemed to me she did a damn good job.

I stood in the doorway dividing the kitchen from the dining area. There were no pictures on the walls, no knick-knacks any where in any of the rooms. Actually, Matty's home looked like a place that had been thrown together in a moments notice.

In all reality, that's exactly what it was.

Matty apparently thought of everything. I wondered when she had time to get beds, and put all the furniture in place, because she had pretty much been with us for the past twenty-four hours.

I really didn't care, I knew she managed to do it just in time to get us out of our house before something worse than an ass whoopin occurred.

Table set, food ready, I helped Matty serve the plates, yet I still hadn't said two words to anyone.

"What would you girls like to drink?" Matty asked.

A choice? We actually had a choice? All we had been drinking was water or Ovaltine, watered down Ovaltine at that. Didn't even know there was anything different we could drink.

I mean, I do remember mom's wonderful Kool-Aid she made daily, but we hadn't had the money for sugar, so we just hadn't had any in months.

"Do you have any Kool-Aid or tea?" Sher asked.

"Yes tea." Matty said, as she took a pitcher of tea from the refrigerator.

"How bout you, Malina." Matty asked.

"Tea." I said.

Matty smiled at me.

"Can I have tea too?" Lori asked.

"No, you drink your milk." Matty said.

I felt guilty as we sat down to eat, guilty wondering if Danny and J.J., and Becky and Carrie were having as good a meal as me and Sher were.

Matty had prepared fried chicken, potatoes, and corn, realizing when I began to eat, just what a good cook Matty was.

Of course it was not my mom's wonderful cooking, but after months and months of eating bologna, it was in fact, very good.

Unable to eat much, with hardly an appetite at all, I just picked at my food. Of course I wanted to eat, but I couldn't.

"Not hungry?" Matty asked.

I wanted to cry, but I held it in.

"I am." I answered.

As I sat picking at my food, I glanced around the room. A living room/dining room combination with furnishings that were quite nice. Not new, just not wore down and trashy as we had at home. A china cabinet in the corner of the dining room, with old plates neatly placed on the shelves. "Yes someone threw this place together." I thought.

My brothers and sisters flashed in my mind, remembering all the fricken disgusting bologna sandwiches we had been forced to eat was quite nauseating. Recalling all the times my stomach hurt from being so damn hungry and eating any tiny amount of bologna that may have been left on the bologna rind. A starving sensation always in the pit of my stomach, a feeling of always being so damn hungry, the temptation to eat the entire bologna rind just to get one more bite of food...

Knowing that, and though mom never had a lot of food to prepare for us, she made what little we had, taste as if it were a gourmet meal.

Forced to eat bologna day in and day out when you crave so much more, knowing it isn't going to come. Let's just say, for six hungry kids it was nauseating to eat the same thing almost every day for four months.

Then I thought of the pictures of starving kids in foreign countries I had seen when Sher would take us all to the library. Thinking, those children had no food, no one to feed them, no one cared.. Supposing we kids in some fucked up way had life a little better than those kids did. It just didn't seem possible.

I had to put it out of my mind, it made me sick thinking of those poor kids, it was just as sickening for me to think of how we lived since mom died.

Then my thoughts went to Sher.

I glanced over at her.

Sher had been very quiet except for her comment to me about the dresser; she really hadn't talked to anyone.

Either had I, but my reason was I just couldn't stop crying. Sher usually the loud mouth, remained very quiet.

Actually, she really hadn't been the good ol Sher since the ordeal with Becky and dad. I wondered if Sher was feeling guilty for not trying to help Becky more than she had. I really don't see what more she could have done to help her. I mean, she couldn't very well have knocked the shit out of my dad for beating Becky so severely with his belt, now could she?

    No one expected it of Sher.

    No one blamed Sher at all.

    Everyone knew Sher had been over worked and beaten down for four months.

    No one expected her to stand up to a monster.

    No one expected it at all.

    No one, except Sher.

7

I really was hungry, and I knew I could probably eat a second helping, but I just couldn't at that moment.

So much had happened, so many changes now.

We weren't discussing any of it at the moment, we weren't talking about Becky or what dad had done or the way we lived..

Actually, we weren't talking at all.

It was so different.

At home, though we would be eating dinner, mom always initiated conversations with us at the table. Doing her best to smile and show us just how much she loved us all.

Perhaps Matty, thinking of her brother as being a monster was not something she wanted to discuss at the dinner table, especially in front of Lori.

Conversation with Matty and Lori was pretty much limited to Matty instructing Lori not to talk with her mouth full, or to drink all her milk.

I picked at my food with my fork, enjoying what I could, but not really having an appetite.

Sher got up for second's, which put a smile on Matty's face, yet she looked concerned when she glanced over at me but said nothing.

I thought of Becky and wondered if she were okay. She had gotten an ass whoopin and beat terribly. I could not imagine the pain her body must be feeling now, something similar to mom's I'm sure..

How does a child cope with such a thing? She had to look a horrible mess, with all the bruises and belt whelps all over her face and body. What I had seen only made me hate dad more.

After we ate dinner, Matty took Lori to Mary's because Lori could not sit still knowing there were two more cousins for her to play with. She had gobbled her food as fast as she could, wanting so badly to run across the street and play with all the kids.

Me and Sher did the dishes, and put the dry ones away. I put my left over food on a plate in the refrigerator, knowing it was not good to throw away perfectly good food. Perhaps I would be hungry later and I could eat it then.

After a few minutes Matty came back from Mary's, not expecting to see that we had already done the dishes and cleaned the kitchen.

She thanked us both, which seemed a bit strange, to thank us for cleaning our own mess. But then again Matty was like that. She was very kind.

Sher told Aunt Matty she was going to Mary's to go see J.J. and Danny.

"Wanna come Malina?"

I shook my head no, a somewhat distant look Sher threw my way as she exited the house.

I was in our room, re-adjusting my things, when Aunt Matty came in our room and sat on Sher's bed to talk to me.

"Are you ok?" She politely asked.

I couldn't help but think if this had been Sher asking such a question, we would have jumped right into our Laurel and Hardy routine of talking shit to one another.

However, this wasn't Sher, this was my aunt, and it damn sure wasn't Liz, so I showed her the respect she deserved.

"I don't know." I answered.

"Malina, anytime you need to talk, I'm here. You can tell me anything."

Nothing was said for a few moments. I was afraid. I think I was afraid to trust anyone, even Matty. She was, after all, my dad's sister, and any thing we talked about, she may feel obligated to tell my dad.

My mind went back to the day dad and Aunt Gloria had taken me to the hospital, remembering if I showed too much emotion, dad might just have me locked away.

Considering Matty already knew just about all the bad things she needed to know, we had after all, just told her all the horrid details of Becky getting her ass whooped. I didn't suppose Matty would be too surprised of anything she may learn now about our living conditions at home.

Knowing my freedom from a psych ward could quite possibly be on the line if I showed too much emotion or talked too much, I was very hesitant, but I needed to try my best to trust her.

I took a chance.

"Aunt Matty, I really did see my mom." I began. Just saying the word "Mom" had me teary eyed, then I began to cry.

I reminded her of the vision of mom I had seen as we were leaving the house.

She listened, getting teary eyed herself, yet letting me talk, not interrupting, or judging me.

I cried as I talked, she listened. She cried also.

Then she said, "Your mom, I believe, really was there Malina. I'm sure she felt you kids pain, from what your dad did to Becky, leaving you kids alone, but not just that, everything, everything you all have been through."

"She loved you kids so much. I believe she was there to make sure you kids were safe, and when she saw that y'all were, she wanted to say goodbye." Matty said, as she cried.

I do believe Matty believed every word she was saying to me.

It made sense, I thought.

"I just miss her so much." I was hysterical again.

"I know Malina, so do I. And I promise you never have to hide your feelings around me. If I'm able to do anything for you girls, I will. Never be afraid to ask if you need or want anything."

I was crying a lot now, Matty was also.

I told her of the day I had gone to the hospital and my fears of dad locking me away. She assured me that would never happen. She was kind and she was trying in her own way to comfort me.

We talked for maybe an hour about mom, the kids, our old house, our new house. It was in fact, also a new home for Matty and Lori.

My head was killing me from crying. It just seemed I could never stop. We would stop talking for a few moments, then I'd start crying. A few times I thought Matty changed the subject just to get my mind off everything, but I always took the subject right back to my mom.

She asked, actually asked if there was anything I wanted to do on Saturday, go anywhere do anything. But really, there was nothing I really wanted to do.

"We'll think of something." She assured me.

Matty brought me some hangers for my clothes and showed me where the towels and wash cloths were, and said anything I wanted in the refrigerator I never had to ask, just get it.

Seems there would be no shortage of food at Matty's, which, after a lifetime of eating bits and pieces here and there, I felt like I had no right to be able to eat what I wanted, when I wanted.

I was feeling so guilty about it, and I hadn't even opened the refrigerator yet.

Matty made me feel comfortable, she made me feel like I belonged, like I mattered.

She wasn't my mom, she had no real obligation to take care of me, but she was. .

8

It was dark out now and getting a bit late. Aunt Matty called Aunt Mary to ask her to send Sher and Lori home.

"Sher isn't here." Mary said.

"What? Are you sure, she left over an hour ago?"

"Yes I'm sure. Well, maybe she went to the back yard with the boys, instead of coming in the house first. I'll go check." Mary said.

"That's ok; I'm on my way to get Lori."

I decided to walk across the street with Matty to say goodnight to J.J. and Danny, and much to our surprise when we walked out the front door...Sher was sitting on the porch, all alone.

I could tell she had been crying. Perhaps all the stress of the past few months had finally caught up with her.

"Have you been here this entire time?" Matty asked.

"Yes." Sher answered.

"Decided not to go to Mary's?" Matty asked Sher.

"I don't know." Sher said. "Once I came outside, it was so shady and comfortable I just felt like sitting here." Sher explained.

Sher looked tired as she spoke, I also noticed, though she was sitting in the shade and talking about being comfortable, she looked flushed, hot, almost sweaty, kind of scared. I remember because I had seen that flustered look before when she would run around the track on field day in elementary school.

Being that she was so fast, she would out run everyone, especially the boys, but the look on her face as she crossed the finish line would be similar to what she looked like at that very moment. Perhaps I was just noticing because I really hadn't paid too much attention to her appearance lately.

Honestly, I just had other things on my mind.

Sher didn't look at Matty or me as she spoke; more or less she stared out into space.

"Ok girls, I'm going for Lori, wanna go?" Matty asked us both.

"I'll go with y'all." Sher said.

J.J. and Danny showed us the room they were sharing with Jake and Mark, Mary's two sons...

Danny was so excited, not even realizing what he had lost. Sher hugged him. Actually, we hugged both J.J. and Danny; they just seemed so different, a bit of happiness in them perhaps. Maybe it really wasn't happiness, perhaps these two little boys finally felt a bit of comfort.

Sher and I stayed in the room with the boys as they showed us where their clothes were, where their bed was, and where they kept their toys. Several times I looked toward Sher as my brothers were talking to her, and though she answered their questions, and smiled at them, she seemed scared. She seemed nervous. Perhaps she was just having one of those bad moments I had everyday all day.

I walked past Mary's dining room and went to the living room. Matty and Mary, sat in Mary's dining room and drank a cup of coffee together; a sight that made me cry remembering the countless pots of coffee mom would drink and share with everyone that visited.

My two aunts sat talking, sometimes a bit of a whisper in their voices. Grown up talk I guess.

Sher stayed in the room with the boys, talking and playing around with all the kids. I could here them all laughing, I could even hear Sher laughing once or twice. When I heard Danny say Sher's name three then four times in a row, I visioned she was again staring off into space. I wondered if she were ok?

I sat in Mary's living room, alone. I looked around thinking how nice of a home she had. Actually, when I thought of Gloria's beautiful two-story home, and even my Uncle Bill's home, it seemed everyone lived very well. Yes, all my uncles worked and provided very well for their families.

I wondered why my dad never had anything. I'm sure my uncles all had mortgages to pay on their homes, my dad did not. He lived free, never paying a penny to my grandma for rent. So why did we live so badly? Why did my mom have to suffer and stretch a penny just to feed her kids?

Questions I would never in my lifetime get answers to.

As my aunts talked, as the kids played in the back bedroom, I sat in the living room and stared.

Then I did what I had to. I cried.

My aunt's both seemed exhausted. They too had been through a lot since yesterday.. No, they hadn't had their asses whooped, but they had been on an emotional rollercoaster ride, dodging dad's suspicious questions. Making up lie after lie to tell him, just to get us out of his house. Then, Mary and Gloria both had to convince their husbands to take on two more mouths to feed, because, it was after all, the right thing to do, wasn't it?

And not to mention, what ever lie or truth Matty had to tell her boyfriend why she couldn't move in with him.

In a way I was glad Matty decided against moving her boyfriend in. Not quite sure how I felt about having a man in the house, since we never had one any way. I'm glad we were all girls living at Matty's.

I had my fill with my dad's ways, and not really knowing this man, I was in no hurry to be living under the roof with a man Sher and I barely knew.

Sitting in Mary's living room, staring at the walls as life went on around me. Matty and Mary continued their coffee drinking and conversations. Sher and all the kids continued carrying on in the kids room, me I lost track of time, besides there was no school the next day. I felt so terribly sad, so terribly lonely though there were nine other people in Mary's house with me at that very moment.

Matty was in the kitchen washing the dishes as Mary straightened up the dining room. Their movements seemed almost routine, yet they had it cleaned up in a matter of moments. We were about to leave when Aunt Mary's phone rang.

I heard Mary say "hello," then within a second or two Mary screamed.

"What? What, is he ok?" She was crying by this time.

She handed the phone to Matty, a completely terrified look on both women's faces.

Matty began crying.

"Ok, ok, I'll take them." Matty hollered into the phone, and then hung up.

All the kids came running into the living room when they heard Mary scream, curious as to what was wrong. Mary was very careful not to say anything in front of J.J. and Danny.

Panicked, Matty and Mary walked outside to the front porch to talk for just a few seconds, leaving me, Sher, and six kids pretty much just standing there..

When they returned, Matty told Mary she was going to leave Lori with her so she could take us.

Take us where? I wondered. And why is she crying?

"Come on girls." Matty said to me and Sher.

We started walking toward the duplex.

Matty was panicked, scared and crying.

"What's wrong?" Sher's voice seemed shaky as she asked.

As we crossed the street, Matty, still crying said.

"Your dad's been shot."

9

I felt my knees go weak, even my heart stopped for a few long seconds.

Sher, who had been walking a step or two behind me and Matty, was now almost running to get into Matty's car. I could hear Sher crying as she shut the passenger car door.

Matty ran inside the house to get her purse and keys. I followed Sher to the car. I assume Matty was taking us wherever dad was.

Matty came out of the house then went back in, then came out, locked the door, then got in the car. It was obvious Matty was scared for her brother because she seemed not to know whether she was coming or going.

As Matty started the ignition, Sher asked, "What happened?"

"I'm not sure Sher. Ray called and said your dad had been shot and they were at the hospital." Matty began.

After what seemed like a very long pause of complete silence, Sher asked the question Matty, even I did not want to hear the answer to..

"Is he dead?" Sher bluntly asked, so much emphasis on the word "dead." A lot of shakiness in her voice, I'm sure not wanting to hear the word "yes."

Hearing Sher say dead the way she did, scared even me. At that very second a horrible visual of my dad being riddled with bullets flashed in my mind, a rush of guilt went through my body, I'm sure my face was read as fire. I was, after all, the one that cussed him, in my mind, damn near every time I saw him or heard his voice.

"I don't know." Matty was crying. I was crying.

Sher stopped crying long enough to ask more questions.

"How bad is he?" Sher asked.

"Ray just said to get y'all to the hospital, because your dad had been shot." Matty volunteered before Sher could ask any more questions. It was obvious Matty had very few details to relay to us, other than, dad was shot, get to the hospital.

Sher began crying even more. I was crying, thinking of dad, the very few and rare times he had been nice to us, to anyone for that matter.

"Where did they shoot him?" Sher wanted to know.

"I really don't know." Matty seemed at a loss for words.

"No, I mean where was he?" Sher seemed annoyed.

"I'm sorry Sher, I really don't know. I'm sure we'll find out when we get to the hospital." Matty tried to sound comforting.

It seemed a bit cruel for Ray to call and let dad's sisters know dad had been shot, yet not give any real details about the shooting or dad's condition. What a horrible thing to put someone through. But I guess some things you just don't say over a phone. Then I retracted my own thought on that, remembering the day mom died and all the countless phone calls Sher had to make to relatives and let them know mom had died. I mean Sher had to just blurt it out, she didn't give relatives time to think about what she was gonna say, she just said "My mom is dead."

So now I was wondering why Ray would not just tell dad's sister over the phone what condition dad was in. Seemed very cruel not to tell them, seemed just as cruel if he had told them. My head was spinning with fear and sadness and regret and hate and love and pity and, I can't even describe everything I felt.

I sat in the back seat, again crying, just as I had not four hours ago.
A terrible thought went through me.
What if he were dead? I mean, to have our only surviving parent die four months after our mom, seemed impossible. That kinda stuff doesn't happen. Even a rotten father was better than no father at all, I thought.

You talk about guilt. This here little girl was suffering a lot of guilt on the way to the hospital. I was literally beating myself up, and I did not like that feeling at all.
I felt of surge of guilt questioning why my mom

had died and not dad. I felt guilt for every time I cussed his ass out, in my mind.

Was I being punished for being such a little bitch about my feelings for my own father. Hey, I didn't impose those feelings just for the hell of it. Everything negative and hateful I ever felt, was due to his actions, not mine.

Didn't matter now, this was straight up guilt, and to tell you the truth, I wasn't cut out for such feelings where he was concerned.

I had never been to a hospital before. Never had a reason to.

When mom gave birth to my younger brothers and sisters, Sher and I were not allowed to visit her. When my grandpa was in the hospital dying from cirrhosis of the liver, again we were not allowed to go see him.

A few times I glanced at Matty's speedometer, and I'm no race car driver but I do believe she was driving way too fast, and I do believe she bolted through a red light or two. I for one, was in no hurry to be in a car wreck just to get to the hospital a few moments quicker. Made no sense. But dad was Matty's only brother, and Sher did love him a lot, and I. Well, my feelings didn't matter. I was beating myself up enough for all of us.

We arrived at the hospital within fifteen minutes.
We were not out of Matty's car three seconds,

when we were ushered into the hospital by at least half the gangsters in town.

Upon entering the hospital I noticed first, the absolute cold, air. It caught my breath, the same way it did the first time we entered the library. Difference, the library smelled of cold air, and new books. This place smelt of medicine, alcohol, and cleaning materials.
The floor was shiny, spotlessly clean. Even the library floor wasn't this shiny.

What the hell was wrong with me, my dad could very well be dead or dying in one of these hospital rooms at that very second, and I was checking out the damn floors.
Oh Malina, you're gonna pay dearly for your lack of concern for your father should he be dead.

There were people all over the place, some coming, some going. Some people were crying, some carrying on conversations as they passed us, some looking lost.
As we walked down the hallway to get to the elevator, dad's men did not step aside for anyone, rather forcing people to stop in their tracks to make way for them. Smack in the middle of all these men, was me, Sher, and Matty.

We rode the elevator to the third floor, squashed in between these men in suits. I couldn't breathe. It seemed they all wore the same cologne dad did, they all wore dark suits and ties, as dad did, sun glasses, though it was dark out, and they all had shiny shoes. Each looking more stone faced then the next.

I felt sick.

I looked at Sher as we rode the elevator, actually Sher looked strange to me, and didn't look directly at anyone, she just stared at the elevator door, waiting for it to open.

Dad's men did not conversate amongst themselves, they did not talk to Matty, and they sure didn't try to conversate with me or Sher. A lot of wanna be Johnny G's all over the place, made me very very uncomfortable.

10

The second the elevator door opened, I could hear dad talking...no yelling, though his room would be at the far end of the hall.

Well, well, well, seems the sixty four thousand dollar question had just been answered.

Nope, he was not dead, and by the rambling on and cussing and hell raising he was doing, I seriously doubt he was any where near death.

As dad customarily did, he was bitching. Every other word I could hear was fuck. Mother fucker this and mother fucker that. I want this mother fucker found...

Dad was not concerned who might hear him, he was not concerned that there were other patients in the hospital, some that could actually be dying, he was not concerned about anything but...of course himself.

I could hear all this bitching and cussing and we still had ten or more rooms to pass before we got to his. And to top it off, his damn door was shut.

I wanted to turn around and run out of the hospital, but being that we were literally squashed in between ten guys, I knew I wouldn't get too far. So I continued walking down the hall with Sher and Matty, feeling a little bit like "Dead Man Walking" on my final walk before meeting with the gas chamber.

One of dad's men knocked on the door to dad's room, twice, but didn't actually open the door, rather waited until someone opened it for us.

Ray is the one that let us in dad's room. Good ol loyal Ray. Of course Ray would be there, "Standing Guard" doing everything he could for Johnny G.

At that very second something inside me felt bad for the idiot that had shot dad. I figured Ray would spend the rest of his life, if he must, just to capture, torture and kill whoever had shot his boss, the man he treated better than a brother, the man he wanted so badly to be like more than any person alive. The man, that if dad had died, Ray would more than likely take his place.

A hand full of gangsters stood near dad's hospital bed, and two guys outside his door..

Dad saw us and smiled, "Hey baby." That handsome betraying smile.

He really didn't look like he had been shot at all, though his arm was in a sling, he definitely didn't appear to be dying.

Actually, he looked like he was high, so I sniffed the air for a second, but I didn't smell marijuana any where in the room.

Smiling, showing off his beautiful white teeth, his beautiful dimples, and his dark glassy eyes.

What I thought was high, was actually the effects of dad on pain medication.

Of course he was given medication for his pain, he had just been shot for goodness sake, and legally, technically, he deserved to be rid of his pain.... So for once in his life, without having to smoke some funny green tobacco, my dad was legally high..

Sher, Matty and I all stopped crying when we realized dad wasn't on his so called "Death Bed."

Dad instructed all his men to move away from his bed so we could hug him, which they did, we did, even his poor stressed out sister Matty.

"Are you ok baby?" He asked of me and Sher.

"Yes," we both said at the exact same time.

"Are you ok dad?" Sher asked.

"Yes baby, it barely scratched me." He said those words like a real wise guy, while looking at his sling, which, even he couldn't see his so called wound because it was so damn small.

I wanted so badly to laugh, because this was the second time in less than a minute he called us baby, confirming, he still don't remember our names.

"Baby" as every one knew, was the cover up name for "Oops I forgot your fricken name again." This was no surprise to me. Being fucked up on pain meds, was the perfect excuse not to remember our names. Again I felt sick.

Some guy I had never seen, was standing near dad, as a body guard would stand near the employer he is hired to protect. Well, technically he was. But was this guy serious? What was this jerk afraid we would do, shoot dad with Danny and J.J.'s water guns.

We're his damn kids for crying out loud. My thoughts as he stared a hole through me with his evil eyes.

"If it's a flesh wound, why are you in bed?" Matty blurted out, trying to sound concerned, but actually sounding more like she was making fun of him.

After all Matty was crying, and had driven a bit faster than she should have so we could get to the hospital quicker, just in case dad's injuries really had been life threatening. And... Matty had after all, tried to sound comforting as she spoke to me and Sher on our way to the hospital so we wouldn't be panicked or more upset than necessary. I mean in all fairness, until we walked in the room we really didn't know just how bad, or not bad, his injuries were. To look at him now, what the hell was the rush?

Perhaps, though relieved dad was ok, she was just so worried... Her question sounded more like a joke rather than concern from his youngest sister.

The big creep beside dad did not laugh at all. He didn't even crack a smile.

Shit, even I was afraid to crack a smile, for fear dad would have me assassinated for making fun of him .

"Well." Dad said. "Seems my blood pressure is a bit high and just as a precaution"... Just then the equivalent to "Nurse Ratchet" walked in, ordering all the gangsters out of the room.

"Who are you?" She asked me. Her eyebrow a bit raised, reminding me when Sher attempted to imitate Elvis.

Before I could say "His daughter," Matty interrupted saying, "These are his daughters," pointing to me and Sher, "And I'm his sister."

"Ok, you three can stay, the rest of you, out." She ordered.

Every last man turned and looked directly at dad, waiting for his instructions. A professional dancer could not have choreographed a better move. Dad merely had to nod his head "Yes" and all of them walked out of the room. No words, no hand gestures, just a simple nod of the head, and one by one they left.

Sure had me thinking, "Oh my goodness lady, you're messing with the wrong guys."

Nurse Ethyl, turns out her name was Ethyl, checked dad's temperature and all his vital signs, with Ray standing right by dad's side, not budging an inch.

"Excuse me," nurse Ethyl could be heard saying to Ray as she attempted to tend to dad. But Ray was not about to move out of nurse Ethyl's way so she could do her job. I watched Ethyl as she scurried around the room, attempting to complete what was expected of her. "Take care of her patient"

She was a rather chunky woman, which reminded me of our old neighbor Jewel.

Once Nurse Ethyl checked all dad's vitals, she filled his water jug with ice and water and instructed dad to "drink it all and get some rest," almost in a patronizing tone.

"Big ass fucking baby." I thought as I watched my dad.

She looked at Ray as if she wanted to box him right out of the room. Ray just stared at her as if he had just looked into the eyes of dad's shooter. Then I realized the mother fucker was looking at all of us with the same evil eye.

Poor old Ethyl, she sure was gonna have her hands full with these two. She's a nurse, for crying out loud, she has rules to follow, guidelines to follow.

Do you think Ray is gonna follow your rules? I thought. These two criminals might just force old Ethyl into an early retirement by the time it's all said and done.

Chunky Ethyl waddled her way out of the room, a walk I remember even my Grandma B had. Perhaps all nurses walk in that fashion. I guess all those hours on their feet, it just happens.

A smell of stale cigarettes lingered behind Ethyl as she left the room.. .

11

Sher and Matty took turns asking questions like, "Where were you when this happened?"
"Who do you think did it?"
"Where are the cops?"
Dad would answer with short quick answers, "at home" as to where he was when he got shot.

"They," meaning dad and Ray, have no idea who did it, but the look on Ray's face when that question was asked, was like..."Just wait, I'll catch that mother fucker, I will definitely catch him, torture the son of a bitch, and leave his ass for dead."

All this I thunk all by myself. I giggled inside me.

And as far as the cops, Lordy he was Johnny G, even the cops wanted him dead, if it hadn't been a cop that shot him in the first place.

It goes without saying the cops sure weren't gonna be in a big ol hurry to arrest anyone for this feeble attempted assassination. Except for a few select cops that dad took care of, the cops could have cared less who shot Johnny G., or why they shot him. It would have been one less gangster for the cops to deal with if the shooter had killed him. One less gangster to arrest, or spend tax payer money trying to send his ass to prison.

It was for certain there were no road blocks being

set out, no detectives out looking for a possible assassin. No one gave a shit, except dad's men.

Naw! As far as I knew this was gonna be Ray's job, and only Ray's.

I felt bad that someone had tried to kill dad, he was after all, my biological father, for whatever that was worth.

All this hospital, medicine, gangsters everywhere, Ray standing there like he wanted to shoot every person that entered the room, especially nurse Ethyl.

I was beginning to feel a bit dizzy. Perhaps I should have eaten all my food at Matty's.

"Yummy chicken." I thought. Damn why didn't I eat all my food? I tried desperately to take my mind out of that hospital room. I mean seriously, can you blame me?

Watching this charade unfold right before my eyes had me thinking of my mom. It should have been my mom recuperating in one of these hospital beds for the butcher job dad did on her face, but no, instead it was dad that needed to spend the night in a hospital room for his blood pressure.

All I could think...Idiot.....You Fucking Idiot....

Then a thought came to me.. Yes mother fucker, I'm sure your blood pressure is high, someone almost got your ass and you're shitting bricks, dad...

I did a real quick process of elimination of who the heck may have attempted to kill the great Johnny G. and failed miserably.

Blank faces of men filled my brain. Faces of men that had got ass whoopins from dad and Ray in the past...could they have been the shooter?
Naw, they already knew what an ass whoopin felt like. They already knew what getting their ass whooped for no reason other than dad and Ray just felt like beating some one up. Nope, couldn't be them, they sure weren't gonna shoot and miss and get worse than an ass whoopin.
Naw, scratch them off the list.

People dad had killed?
Dummy Malina! They're already dead..Haha! I forgot.

One of dad's men?
Are you kidding, they would have already left the country.

Sal?
Naw, dad was making money for him at the garage.

Ray?
He was in fact the next in line to take dad's place? Nope, he's about the only person that really, really loved dad.

Then I got comical...

Nurse Ratchet? No way, she barely met him. Maybe in a day or two, after having to put up with dad and Ray she will definitely wanna shoot both of their fucking asses.

Danny?
Naw, too little. He would have shot dad's knee caps, not his shoulder.

Becky?
Hum? Revenge for the beating she had endured. She sure did have a motive.

Sher?
Are you kidding... she loved dad as much as Ray. No, she loved him way more than Ray.

Me?
Nope not me. You can bet your life if it had been me, I would not have friken missed.…... Fact.

Ok Malina you're fishing now. I shook my head to get all those wicked thoughts out of my brain just as dad looked right at me and asked, "Are you ok?"

I shook my head again, this time in response to dad's question. I must have looked as if I was having a seizure or something with all the head shaking I was doing.

I did after all, have a bunch of voices going off in my brain, going from "who did it" to half ass listening to what they were all saying.
This was a lot of fuckin bullshit to try and absorb.

I gathered this much.
Dad had gone home alone. The porch light wasn't on because we kids weren't there to turn it on. As dad got out of his car someone shot him and disappeared in the night. Not much more was said about it.
I mean really, they're gangsters, they don't shoot and tell.

And for the record, everyone knew the cops weren't gonna waste the man power to find who ever did this.
Why? Once they found the jerk, dad would only have Ray kill him.
I tried to pay attention to what was said but neither dad nor Ray was going to tell of their plans to kill whoever.
It was inevitable someone was gonna die for this bang bang, shoot and miss bull shit.

12

I sat there watching all these men running around like they really didn't know what to do. If there were any of dad's enemies lurking around, they sure knew how to get this organization of his out of whack.

Sher cried off and on while we were in dad's room, dad assuring her he was "just fine." It seemed every time Sher looked at dad she cried even more.

I wondered why she was so terribly upset, I mean come on, I knew she loved him more than me. I knew he loved her more than me, but really Sher, the mother fucker was ok, so what's up with all the tears. He's alive, he's still being a fricken jerk, so calm the fuck down.

But she didn't calm down and at one point she got almost hysterical, that Matty had to take her out of the room to calm her down, unfortunately leaving me alone with dad and Ray.

Now that... was a fuckin creepy feeling.

Me all alone in a room with number one and number two "KILLAS." That was an intimidating feeling to say the least, daughter or no daughter.

I mean really, I am the child that pissed my pants my entire life every time I saw the man, no every time I heard his damn voice. Now I was left alone with him and his right hand man. Who the hell gets that damn unlucky?

If dad hadn't been so concerned about the scratch on his arm, he could have been a real ass hole and taken full advantage of the fact I was a cry baby and scared to death of him. He could have really fucked my day up with his intimidating ways.

Thank goodness for me he cared less about mentally tormenting me at the moment, only caring for his bullet wound, which in all fairness looked more like a B.B. wound than a shot from a 9mm, or sawed off shotgun. Get real dad.

Damn I need to quit thinking bad thoughts, one day one of these bastards is gonna read my mind.

Sitting in dad's room, with absolutely nothing in common with these two murderers.... Hold up, I said murderers, simply a word I used to describe them. In all fairness, though they had been accused several times of murder, neither of them had ever been convicted of any murder, or at least no conviction that could hold up in court. I mean seriously how can you convict a so called killer when all the "Witnesses" were droppin like flies.

Without a doubt neither dad nor Ray was gonna attempt to comfort me. If I wasn't so worried my dad would find something to bitch about, where my appearance was concerned, I would have left the room the second Sher and Matty did. But I wasn't gonna give my dad the satisfaction of humiliating me just because I wanted to get the heck away from him and Ray.

It's a fact, should I have attempted a hasty departure from the room, dad would have started in on me before I would ever have made it to the door, which was about seven feet from where I was sitting. I did not possess the quickness of Sher, so sure enough dad would have bombarded me with question after question, preventing me from getting out of his sight.
"Did you brush your teeth today?"
"What's wrong with your hair?"
"Your dress is too short."

Those are just a few of the nice things he would have bitched about.
Technically, I had no one on my side, no one to protect me.
Nope….. I stayed put!

Remembering very clearly my dad had an unlimited list of unanswerable questions he could ask, just to get you to answer the same question over and over.
He just had to keep everyone on their toes. Even from a hospital bed.
It would be just like him, out of nowhere, to ask a question like "Who was the 10th president of the United States….

Really fucker?

You know damn good and well I don't know the answer to that. Only a history buff could answer that on a seconds notice. Remember, I'm the daughter that hated school. I'm sure somewhere along the line I learned or was taught the names of all the presidents, but in all fairness, how the hell could I remember them. I had more important things in my life, like hiding machine guns from the F.B.I. and watching dad roll joint after joint. How the fuck could I remember history shit when there was so much more going on in my life?

Besides, not even dad and Ray combined could answer that question. I seriously doubt they even knew who the current president was, let alone a president a thousand years ago. Even if I did know, by some miracle, I would have got an ass whoopin, because if dad didn't know the correct answer himself, then he'd assume I was making it up, thus beating my ass for making a fool of him.

In other words, play a fricken mind game. It was remarkable the way his brain worked.

So remembering my dad's wittiness in attempting to catch one of his kids in a lie, or if he thought someone was lying, let's just say, getting tangled up in his bullshit while I sat defenseless, alone, no one in the room to protect me, was not on my to-do list.

I knew for sure Ray would not have had my back, so to say. So, no damn way. I was not about to put myself in the line of fire.

After about ten minutes Sher and Matty returned. That was probably the longest, quietest ten minutes of my life.

The look of love in Sher's eyes as she glanced at dad upon entering his room. Perhaps one tenth of the look I always had for my mom. She obviously couldn't help but love him.

13

Dad assured Sher over and over he was ok.

I remained quiet, letting Sher and Matty ask all the questions they wanted, which eventually seemed the same questions were being asked over and over, Matty more so out of loyalty, Sher asking the same questions over and over out of love.

Me? You guessed it. I said not one friken word. But I sure thought a lot of words, most of them cuss words. It was my way of coping.

Several times I glanced over at Ray and his roaming eyes were looking at Sher, then Matty, then me, then of course he looked at dad. The second and third time I saw his beety little eyes look my way, I got scared and looked away, which, if I remember my gangster handbook well enough, I believe to a gangster, that is a sign of guilt.

He didn't seem like the fun, happy, kind Ray I once knew, but then again, the kind, fun loving Ray I once knew was gone in my eyes since the day he stood there like a worthless piece of shit, and didn't attempt to prevent my dad from slapping the hell out of Sher, all over a fuckin piece of paper.

Again I remembered why I hated Ray. He seemed now, what he had always been, a heartless, ruthless gangster that cared about no one but his boss.

I watched him for a few moments.
 The fourth time his creepy eyes met mine I wanted so badly to jump up and say "Fuck you Ray, I didn't shoot this mother fucker right here, if I had, you'd be burying his fuckin ass."
 Just a thought, from a scared little girl to a low life criminal.

 Nurse Ethyl returned within fifteen minutes, this time carrying a tray of food for dad. It smelled good, it even looked good.
  Come on now, anything would look good and smell good compared to the shit me and my brothers and sisters had been eating. Other than the cafeteria food at school and the food Matty had just prepared for us a few hours ago, we literally had been eating pig slop. Stray dogs had better meals than we had.
 Dad, such a jerk, started scarfing down his food, as if he too hadn't had a descent meal in months.

 The hospital cafeteria had long since been closed, but somehow, nurse Ethyl managed to get dad a plate of food. I wondered why? Why did she give a shit if he ate or not?
 Goodness did she already get the scoop on who the gangster was in room 301, and knew her life could very well be on the line.

 We, meaning me Matty, Sher, and Ray all sat and watched dad eating, as if we four had absolutely nothing better to do. What a fuckin sight we must have been?

There was a knock on the door, which, when I think of it, the second someone knocked; me, Sher, Matty and even Ray the killer, stopped staring at dad.

The trance broken.

The knock, I suppose, startled us and kicked us back into reality.

My goodness he was eating a plate of food, not performing open heart surgery.

Un-fricken believable.

Ray opened the door and in walked a man, a small man, with thick rimmed eyeglasses. He was a very short man, wearing a trench coat though it was not at all cold out side. He wore a hat and had a briefcase, which he was holding with both hands. Perhaps it had liquid nitrogen in it, because he held it so close to his body. He was an odd looking man, not at all what I would suspect would be the leader of an organization, if that were in fact what he was. But my instinct from being the daughter of a low down rotten gangster, told me this wasn't just any ordinary man.

Dad stopped eating for about ten seconds to look up at him.

Actually, dad was eating so damn fast, I thought for a split second the mother fucker ate his finger off. I sooo wanted to laugh.

Shhhh Malina, such thoughts.

The man did not smile, he said not one word, just went directly to dad, shook his hand, then kissed dad on his cheek.

Gangster bullshit rules of respect, I suppose.
Dad told him to have a seat, Ray retrieved a chair for him and placed it very near dad's bed. Dad put his fork down, drank some of his tea, then looked at me, Matty and Sher and said "Matty, take the girls out to the visitor's lounge.."

We said nothing, just did as we were told, of course. Not one word was said by dad, Ray or this strange man while we were in the room, not even once we got out to the hallway could dad's deep loud bitchy voice be heard.
I for one, was not gonna try and eaves drop. Best I could figure, they were gonna put their heads together about dad's shooter.
 Two of dad's men were in the hallway, one on opposite ends of the hall, just standing there, staring, still wearing sunglasses. I guess they were supposed to be intimidating. Really, sunglasses, late at night, in a hospital. What a dead give away, who they were, what the were.
There was nothing "Incognito" about these idiots.

14

Matty asked one of the nurses at the nurses station if there was a waiting room nearby. The nurse said nothing, just smiled and pointed down the hall.

We walked down the hall, passing room after room. Sher and Matty a few paces ahead of me.

Some doors were open to patients rooms and I could see into their rooms. Some doors were shut.

As I passed one room I noticed there was a very old lady sitting in a wheel chair, looking out toward the hallway. Her eyes met mine as I walked slowly past her room. I did not stop and stare at her, but as slow as I was walking, it was easy for me to view her entire room. Her face had wrinkles like I had never seen before. Deep wrinkles that looked almost like someone had slashed her face. She did not move her head, only her eyes roamed. It seemed such a sadness in her tired old eyes.

Her room was dimly lit, which made her look even more scary to me. She watched me, I watched her, till she was no longer visible to me.

Goose bumps were over my entire body.

As we approached another room, a man lay in his bed, moaning. A deep painful moan which could be heard long after we passed his room. He wasn't yelling or calling out to the nurses, only moaning..

I wondered what was wrong with him? Was he in

pain because he was suffering a deadly disease? Had he had surgery and needed more pain medicine? I felt very sad for him. I wanted to cover my ears to drown out the sound of his moans.

The next room we passed, there were two women, a young woman and an older woman, I suppose were hospital housekeepers. Both women in the room, busily cleaning up what appeared to be vomit on the floor next to the patients bed.
 I couldn't see the patient because the housekeepers had drawn the curtain around the bed. A nurse entered just as I passed the room scurrying around, doing what nurses have to do. I heard someone gag, which made me almost gag. Not sure if it were the women cleaning the mess, the nurse that had just entered the room, or the patient himself.
 We continued down the long hallway, to the visitors lobby. I wondered if this were the same hospital my mom had been in when she had given birth to Becky, Carrie, J.J. and Danny. I wondered if this was the same hospital my mom rode the bus home after having Danny because my dad couldn't or wouldn't be found to drive her home.
 So much I wondered.
 Naw no way, dad wasn't about to be in a county hospital. This was not the county hospital. My dad was above that.

The visitor lobby appeared to be a very comfortable room, not brightly lit like dad's room.

A few dark green leather sofas, and matching leather chairs placed throughout the room. A coffee table in front of each sofa, and lamps on end tables at the ends of the sofas. It appeared as a nice large living room might look in an upscale home on the upper west side of town, not all sterile and shit like a hospital.

It seemed the objective in this room was to make family members comfortable while waiting to visit their loved ones, since no one could actually stay in the room with the sick family member.

There was a T.V. in the corner of the room, on, but the volume was muted. Four to six people sat huddled together talking, perhaps discussing their loved ones. Relatives maybe; or just strangers that had recently met and had the misfortune of being in the hospital at the same time.

They each looked up as we entered the room, one or two of them smiled as they glanced at us. I wondered if they were discussing my dad and his unruly behavior. I hoped not.

Comfortable, cushiony, high back chairs were lined up against the wall nearest the door. Sher and Matty sat down, with one empty chair between them, not sure if I was supposed to sit between them or find a chair of my own.

Matty looked tired and stressed. Sher, again not saying anything, just, I couldn't help but wonder what the hell was she thinking.

I sat on the chair next to Sher, leaving the space

between Matty and Sher. I looked around, wishing I were anywhere but there.

Me, Matty and Sher didn't talk to one another while we waited. After a few minutes Matty got up to call Mary on the hospital phone, I picked up a magazine from the end table, mostly just thumbing through the pages. Sher still just sat there, an empty look on her face.

Apparently no one answered at Mary's because Matty never said a word. I saw her dial Mary's number a second time, same result each time. No answer, then she came back and sat by me and Sher. Again nothing was said by any of us.

I contemplated saying "What a waste of our time" but rejected the urge for two reasons. First off, Matty was his sister, and though I really knew nothing about how they were raised, I knew how I felt about my own brothers and I sure the hell wouldn't want anyone talking shit about neither of them. But of course Danny and J.J. were wonderful little boys. I had no idea how good or bad of a brother my dad was to his sisters, none the less, I'm sure Matty, out of respect, didn't want to hear any negative shit I had to say about her only brother.

Second reason, Sher. She looked as if she were about to burst. Burst out crying or just maybe she was so stressed and she needed to hit someone. Hit someone and hurt them.

Now, it was a given she had the capabilities to beat the hell out of several people at one time. She may have been very beautiful but the bitch could hit and the way I saw it, she was about ready to unload a lot of stress on someone. And if I were stupid enough to say just the wrong thing at just the right time, well I would probably have to be recuperating in a hospital bed, and the fuckin thought of recuperating in the bed right next to my dad, fuck that shit. I kept my big fuckin mouth shut.

Finally Matty spoke. "Are you girls hungry?" She asked.

Don't recall hearing those words spoken to us since mom's funeral, visualizing my brothers and sisters, my self included, devouring any meal we ever had. Never had to ask us twice.

But then in all fairness we had just eaten a few hours ago and it didn't seem appropriate to make a fucking animal of myself as I had just witnessed my own father doing.

Damn I wish I had my left overs now, I'd scarf that shit down for sure.

"No." both Sher and I answered. I knew I was lying. I was friken hungry.

So we sat and we waited. I thought of the nurses in the hospital. I thought of all they must do for each patient. Watching the nurse tend to the patients, watching the housekeepers do what they needed to do whether they liked their jobs or not, and even watching poor ol Ethyl tend to the likes of my dad had me remembering when I was real young I told my mom and grandma B I wanted to be a nurse when

I grew up.

   Periodically throughout my life my mom would go to the nursing home that grandma supervised.. Usually we would go to borrow money from her. I always loved to go there and watch my grandma with her kind words and the love she showed towards each and every one of her patients.
   Always a smile on her face, her perfect white false teeth, and her gentle laugh. She called everyone sugar or honey. Not because she forgot their names or ours for that matter, but because to her, everyone was sweet. Everything she did, made me want to be a nurse more than anything in the world.
   All the old folks at the nursing home loved grandma, and she them. Even the other nurses loved her because she was so kind and cheerful.
   Being a nurse was all I ever wanted to be, until I saw the toll, being a twenty-four hour nurse to my grandpa, took on my grandma as he suffered dying. I retracted my love for the thought of being a nurse then. So much pain to watch someone die. And working in a nursing home I'm sure my grandma dealt with a lot of death. But to actually watch her get wore down by the stress of taking care of her dying husband, well I might have been a mere kid, but watching grandma almost disintegrate into nothing because of all the weight she lost and the horrible circles around her eyes, naw, it wasn't for me.
   I simply just changed my mind.

15

Perhaps half an hour passed when one of dad's henchmen came in and told us we could go back to dad's room.

We walked back slowly, me not really wanting to pass the same rooms again, dreading what I might see and hear.

I noticed first the room with throw up, had all been cleaned and the man in the bed appeared to be asleep.
Yes, he was asleep because I heard him snoring. His room, as I walked slowly past it, smelled a little strong of cleaning liquids, but then I guess that was necessary. Gotta really appreciate the nurses and the housekeepers for the jobs they do.

We were now approaching the man's room that had been moaning, remembering the sounds he was making, a frightful pain in his moans. Now it seemed he was asleep, either medically induced, or exhausted from so much moaning. I glanced at him, his eyes were shut, as he took deep, slow breaths, almost as if he was taking his final breath.. I got scared.

I was now approaching the old woman with all the wrinkles on her face. I glanced towards her, she still sat in the same spot she had been maybe thirty minutes before. Still staring in my direction, the only thing moving on her, again were her eyes.

I wanted to smile at her but before I did, she did. Perhaps she was paralyzed from the neck down and couldn't move anything but her eyes and lips.

An overwhelming urge came over me to stop, go into her room and talk to her, because I felt very sad for her. She just looked so lonely.

I stopped in her doorway, but at that very second dad's henchman cleared his throat as to say, "Come on kid."

I smiled one final time at the old lady, knowing I would never see her again. She smiled a second time, then closed her eyes.

I got really scared thinking she just died. I took two steps toward my dad's henchman, then took those same two steps going backward. I went back to her doorway, looked in her room. I suppose she sensed me there, she opened her eyes and smiled at me one last time. I just had to make sure she hadn't died right there before my eyes.

Walking down the hallway I realized, though the hospital was clean and cold and didn't smell of anything but medical stuff, it felt of sickness and death.

It seemed to me you get one of two things from a hospital, you are either sick, or dying, which in all fairness those are the only two reasons to be in a hospital in the first place...Right?

It is either your cured, or you die.

Doctors either fix your ailment, or pain or disease and you go home. Or you can't be cured, you can't be fixed or saved and unfortunately, you die.

For some you leave the hospital with a smile on your face, for others it is sadness and unhappiness and death.

That's it. There is no in between.

So it is either the best place to temporarily be, or it is your final place to be, eternally. Toss of the coin it seemed to me.

What a horrible thought. What a horrible predicament, or in the case of having your life saved, or being cured, what a wonderful place to be.

Just seems my life got more and more difficult. Here I was in a place I didn't want to be. I was dealing with the shooting of my father, in all fairness would probably end in the murder of a lone assassin.

When does it ever end? When would life be in my favor? At that moment I again questioned God.

I was weary and tired.
I was nauseous.
I wanted out of that hospital.
I wanted to go home.
I wanted my mom.

16

I hurried to catch up with Matty and Sher who were just getting to dad's door.

Dad was now sitting in a chair, almost like a king sitting on his throne, Ray sitting in another chair facing dad, the strange little man now gone. Dad and Ray were talking, some serious gangster shit I'm sure, but stopped the second we entered the room.

Of course he wanted to know where we had been and what we had done. Geez, he's the idiot that sent us out of the room, what the hell did he think we had done?

Matty informed him we hadn't left the floor, merely sat in the visitors lounge.

"Did anyone try o talk to y'all?" Dad asked.

Matty assured him nobody bothered us at all.

Small talk between dad and Matty. He never once asked us about moving to Matty's. Not once did he ask or offer Matty any money for taking us in. Really the conversation was mostly about, no, was entirely about him.

I believe we had out stayed our welcome with dad. He seemed to be getting a bit bitchy. Or should I say ... bitchier.

We stayed long enough to confirm he had no life threatening injures, would not die, and probably would be released tomorrow morning, and be at Sal E's bar by tomorrow afternoon, reliving and retelling his story over and over and over about some mother fucker trying to kill him. And like robots everyone in the bar would listen carefully ooohhh and aaaawwwwing him the entire time.

Finally, we took turns hugging dad good-bye. Not once dad saying neither mine nor Sher's names. Sher must have felt like shit knowing how much she loved him, he never once called her by name. I could have cared less if he said my name or not.

Actually he probably only said my name once in my life, the day he read my birth certificate, I'm sure only to confirm Guetarro had been spelled correctly.

What a fucking exhibition this was...

As we walked past the army of henchmen I thought..."Oh my, these guys act as if the president himself had been shot. I suppose to them, he was the president.

Ray instructed two of dad's men to walk us out of the hospital and to Matty's car.

Just as we got on the elevator I heard nurse Ethyl saying, "You men have already been told, it's way past visiting hours, and our Mr. Guetarro needs his rest."

Our Mr. Guetarro? I thought. Only thing missing from this visual was Ethyl shoving a loli pop in his friken mouth.

My feet could not get me to the elevator quick enough.

Sure enough, as I knew, all dad's men ignored her.

Only Johnny G. gives orders. And of course just as the elevator door closed, I again heard dad cussing and yelling.

I had a horrible vision of this poor old nurse being tossed out of one of the hospital windows, just because she was trying to do her job.

As we left dad's room I thought about dad, the way he carried on, Ray being protector, and all dad's men doing... well whatever dad told them to.

I thought, as much as I hate my dad's ways, and as much as I hate him for the horrible husband and father he was, I really didn't want him dead. I really didn't. Not that anyone would ever believe me. But then I gave a shit less who would believe me, or who cared about my feelings.

One must really hate someone to shoot them, to attempt to kill them. Me for one, I had more than my share of hate for everything my dad ever did wrong. But to want him dead. No not even at thirteen years old did I want that to happen.

I guess dad escaping death by a dumb ass shooter would be in his favor, for now.

As the elevator door closed, I again watched Sher. She looked so sad, like she wanted to start crying again, she made no eye contact with me or Matty. I really didn't get it, you know being that upset over a scratch on his friken arm, but then maybe the thought of her losing her precious daddy was just too much for her.

Once we exited the hospital, dads men were gathered outside, huddled around, smoking, talking, looking every which way. They watched us as we walked to Matty's car, actually two of them escorted us, then watched us as we drove off, pointing us in the direction of the nearest exit.

As we passed the hospital door where some of dad's men stood, I glanced toward the enormous glass doors and saw Ray walking outside to greet someone.

More gangsters? I thought.

Goodness gracious, such a fuss over a damn flesh wound.

But I was wrong. It wasn't another gangster. Not a gangster at all.

This was a woman, and from where I was, it didn't seem to be just any woman either. It appeared to be the same woman I had seen with dad a few times, his girlfriend, I called her to myself.

She didn't see me, neither did Ray. She just smiled as Ray opened the door and led her into the hospital. I looked at her real good as we drove past them, just as she stepped into the hospital, she stopped and looked back.

I saw her face very clearly. I saw everything.

There was no mistaken this woman, it was her, without a doubt.

I could only stare as my eyes filled with tears, wondering if my eyes were deceiving me.

I couldn't believe what I was witnessing....This fucking bitch was pregnant.

17

I literally wanted to be sick. That so called "girlfriend" of dad's wasn't a few months pregnant, she was a lot pregnant. Pregnant enough for a stupid kid like me to know, this wasn't a pregnancy of one or two months. By the looks of it, the bitch was about to pop.

I didn't know what to say, I didn't even know how I felt about this situation. No, I take that shit back, I knew exactly how I felt about this fucked up situation.

I gathered this much.
This useless father of mine, was not only fucking around on my mom, but now, he was gonna be a daddy again.
Daddy? You call that a daddy?
Did this bitch think dad was gonna be a "Father of the year" type of dad to her kid?
Did she think he would treat her kid any better than he treated us?
Did she think her kid would be born with a "silver spoon" in it's mouth? Really?
What the fuck was wrong with her?

Maybe, just maybe, I was jumping to the wrong conclusion here. Maybe this wasn't dad's girlfriend after all, and maybe, just maybe, it wasn't his kid she was pregnant with.

Who the hell was I kidding?

I had seen her a few times with dad, and now, just like a loyal wife, she was going to visit his ass in the hospital. Then to make matters worse, to see Ray greet her at the door as if she were a queen, worse yet, as if she were his new wife.

Ray, you disloyal ass mother fucker! Disloyal to my mom, and my mom's memory.

What a miserable sight that was.

I mean really, Ray stopped "Holding the great Johnny G's hand" long enough to escort dad's bitch from the parking lot to his room. He actually stepped away from dad's bedside long enough to play tour guide.

Wasn't Ray concerned nurse "Ratchet" might just inject dad with a lethal dose of strychnine?

Whoever the fuck this woman was, whatever the fuck she wanted, I couldn't stand this woman, and as mean as it sounds, I couldn't stand her baby either.

I cried wondering if my mom knew of this woman, of this unborn baby. Then I recalled, is this what had almost pushed my mom over the edge, when she told dad she didn't know how much more she could take?

It was apparent this woman was messing with my dad when mom was still alive, but how dare her just show up, as if this were her place to be by his side.

Though I personally did not enjoy being at the hospital, watching dad make a spectacle of himself, I felt completely disrespected by this woman's mere presence.

What a fuckin joke!

No one gave a shit if I felt disrespected. Who the hell was I kidding?

The vision of that very pregnant woman flashed in and out of my mind all the way back to Matty's.

Sher cried the entire time, I cried off and on.
Matty told us both not to worry, dad would be ok. Ok???...... Ok????

Did Matty think for one second I was crying for my dad? Did she really think all my tears were for my cheating, dishonorable, scum bag father?

Of course she did.

Matty, nor Sher had seen that woman being greeted by Ray, I had. Sher hadn't seen that woman sitting in my dad's car on one of dad's rampage days, I had.

Or, was it possible Sher and Matty had already been informed of this woman, and no one bothered to tell me.

Oh fuck this, my mind was about to explode. I cared less of my dad, his so called bitch, or their kid.

All I cared about was my mom.

When we got home, Matty went to Mary's to get Lori, and to tell Mary of dad's condition. Sher and I went to our room.

The evening's events were scrambling around in

my head. Watching my dad lay up in that hospital bed like he had been shot up at the "Saint Valentine's Day Massacre" and had been the lone survivor.

Listening to him yak, and cuss, and bitch non-stop about.. well whatever the fuck he was yakking about.

Not to mention, all those body guards. What the fuck were they protecting? Surely an assassin would not be stupid enough to attempt to "finish him off" right there at the hospital.

I was disgusted about everything I had seen and heard. To be witness to my dad and his shenanigans at the hospital was one thing. But to see his bitch being led in the hospital pretty much put the icing on the cake for me.

As much as I tried I could not get the vision of dad in that hospital bed out of my mind, thinking, my mom should have been the one in a hospital bed when he damn near beat her to death. Not this miserable excuse of a man loving the sympathy he was getting from all his men, by laying up in the hospital being catered to hand and foot, with nothing more than a scratch on his arm.

High blood pressure indeed! Someone almost got his ass, and he knew it.

Was I feeling sorry for him? I wondered.

Naw! No way! He had a flesh wound for goodness sake. The exhibition at the hospital was so unnecessary. Yet, it seems there were quite a few men there that loved and wanted to protect him.

Actually, I had seen the charade people put on for my dad the few times he had taken me and Sher to Sal E's bar. I had seen men hug him, kiss his cheek, laugh with him, carry on like they really really loved him. I would be witness to women standing so close to him, just to get his attention, possibly wanting to be the next bitch he fucked around with. People loved him. They wanted to be near him..

I would learn my entire life just how much people loved and respected him.

Everyone but me.

Nope, I was not feeling sorry for him at all. What was going through my mind the entire time was my mom.

18

Sher had been extremely quiet since we left our house, and though I did not enjoy being on the receiving end of Sher's torture, cause she loved to pick on all five of her brother's and sisters, she really didn't say much on the way to the hospital or at the hospital, other then the repeated question she asked over and over to her daddy.

She was equally as quiet on the ride home from the hospital, except she cried a lot. Perhaps the thought of losing her precious dad was just to much for her.

I considered asking her if she were ok, but I knew that would be like opening the flood gates of verbal torture she would unleash on me because, in all fairness, she probably needed someone to take all her frustration out on. I'd be the logical choice.

We were in our room preparing for bed when Matty came in, trying her best to initiate a conversation with us. "So girls what would you like to do tomorrow?" she asked.

"Park!" yelled Lori from the other room attempting to get in on the conversation.

I remained quiet...

"Can we go to the house?" Sher asked. "I want to get mom's sewing machine, so I can make some skirts for the girls." She told Matty.

"Sure." Matty said. I don't work tomorrow, so

whatever you girls would like to do, just let me know."

Well it was certain, one thing I did not wish to do was a return visit to the hospital. Two days in a row, dad, Ray, henchmen, bullshit gangster rituals, no fricken way.
Sill I said nothing.

Matty and Lori said their good-nights and went to their room. Sher had already begun her shower and was ready to go to bed.
I wondered if Sher was going to have a good nights sleep knowing she was not going to have to worry about breakfast for six, lunch for six, dinner for six and all the responsibilities that had been piled on her shoulders since the day mom died.
Once she showered and went to bed, she fell asleep the second her head hit the pillow, and just like clock work she covered her head with her pillow just as she had done robotically every night of her life.

I got my things and went in to take a shower, something I had never done in my life. Such a simple task, taking a shower! But for me it was a milestone.
The second the water from the shower hit my face, I panicked. I really panicked enough to turn the water off for a moment.
The horrific memories of the day at the lake when dad chunked me in the water, all came back to me. I

had to turn the shower off because I was choking, a little bit of dejavu perhaps.

I knew for a fact I couldn't actually drown, for goodness sake I was standing up in the bath tub.

You can't drown standing in a shower, there was no water filling up in the tub. The water was merely hitting me in my face and running down the drain.

Didn't matter at all, those horrible memories of almost choking to death in the lake were there with me in the shower.

To me, the tub was full, I was drowning, and my fricken dad was standing there smirking at my fear.

I slowly turned the water back on, then I began to cry. Not only was I reliving the drowning episode, I relived my mom coming to my rescue at the lake that day and saving me as she seemed to do on a daily basis my entire life where my dad was concerned. Only now, she wasn't there to save me. She wasn't there to comfort me, make all the bad go away. I was having to deal with this all alone. So I cried and I cried.

Eventually I continued with my shower and survived. As much as I thought I had looked forward to a shower, all it did was hit me like a ton of bricks. I cried all through my shower and I cried when I got out of the shower. I cried as I sat in Matty's dark living room, towel drying my hair.

Sitting all alone in a living room I had paid no attention to when we arrived. Yet in the dark I could see the two sofas, the TV, the lamps, even the black throw rug under the coffee table, which reminded me of the rich house game we girls always played.

I wanted to scream for my mom but knew it would do no good. All it would do was frighten Lori and startle Matty.

Sher, she probably wouldn't have even heard me, after all remember her head was covered with her pillow.

Not quite sure how long I sat in the dark living room, crying, longing for my mom.

It had been a terribly emotional day again. The emotions of leaving our house, seeing my beautiful mom at the door, then going to the hospital and being forced, out of loyalty to deal with all my dad's dramatics. Yes, this was another one of those days I just wished I didn't have to go on anymore..

I finally had it in me to go to bed. I was exhausted, I mean really friken exhausted.

So much guilt inside me for having my own bed, so much guilt in me for having a good meal to eat. It just didn't seem right.

As I walked back to mine and Sher's bedroom I would feel guilty, ashamed that I would be sleeping alone in a new bed, my own bed. Realizing there would be no ones foot in my mouth, no one breathing in my ear. No one smacking me in the face, or in my gut with their foot as they rolled over in their sleep. There would be no one getting up in the middle of the night to go piss and waking me..

But as I lay in my bed, with what seemed like new sheets, and a new bedspread, my thoughts were, I would gladly go back to my nightmarish childhood, all the horrible living conditions, all the abuse, all the fear, all the unhappiness that had been a part of my life, just to go back to be with my mom, to have my mom alive and with me..

I'd gladly go back and sleep in our fucked up bed with springs gouging my back, eat crumbs for meals, piss myself every time I saw my dad, or heard his voice.

The comforting, loving feeling I always had just knowing mom would be in the next room as I slept. Or the love I would feel every morning when I would wake, go to the kitchen and see her beautiful smile as she prepared the best breakfast she could.

God what I would give to go back.

I lay there a few moments, wanting desperately to scream as loud as I could. I reached over, turned off the lamp, and so as not to wake Sher, I too put my pillow over my head and I cried and cried, saying "Mama, Mama," to myself over and over.

I tossed and turned, tossed and turned. At one point I started to get out of bed to go to the restroom, but for a second I didn't realize where I was.

I began to cry again, fearing my cries would wake Sher, Matty and Lori. I couldn't hold my feelings in. I couldn't pretend I wasn't in pain. Unable to hold back my cries. I did just that. I cried.

Matty came in and asked if I was ok?.

Why do people ask me that? Doesn't everyone know I'm not ok?

When I didn't respond Matty asked if I'd like to talk.

"No". I responded

"Ok." She said. "But if you change your mind, I'm just in the next room."

I felt bad for saying no to her, but I knew she had to be tired and she herself had been through a lot. Moving us out of our house, dealing with dad, she already had a lot on her plate.

All the day's events flashed in my mind. I thought of the kids. I had seen Danny and J.J. at Mary's, but hadn't seen or heard from Carrie and Becky. It was barely the first day separated from everyone, though it seemed forever. I contemplated getting out of bed and calling Carrie and Becky, just to see if they were ok, but I knew it was very late and I didn't think uncle David would appreciate me waking everyone up.

Matty went to the restroom, then I heard her in the kitchen getting a glass of water.

"Goodnight!" she whispered as she passed my bed, then went to her room and shut her door.

I lay awake, in the dark, staring at nothing.
My head pounding.
My eyes swollen from crying.
My heart broken.

19

Seems every morning since my mom died, I would wake to the same thought. Perhaps it was all just a nightmare. Perhaps I would wake and the nightmare would be over and I'd wake to the love of my mom. Everyday I would wake begging the nightmare to be over, ever morning I would wake to the reality, she really had died and I was forced to live without her.

The next morning I woke to the smell of breakfast being cooked. Though my mind knew this was not the customary breakfast my mom prepared, for a split second I imagined I was back home and my mom was in the kitchen preparing a wonderful breakfast, the kind that she seldom prepared for dad, because we rarely had bacon and eggs.

I thought it, but only momentarily. My thoughts were interrupted by Lori running to my bed, her face inches from mine, and whispering "Malina, are you awake."

"Lori," aunt Matty somewhat yelled from the kitchen, "leave her alone, let her sleep."

"It's ok aunt Matty, I'm awake." I looked over at Sher's bed and she wasn't there.

"Are you looking for Sher?" Lori asked.

I smiled at her, "Yes."

"She's in the living room talking on the phone," she giggled.

I got up, went to the restroom cleaned my face and brushed my hair. The same routine I did everyday my entire life. By the time I got out of the restroom Matty had finished preparing breakfast. I went to get a pair of shorts and a shirt from our chest of drawers to wear, just as Matty and Lori sat down to eat.

"Breakfast is ready, Sher and Malina, if y'all would like to join us." Matty said.

As I walked to the restroom to get dressed, Sher was just sitting down at the table. I changed my clothes and went in to join them. Again wondering about my brothers and sisters.

After we ate Sher and I cleaned up, then Sher asked Matty to take her to our house.

I didn't want to go with them, instead offering to watch Lori so Matty could take Sher. It wasn't that I didn't want to go to our house, of course I wanted to be there. But the reasons I would want to go would be to be there with my mom, or at least visualize her in the house, cooking, dancing, sewing, laughing.

None of this would be so.

To go just to assist Sher in retrieving her machine, would mean I would have to relive yesterday's emotional roller coaster. I just didn't have it in me to do that.

Once Sher and Matty left, me and Lori were sitting at the dining room table. Lori had her crayons and coloring book, actually she had several coloring books. She thumbed through every page until she found just the perfect picture. I watched her as she intensely tried to stay within the lines of the picture she was coloring.

"Do you wanna color?" She asked me.

"No thanks." I said.

"Do you like to color?" I asked her.

"What happened to your mama?" Lori looked up at me.

I think I turned a shade of pale. Tears filled my eyes. At first I said nothing.

She looked back down to the page in which she had been coloring," My mommy told me she is in heaven. Is she in heaven Malina?" Lori so innocently asked.

A lump in my throat. I didn't know what to say.

My first reaction was to run out of the house, and just keep on running. My second was to run and hide in the restroom and cry.

I did neither.

I looked at Lori and said, "Yes she is." The lump now stuck right in the middle of my throat.

The memory of J.J. asking where mom was just a few short months ago, and my inability to answer him then, as I was unable to answer Lori now.

Remembering that Sher had to intervene then for me, wishing she was here now to do the same with Lori.

Lori again looked at me for a second, then looked back down at her coloring book and continued coloring. The conversation ended as mysteriously as it had begun.

Lori was so young. I really didn't know how much Matty had told her about death, my mom, our entire situation. But I did know, I could not answer all Lori's question, had she continued to ask them. I was glad she was more interested in coloring than carrying on our conversation.

I didn't have to concern myself that I may give Lori the wrong answers to any of her questions. At that moment Matty and Sher returned.

Sher had her machine and more of her things. She put them away, tidying up only her side of the room. She had strategically placed all her belongings on her side, nearest her bed. It seemed her side looked full, looked lived in. Mine, on the other hand looked empty. There was nothing on my side, just my bed. I guess it looked how I felt.

Again, I cared less...

I sat in the living room, staring at the T.V. that was on, though we weren't actually watching it. The sofas were positioned perfectly for me to sit and stare out the window.

With the front door open, the screen door latched, I hadn't remembered we were living in a duplex, and at that moment a man and a woman walked up to the porch and began to open what was actually their front door.

I could see them perfectly, they could see me also. The woman unlocked the door, while the man held two bags of groceries. I hadn't seen or heard a car drive up, making me believe they were walking from the grocery store.

Then I heard the laughter of a small child, a little bit younger and smaller than Lori. She pressed her nose against Matty's screen door to look in. She saw me looking at her, smiled and said " Hi, I'm Chelly."

I smiled at her.

She was a beautiful child, with big eyes and hair that went all the way down to her waist. Almost like mine.

Just then the man yelled, "Michelle, come here." And with that "Chelly" ran into their apartment and closed the door.

It was strange having someone live that close. This wasn't an apartment complex. This was an old house that had been converted into two apartments. From the outside it looked like one big house, but it was in fact two separate apartments.

I continued looking out of two of the five windows in the very large room.

Matty and Lori were at Mary's.

Sher was on the phone talking to one of her friends, well actually she was trying to whisper on the phone, having me wonder, was she talking to a boy, or a girl. There was no way I was going to ask.

I stared out of the windows for a few moments, then told Sher I was going to Mary's to see Danny and J.J.

Sher remained on the phone, whispering, and in her own world.

20

As I walked across the street I could hear all the kids laughing and screaming from Mary's back yard.. I didn't bother to go through Mary's house to get to their back yard, I just opened the gate and went directly to where all the kids were playing.

The second Danny and J.J. saw me they ran to me and hugged me. I wanted to cry.

The side door to Mary's house was open. I could smell coffee, and I could hear Mary and Matty's voices, though I could not hear what they were saying.

I sat on Mary's back porch and watched all six kids playing. Danny, J.J., Lori, and Mary's three kids.

Danny and J.J., in spite of all they had been through actually looked happy, if that were possible.

There I sat wondering what thoughts actually went through their little minds..

I thought of Lori asking me about my mom, remembering I almost got hysterical when J.J. asked me about her. I wondered did my two little brothers realize how drastically all our lives had changed? Did they realize they would never see our mom again?

Did they miss our mom?

Of course they did! They had too.

Surely they hadn't forgotten her so soon?

I think confusion is a good word. They were young. I'm sure they missed and remembered her.

Possibly they didn't realize what death was.

Perhaps they thought death meant, gone for awhile. Maybe they thought she would be returning, and maybe, just like me, they were in shock, and didn't know how to ask. I wondered were we all in shock and just simply didn't know how to talk about it?

Matty, I'm assuming was able to discuss it with Lori because Lori wasn't emotionally attached as J.J. and Danny were.

I know what I was feeling. I couldn't be happy like them. I couldn't smile and laugh and play around. All I could do was cry and beg for my mom's return.

Maybe it was good they didn't understand. The pain might be less if it were an uncertainty. Maybe dealing with life the way they were, would be the easiest thing for them.

For them, not for me.

I would never want any of my brothers and sisters to feel the pain I felt. I knew I could never explain to them what I had witnessed, what was bottled up so tightly inside me. I knew there would be no way to make them understand what we lost when our mom died. I didn't think I could ever explain any of this to them, and to tell you the truth, I would never try.

So I sat and watched these six kids, laugh and scream and fall to the ground, rolling around on the grass playing. I watched them come alive with happiness.

How wonderful they must feel.

Not wonderful that any of this happened, but wonderful that they had some kind of magical emotion in them, that allowed them to all just be kids.

Thinking back on my life, though I had many happy, loving memories of my mom, seems I was always walking on egg shells, wondering when my beast father would come home and terrorize us. Seems I never got to just be a kid, because I was always afraid. It just wasn't fair. Life was not supposed to be like that.

Should I sit Danny and J.J down and ask them if they remembered mom, if they knew what death was and what it meant? If Lori could ask about my mom, then I wondered if my brothers felt the same but were afraid to voice themselves.

I thought of explaining to them, this was all real, this was our new lives, the beautiful mom that lived with us in our old house, was our mom, and we would never see her again.

I thought about it.

But there was no way to explain any of this, and worse than that, there was no way to explain, mom was gone and it was forever.

They were just so young, so innocent to fully understand the loss of our mom and not understand what they had lost.

21

No, My decision...I would not question them about anything. I would never want them to hurt like I was hurting. So I left them alone, to play and laugh and enjoy the life they now had.

Teary eyed, watching them play tag, Danny getting frustrated because he ran so slow, the bigger kids easily catching him. I believe J.J. deliberately would get caught, just so Danny could, unfreeze, giving Danny the opportunity to play.
Always the loving protector, J.J. was, no matter where they were, or what they were doing. J.J. looked out for his little brother, good and bad times.
Still sitting on Matty's porch, I could hear someone behind me standing at the door. I didn't look back to see who it was, it could only have been Matty or Mary.
Then Matty said, "Come on Malina, let's get Sher and go for a drive."
We left Lori with Mary, then walked across the street and yelled for Sher to "Come on."
Sher came to the door when she heard me and Matty yelling for her.
"What?" Sher growled, in a bit of a Johnny G tone, frustrated I'm sure because our yelling out her name caused her to hang up the phone, and when she saw that our yelling was not due to an emergency, it pissed her off.

"Get my purse and keys from my room and come on." Matty said laughing as we both got in the car.

I knew how bitchy Sher was about riding shotgun, so I got in the back to save myself from getting my hair pulled or what ever Sher would do from the back seat if I had gotten in the front seat.

No, I would let the queen sit up front with Matty.

Sher locked the door and was off the porch and down the four steps, with just one leap, me remembering her long legs, I laughed at the sight of her.

Matty drove an opposite direction Sher, or at least I was accustomed to, which was south, towards our house. Instead she drove north, seemed strange because I had never been in that direction. She was driving away from our high school toward neighborhoods we had never seen.

Nice houses with perfect lawns. People outside cutting their grass, kids playing with water hoses. Matty showed us the park nearest the duplex, then just took us on a joy ride, I guess you could call it.

I think Matty's objective was to keep us occupied, trying to show us things we quite possibly had never seen before or take us places we had never been. It's impossible, I thought. Impossible to keep my mind occupied when every few seconds my thoughts would go back to my mom.

We passed a grocery store, then Matty turned the car around and doubled back and asked if we wanted to go grocery shopping with her.

This was a big grocery store, not like the small neighborhood one we were accustomed to. Our old neighborhood store had parking spaces for less than ten cars, this one had well over one hundred parking spaces.. it seemed
We would actually use a shopping cart to carry all the things Matty would purchase, remembering the damn lousy ten dollars dad always gave us for groceries, we were able to carry the shit in our hands, easily.
Sher was a lousy cart driver because she kept running into my heels, without saying "I'm sorry Malina." Nothing, no apologies what so ever, so I smartened up and walked behind them.
Matty put fruit, and bread, milk, cereal, canned food, sodas, ice cream almost everything imaginable.
I had never seen such shopping.
She filled the buggy up, knowing exactly what she wanted from each aisle. She didn't have to stop and think about what she wanted to buy, she already knew.
"You girls can get what ever you want." Aunt Matty said.
I didn't dare, because there was no way to know what to pick, with all the food in my face, aisle after aisle.
Sher got herself her own pack of gum.
Gum?
With all this food, everywhere, and the

opportunity to get whatever she wanted in that entire store, I wondered why gum?

Sher looked at me and winked, "In case I kiss a guy!" She whispered.

We both laughed.

Then Sher grabbed a package of candy bars and put it in the buggy.

"Here aunt Matty, Malina wants this." Sher said as she put a pack of Snicker bars in the buggy.

I had never had a Snicker bar before. It was rare to eat candy in our household, except for the candy we bought with the money we saved from drawing pictures, or of course, Halloween candy. There was just never enough money for such things.

Matty was in line to pay for the food, Sher and I stood there looking around the store as we waited on Matty.

We loaded everything into the trunk of Matty's small car. Before Sher closed the trunk, she grabbed the pack of Snickers from the grocery bag and threw it in the back seat with me.

"Here changa!" she said.

I wanted to cry when she called me changa. Not because it hurt my feelings to be called that, but the fact that she hadn't called me that in awhile.

Six Snicker bars in one pack. I wasn't sure if I should wait till after we ate lunch or supper to try one, or open them now and experience what a delicacy these things were.

"Open them up stingy." Sher smiled.

"Yeah, we both want one." Matty laughed.

I was about to eat the best tasting candy I had ever had. I handed one to Matty as she drove, and tossed one to Sher.
We each ate it as we drove home to Matty's.
"Good?" Sher asked from the front seat, a big smile on her face as she turned and faced me.
I laughed. She knew damn good and well that Snicker bar was very good.

When we got to Matty's the three of us put the groceries away, then I stood back and just stared at the over stocked cabinets. Looked like a little mini mart. Something I had never seen in an actual home. Cabinets full to the max.
Dad never provided such luxuries, and poor mom never made enough money washing and ironing clothes to afford these luxuries either.

Matty prepared sandwiches, chips, pickles and we drank soda for lunch.. Can you imagine an entire soda just for me. That was unheard of in the Guetarro household. I never even remembered drinking a soda while growing up, but I guarantee if we did, one can would be divided into six equal amounts, same as the can of chicken noodle soup would be.
I recall mom splitting one can of soup six ways. Before serving it to us she would add three or four cans of water to the pan, so there would seem to be enough. Hungry.. we never could tell the difference that it was so watered down.
Sher and I weren't used to eating at appropriate

times, we couldn't even eat if we were hungry. We only ate if we had food.

A simple meal Matty had prepared. Simple and cheap. Who would ever have known you could eat a good nourishing meal, for such a cheap price.

That was a shame, a damn shame.

22

It was Saturday night, and Matty was home spending time with her daughter and her two "new daughters."

We all watched the TV, front door open so Sher stepped out on the porch a few times just to get a breath of fresh air.

She seemed almost anxious, like she had to much free time on her hands.

It was nine p.m. and she would just be getting the kids situated for the night, if we were at home.

She didn't have to worry any more who had brushed their teeth, who needed their clothes washed, who might be hungry, or was the front door locked?

All those responsibilities were gone.

Other than helping Matty around the house, she had no responsibilities at all

As quickly as the responsibilities had been thrust upon her, they were now our aunts responsibility.

Any other teen would be grateful.

Not Sher! I think she felt that all her brothers and sisters were still her responsibility. Maybe she was still blaming herself for what had happened to Becky.

Maybe she felt she hadn't done enough for all of us, though Sher did more than any adult had done since mom died.

She sat on the porch, to me, looking sad, almost lonely....I wanted to cry for her.

Over the past four months I had her to comfort me. Over the past four months she had done it alone, no one to comfort her.

How different things were now.

Just two days ago, there was so much to do, so much to worry about. I wondered how she ever got any sleep, when did she sleep? She was doing just as mom had, with no help from anyone.

I mean, how the hell did Sher, like mom, manage to feed us all on the few miserable dollars dad would periodically give her to take care of the six of us? Where the world did Sher ever get the strength to do what she had been doing?

I rarely saw her cry. Perhaps had she broken down and cried, all her strength would have been drained. Perhaps if she had given up, we would not have survived as well as we had.

Matty and Lori continued watching TV, Sher paced a few times, then went back outside and sat on the porch.

Sitting close enough to the window as I had earlier in the afternoon, I could see out the window. Visible was every car that passed, every person that walked by.

Sher, still sitting outside, was now talking to someone. There hadn't been a car drive up, then I realized it was "Chelly" because she was giggling.

I got up and walked to the door, the couple that lived in the duplex and Chelly were again just getting home. Apparently Chelly saw Sher and initiated a conversation with her.

I heard Sher laugh out loud, indicating Chelly was getting Sher's attention. The couple went into their apartment taking Chelly with them.. A few seconds later I heard their TV on a bit loud. I could also hear Chelly laughing.

Sher remained outside.

Perhaps another hour of watching the television, and Sher going back and forth from the sofa to the front porch, Matty and Lori said their good-nights and went to their room.

I remained on the sofa, Sher outside.

After about another twenty minutes Sher came in, locked the door behind her and announced she was going to take a shower and go to bed.

I remained in the living room, still staring out the window. A calm fresh breeze blew through the open window, the white curtain blowing in the wind.

The night was calm now, no cars passing, no people walking by.

I heard a car door, but didn't see a car anywhere. Within a few seconds I saw the reverse lights of a vehicle backing out of their driveway. It was at least six houses down the block. Such a quiet neighborhood. Quiet compared to ours.

Our neighbors must have gone to sleep, because I no longer heard their TV either.

No noise was coming from Matty's room indicating that they also were asleep.

Sher was rummaging around in our room, then I

heard her start the shower.

I lay on the sofa with just my thoughts, so much on my mind, reliving everything we had been through. My concentration was broken with a very familiar sound. A sound, I hadn't heard or paid any attention to in months.

Almost a mile away now, I could hear it just as if I were back at home.

The train. The horribly loud train. Rail road tracks, just three blocks from our old house, just as well could have been in our front yard, it was just that loud. Seems the trains ran a gauntlet twenty four hours a day, seven days a week.

Trains can't tell time, as big and loud as they are they seem to have a mind of their own, though there is an engineer behind this massive contraption. They don't care if you're asleep, if you're trying to get to work on time, or trying to get home.

They are loud, slow and they blow the shit out of their whistle or is it a horn? I never have known the correct term for that loud ass sucker.

It was a menace for years.

If I was sound asleep, I would immediately wake from the loud train whistle, which seemed to me, at two a.m. the engineer purposely blew that damn whistle longer than he did during the day.

Ok I get it, they gotta blow that whistle to warn any dumb ass that might attempt to cross the rail road guard illegally, but it seemed to me the engineer kept that whistle blowing from one end of town to the other.

Asleep or not, if you lived in North side you heard that whistle no matter where you were or what you were doing. I could not understand how the heck the folks that lived 200 feet from the rail road tracks could stand that noise late at night. Perhaps it was just something you would have to get accustomed to no matter where you lived.

So many nights we would sit out on our porch, looking for light bugs, looking for shooting stars, or just sit and enjoy the evening.

One could always depend on the train whistle.

Memories of Danny and J.J. covering their ears as the whistle was blowing, Carrie and Becky not phased by the noise at all, full concentration on their game of jacks was not gonna let that loud noise interfere with their game just to cover their ears.

Mom smiling at Danny and J.J. as they screamed as loud as they possibly could while covering their ears, which looked more like 2 little boys with their mouths wide open while holding their ears, because we could not hear their screams over the loudness of the train.

Only if the train whistle stopped abruptly before J.J. and Danny stopped screaming could we hear just how loud those two little boys actually were.

Mom's laughter as she would stand at the door way watching them. Her beautiful smile, her delicate laugh, her undeniable love for her kids, all the memories of these things were here with me, as I lay in the living room at Matty's.

Even from the sofa, over a mile from the railroad tracks, I could hear the train. Such a bittersweet sound.

I cried. You bet I cried. Seems any little thing could jolt my memory right back to where I wanted to be, back at home, with my mom.

I don't even remember turning off the T.V. or going to bed that night. But at one point perhaps I dozed off on the sofa, probably enjoying the cool breeze from the open window. Perhaps in a trance I went to my bed.

Strange, it was not easy to fall asleep in comfort. Really, so many years sleeping a certain way it was not easy to change my sleeping habits. Though dad had purchased, or stole, new, or almost new beds for us, right after he beat the living crap out of my mom.

Yes, the rusty spring stabbing us in the back every night were gone, but the squashed sardine feeling continued, me Becky and Carrie continued sleeping together. It was not easy for me to adjust. I suppose the worst thing for me was knowing, I may be sleeping in a comfortable new bed now at Matty's, but I would wake to an empty heart. And that was not worth sleeping in any new bed anywhere.

23

It was now early Sunday morning. Aunt Matty woke early to go to church.

With all Matty did, preparing her self for church, getting Lori up and ready also, she still found time to make breakfast for me and Sher. I'm pretty sure she knew we didn't know how to cook a descent meal.

Actually cereal and milk would have suited me just fine, but it seemed Matty enjoyed full breakfasts on the weekend. Now I wasn't sure if Matty was doing all this, just for me and Sher, or was this customary for her to go all out with the breakfast menu.

Trust me, I wasn't about to complain, but I didn't want Matty to do more for me and Sher than she necessarily had to.

She had explained there was so little time during the regular work week for her to make breakfast, so she said we should make cereal with toast if we wanted, in the mornings for ourselves, because she would be long gone by the time we got up.

Actually so would Lori, because Matty dropped her off at Mary's house before she went to work, so Mary could take Lori to school with Mary's kids, and it was Mary that would pick up Lori after school and keep her till Matty came from work.

This was the second morning I woke to the smell of a good breakfast.

I could hear Lori in the kitchen sitting at the small breakfast table. Matty placed Lori's food in front of her and instructed Lori to eat all her food so they could go to church.

I heard Matty tip toe past me

"Aunt Matty you don't have to tip toe, I was already awake, and Sher, well you can see," I said as we looked over at Sher and sure enough her head was covered with her pillow.

We both laughed.

I wondered how the heck Sher could sleep with her pillow over her head, all night, every night. Didn't she need fresh air to breathe properly? Surely she inhaled very little air with that pillow completely covering her face.

"I made breakfast, if y'all are hungry. Matty said.

"I sure am." Sher said from underneath her pillow.

Matty continued to her room, no longer tippy toeing.

"I take Lori to church every Sunday if you girls would like to come along, I'd be glad for y'all to join us." Matty said from her bright sunny room.

She had opened all the curtains in her room, and it lit the room up, actually it looked almost too bright.

"Thanks, maybe some other time." I told her.

"Me too." Sher said.

Lori finished up her breakfast and hurried past me and Sher as we both remained in our beds.

I didn't want to get out of bed yet, giving Matty time to get herself and Lori ready, knowing there was just one restroom and not wanting to interfere with their Sunday routine.

Within twenty minutes Matty and Lori were out the door, Sher and I taking turns in the restroom brushing our teeth, our hair and you know, the morning routine.

Church? Wasn't sure how I felt about going there again. The last time I had been in church was when they had the service for my mom, right before burying her.

Matty was going to the same church, actually it was the only church in the neighborhood. Nope I wasn't in a big hurry to go there again. But if it turned out to be one of Matty's house rules then I knew I would eventually have to go.

I put that out of my mind for the moment.

I thought of the only time I had really been interested in the bible, holding on to it's every word, was the night mom died, the night she read a chapter to me and Sher..

It seemed like God was punishing us. It just didn't seem right, to read and believe, then within hours we had no mom, we had the worst thing to ever happen to us, the death of our mom.

No, I was not in any hurry to go to church, for now, my faith was questionable, very questionable.

If I even had faith at all.

Sher and I ate the breakfast Matty had prepared..

Once we finished our breakfast, we cleaned up the kitchen, straightened up our room, made our beds then went to watch TV.

Neither of us really watched the TV, more like stared at a meaningless screen.

"Seems there isn't much to do around here, is there Malina? Sher asked.

"No!" I answered,

"You don't like it here?" I asked.

"I mean yes, I like it, but it just seems like I should be doing something, beside starring at a TV." Sher complained.

"Like what?" I asked.

"I don't know, taking care of all y'all, something, anything." Sher said.

"But you already did Sher."

"Well I damn sure didn't do such a good job, now did I?" Sher was quick to say.

"Sure you did." I answered.

"I'll bet you a million bucks Becky wouldn't say that." Tears were forming in Sher's eyes, but she was very hasty to look away.

"That's not your fault." I was quick to defend Sher.

Now I was getting pissed at dad again.

"You know, I should have helped her. I should have called the police." Sher's voice seemed to crack.

"You did the right thing, you called Matty," I said.

"Yeah maybe." Sher said. A very distasteful look on her face.

"Sher, you did the best you could, I sure couldn't

have done it, not without you."

I wanted to cry just thinking if I had been the oldest and forced to take control. There was no way my meek ass self could have done it.

Never, I thought.

"You twerp!" She said as she threw the cushion from the sofa and hit me in the face.

"Look at this place, clean as a whistle." Sher said, as she wiped the coffee table with her finger, and showed me not a speck of dust on her finger.

"And you're mad at that?" I asked.

Like, really Sher this is a bad thing?

"No, I'm not mad stupid." She said.

"Don't you remember, we cleaned for hours at home and it never looked clean at all, and now we don't even have to sweep this place, and it's spotless."

"But you sound like you don't like it here." I said.

"I do like it here, but come on Malina, wouldn't you rather be at home?"

"Of course I'd rather be at home. I can't believe you just asked me that Sher. But I'd rather be at home with mom, not alone, watching you do it all."

Now I was the one getting teary eyed, and I think Sher knew where this was leading, so she tried to turn the conversation around.

"I don't know, I guess I'm just feeling bad for Becky and dad and....oh shut up leave me alone." She sounded like she wanted to cry again, and we all know ol tough ass Sher wasn't about to let anyone see her cry.

24

Sher went out on the porch, I'm sure, to avoid the fact we both were probably about to cry.

"Know what you need sista?" I followed her outside trying to cheer her up.

"I'm too young for that." I believe she was trying to make a joke.

I laughed, "You need a job!" I looked over at her, I had her attention... I continued.

"You, my big sista, need a job." I smiled.

"You need a job to give you something to do."

I saw a tiny sparkle in her eyes.

"Where the heck am I gonna find a job? What kind of job could I possibly do, I have no experience at anything?"

"I don't know, you took care of us. Why don't you go try and work at the day care on the next block." I suggested.

"How do you know there's a day care on the next block?" Sher asked.

"I saw it when I was walking home." I felt proud to know something she did not.

There was a few second pause, then Sher said.

"You're right." She was smiling.

"But I ain't working at no damn day care. Crappy ass diapers and all."

We both laughed.

"Hey you know what Malina! I'll bet the counselors at school might be able to help me find a job. I'm a sophomore, fifteen, soon to be sixteen, maybe they can help me find something."

She turned and smiled at me. "Hey you're a good little changa." She teased.

Changa...Yikes, I looked at my arms and I wasn't wearing a sweater. All the years I suffered in the summertime wearing a hot fricken sweater to block my ugly hairy arms.

All we had been through, all the pain, and now for some reason I completely forgot I even had a complex about my arms. Something I had spent all my life trying to cover up, now seemed such a minor issue.

Sher laughed at me, not too much though. She still knew I was a cry baby and too much making fun of would have had me in tears. She joked just enough to get a laugh, but not enough to make me cry.

We sat on the porch a bit, then Matty and Lori returned just as Lori's dad drove up to pick up Lori for the day.

Lori seemed excited to go with him, vigorously waving bye to me and Sher as we sat on the porch.

Once Lori left, Matty got her purse and keys, she too was leaving.

"I'll be back in a few hours." Matty smiled as she got in her car.

Me and Sher both smiled back, she didn't owe us an explanation but we both kinda figured she was going to visit her boyfriend. I mean after all, we had robbed him of a place to live.

Neither Sher nor I made any sly remarks about

where and what Matty was up to. It wasn't our business.

    Barely noon, we had the entire day ahead of us.
    Sher got on the phone a few times, I really didn't pay attention to who she was talking to. I felt Sher needed some privacy so I went to Mary's to check on the boys.
    When I got there Mary was having her first referee call with the four boys. Seems someone hit Danny, he was crying, and J.J. was comforting him.
    I listened as Mary talked to all of them, explaining that this was going to be Danny and J.J.'s home and that Mark and Jake couldn't be stingy and not share their toys, but that they also could not hit one another.. She seemed fair. No partiality.
    Danny stopped crying and within ten minutes all four boys were in the back yard rolling around on the ground as if there had never been any kind of problem at all.
    Katy seemed lost without Lori so she sat beside me on the sofa.
    "Where is Matty and Sher?" Mary asked.
    "Sher is on the phone and aunt Matty left." I answered.
    "Where did she go?" Mary asked.
    I looked at her, she was smiling.
    "Honestly I have no idea." I smiled back.
    Mary's phone rang, I gathered it was Aunt Gloria because I heard Mary ask how Becky was doing.
    Small talk, a few comments about dad and his

hospital visit, then Mary said "Hold on."

"Malina, Becky wants you."

I got up from the sofa and took the phone from Mary.

"Hello." I said.

"Malina?"

It was Becky, she sounded scared.

"Yes. Becky, are you ok?" I asked.

"Ye..., no...Well I have a black eye and my body hurts." Becky said in a quiet voice.

I wanted to cry, I choked back my tears.

"Hey Malina, I have your change purse. You know the one you got for Christmas."

I hadn't even noticed it was missing.

"Oh, ok Becky, I'll ask aunt Matty to take me over there one day this week and get it."

"Ok. Where is Sher?"

"She's at Matty's."

"Where is Carrie?" I asked.

"Right here next to me."

"Are y'all ok?" I asked.

"Yes." Becky said.

"Are y'all getting along with the girls?"

"Yes." Becky said. "Everyone is nice. You know how scary uncle David is sometimes, but he ain't like dad for sure." Her voice sounded like she wanted to cry just saying the word dad.

I'm sure a ton of flashbacks of her ass whoopin was goin through her mind. Surely she relived it over and over, hell I did and I only witnessed some of it.

"He's nice, so is aunt Gloria. All the kids are nice,

and aunt Gloria, she sure can cook."

I laughed, because one of my guilts was wondering if they were eating good, I mean I knew they were, yet their faces would flash in my mind throughout the day, thinking of those bologna sandwiches and all of our dislike for having to eat them.

"No more bologna?" I asked

" No." Becky quietly said.

"Us too, no more bologna. That's a good thing huh?" I asked.

"How are the boys?" Becky asked.

"They're good, they're outside playing." I assured her.

"Oh ok, well I guess we'll see ya!"

"Ok." I said. "And y'all mind Aunt Gloria and Uncle David."

"We will."

And with that they just hung up.

I wasn't sure whether to cry for them or be happy. One thing was certain. Dad surely wouldn't go trying to harm Becky while they were at aunt Gloria's. Not that uncle David was a bad ass that could kick dad's ass, but one thing dad didn't want was his kids back. And should he go trying to throw his weight at Uncle David's house, well he could very well find himself being escorted away with his kids.

Dad wasn't stupid he wasn't about to rock the boat. Uncle David was doing a good thing for his wife's brothers kids. And if the worst thing Becky and

Carrie would have to endure at Gloria's was uncle David's intimidating and timely snap of his fingers, to shut every one up, then hey, that was well worth having to endure.

I was sad for my sisters, but then again I was happy for them. They were eating good, they had a roof over their heads, and they were safe.

For that I was pleased.

I stayed at Mary's awhile talking with Katy. She took me to her room to show me her elaborate collection of Barbie dolls.

She was the only girl and it just seemed she had every doll ever made. Her room was tidy and had more toys than I had seen at the department store when I had gone Christmas shopping with mom. Katy proudly showed off all her things. This was a room I was sure no one was ever allowed in.

Katy was the perfect little girl. She didn't really like to play with all the boys. At least not as much as Lori. Aunt Mary encouraged her to play outside with the other kids but it seemed Katy preferred to be inside with her mom.

Katy, it seemed, possessed every toy a little girl could ever dream of owning, from dolls to miniature stove and ice box, to a little vanity to put her pretend make-up on. Yes, a little girls paradise. But she just seemed to be lost without Lori there to play with her.

25

When I got back to Matty's Sher was still on the phone, laughing and carrying on. What the hell do people talk about so much on a phone? I wondered.

Hi and bye is all I'd say, I suppose.

I went to the kitchen to fix myself a sandwich. But this time no bologna and for sure no damn watered down Ovaltine. It was turkey breast, chips and a soda. This, though simple, seemed a delicacy.

Sher saw me preparing my food.

"Make me some." Sher yelled from the living room.

Initially I was gonna refuse her loud demand, but what the heck, I sure didn't want to start a fight with ol bossy, so I obliged my queen sister's demand.

Sher ate in the living room so she could remain on the phone. I sat in the kitchen at the small breakfast table and ate alone.

Sher and I spent most of the day going back and forth to Mary's to hang out with the boys.

I told Sher of my conversation with Becky and Carrie, which prompted her to phone them the second we got back to Matty's.

A smile on Sher's face as she talked first to Carrie, then a horribly sad look as she talked to Becky.

I looked away from Sher as she talked to Becky. I was afraid her conversation was getting too intense and she may cry, then her embarrassment of me seeing her cry would only have her wanting to beat the crap out of me for not looking away.

Pretending to be thirsty and wanting ice cold water, I went to the kitchen just to get away from Sher's haunting looks.

Ten perhaps fifteen minutes on the phone with our sisters, Sher hung up and went directly to the restroom. I knew exactly what she was doing.

She was trying to wipe away her tears before I could see them.

Didn't Sher know what a fuckin coward I was? I would never call her out where her emotional side was concerned.

Hey, if she got teary eyed over our sisters, then good for her. But I knew I was not about to get in a wrestling match with Sher, one I knew for a fact I could not, would not, ever win.

Trust me, Sher had every bit of privacy from me she would ever want. This here little dumb ass girl knew when she was defeated. I didn't need to have her prove she could kick my ass. It was an understatement I would never ever in my lifetime want to prove wrong.

Eventually Matty then Lori returned. Lori wasn't out of her dad's truck ten seconds and she wanted to go to Mary's.

"No, Lori tomorrow is school. We need to get you ready." Matty insisted.

Lori put up a small fight, expecting to get her way but as I say Matty played no baby games with Lori.

As we were getting ready to go to bed, Sher lay down on her bed, and said "I forgot to tell you, I saw Ray yesterday."

"Where?" I asked.

"He was at the house."

"What house?" I stupidly asked.

"Ours dummy." Sher rolled her eyes, like I was the stupidest fuckin kid in the world. And boy did I feel like the stupidest fuckin kid in the world.

"What was he doing there?" I asked.

"He said he was on his way to get dad from the hospital, and he stopped by to "Investigate."

"Isn't that the cops job?" Again another stupid question I asked.

"Really Malina, you really think the cops give a shit about him?"

I did not say one word in response to her.

"Yep he was looking all over the place." She said.

"Did he find anything?" I asked.

"Well he didn't find a written confession, if that's what you're wondering?

Damn this bitch was a smart ass...No I was not wondering, remember this is your fucking daddy Sher. I just have his name, or so I always felt. Again Malina ain't no dumb ass.

As with dad and Ray I would cuss the mother fuckers to hell and back, in my mind only. And considering Sher had been a bit bitchy herself lately I was doing the same with her, perhaps she sensed what I was doing, but she, like dad, could prove nothing. So again in my mind, I'll say whatever the fuck I please and no mother fuckers gonna tell me different.

Yes, I was scared she would figure me out, so with Sher I tried to control my thoughts, knowing damn good and well my facial expressions were gonna give me away one day.

Sher looked at me like, Ok, I'm sorry I'm being a bitch, yet she sent no apologies my way.

"He did in fact find a bullet casing." Sher said.

"What is that?" Old dumb ass Malina just had to ask.

"It's part of the bullet, the part that flys out of the gun when you shoot it".. She sounded like she knew just what she was talking about. Of course.

"How scary. I feel sorry for the person that did this." I said.

"Yeah me too." Sher said.

"You know Ray's gonna do what ever he has to do to kill whoever." She said.

"Yes I know, and that's scary," I said

"Ray said it wasn't a professional hit." She said.

"What's that?" I asked.

"In other words, who ever shot dad wasn't a professional killer." Sher explained.

"How the heck does Ray know that?" I asked.

"Because dad isn't dead." Sher explained.

"If there had been a contract out on dad, either by another gangster or possibly a cop, dad would be dead right now. The fact that he is alive showed that it was a dumb ass, that did it, according to Ray." Sher said.

"And for that Ray doesn't want us around there for awhile. He says that person or persons could just go back anytime."

"That's really scary." I said.

"Yes, it's also because Ray is a "Mean mother" she stopped. Then laughed to herself. Then I also laughed.

"Why you laughing? Sher asked.

"Cause Ray is so damn loud, I can't imagine him creeping up on anyone."

"Yes." Sher laughed out loud. "Except maybe a deaf person." We both laughed.

Seems Ray "Tha Killer" was on his own to find a would be assassin. The love he had for dad, his determination to find the idiot that shot dad, and his killer instinct, it was definite, he would never give up.

26

It was time to prepare for school.
Yes, I hated school, even more now, but I knew there was no way of getting out of it.
Sher already in bed, Matty and Lori also asleep I did the routine of preparing my things, got me a snack then went to bed.

My mom's face in my mind as I lay in the dark, thinking of how busy her life had been with all six kids, dad's bullshit ways, and ironing and sewing everyone's clothes.
It seemed she never had time to rest or time for herself. I remembered a few days after she died, when I was laying on my bed, she came to me, so it seemed, and promised me she would return.
I knew she would not return in the flesh, but hoped she would return in my thoughts, in my dreams.
She did return, just as we were leaving our house. And that, no matter what any one ever tries to tell me, was real.

I closed my eyes, and cried. I whispered her name several times hoping that if I said mama enough, I would be blessed with her return. The loneliness just never left my heart.
I thought of the life I had, all the pain, missing my mom, thoughts of my dad and all his gangsters and I

thought for a second, how different it now felt to sleep in a house that had no apparent danger.

Perhaps this is how most people sleep. It sure wasn't how my mom got to sleep, ever. So for the third night in a row, in a new place to call home, I cried myself to sleep

When I woke the next morning, Matty and Lori were just leaving. Sher was already in the shower. I lay in my bed a few moments dreading the school day ahead.

I considered faking being sick as I had so many times in the past, but what point would I prove. I didn't have my mom to fake being sick for so I could stay home. Now to fake would just be so meaningless.

Sher came out of the restroom very quickly, like she had seen a ghost or something, then glanced over at me.

"Hurry if you want to walk with me to school." She seemed to growl.

I covered my head, so as to not see the look on Sher's face, which was a dead ringer for dad's when he'd just be getting home and be in a very bad mood.

I almost stupidly made a comment to that fact, but covered my own mouth cause I knew once I opened my mouth Sher would pounce on me.

Getting on Sher's bad side at seven-thirty on a Monday morning wasn't exactly what I had planned for the day, so I said nothing, did nothing.

Now, I know I could have faked being sick for thirty minutes or so, just till Sher left the house so I didn't have to deal with her "Johnny Guetarro" mood.

I more or less crawled out of bed dragging myself to the restroom, Sher in the kitchen, I'm assuming fixing herself breakfast.

By the time I got out of the restroom, she was fixing her hair.

"Are you coming?" She asked.

I looked down at my clothes, which was still my pajamas, but I didn't say anything.

"Damn Malina, hurry up." Sher growled.

Now keep in mind, this was ol bossy, and though she could very well beat me up with no effort at all, not even if this bitch did hit me was I going to school in my Pj's just because she didn't have any desire at all to wait on me.

I mean seriously, I just friken woke up. I barely had time to wash my face and brush my teeth. Did she expect me to just walk out the door dressed the way I was? Not put a brush through my hair? Go barefoot?

Sure I friken hated school, but there is no way I would go looking like more of a damn fool then I already did.

"Sher you can go on without me. I'm gonna make me some cereal, brush my hair and then get dressed. Go on, I can get to school by myself. I'm not a baby."

I cringed for a second suspecting she may throw her brush at me, or any object she could get her hands on, cause I sure as hell wasn't looking her in the eye when I became so fucking brave so early in the morning.

Oh no, what had I said? Damn Malina, you and your big mouth.

Actually I was tempted to say "Bitch don't fuck with me this early in the morning! Get the fuck outta here and go on to school with out me."

But come on now, you all know there was no way I would talk shit to Sher. It was just a stupid thought.

"Oh really now?" She said.

Yikers, what the hell, did I just think something out loud that she actually heard?

Then out of no where she smiled and said. "Ok."

Almost too fricken happy not to have to wait on me, walk with me or be seen with me for that matter.

I was relieved when she left. There was no need to rush me or be rude, we had plenty of time to get to school, and by the way, we were a mere three blocks from the school, but to bring that subject up would only have insulted her intelligence.

The fact that I was a wimp all my life, pretty much kept me from voicing my feelings. But one thing was certain. I hated hearing anyone cussing and talking shit first thing in the morning.

With mom it was always "Good morning" hugs, kisses and smiles no matter how rough her life with dad was. She never took her frustrations with dad out on her kids.

Dad on the other hand began and ended every day with "What the fuck" "Are you stuuuuupid or what?"

"Where the fuck is......" Well you get the idea.

Needless to say, a very fucked up way to begin any morning. I hated hearing his bitching mouth first thing in the morning, but like I said being a wimpy ass kid, there was no way to voice my feelings.

Now here before me was Sher, a mini reenactment of my dad's behavior. Of course I would not ever say anything to Sher, but I damn sure could talk shit in my mind.

Seems to me, or so my theory goes, the way you begin your day, is pretty much how it will go all day long. You start it fucked up, it more than likely will be a fucked up day. But if you start it with love and kindness, well seems you pretty much got a running start on a positive day. Right???

Of course in our household no matter how many good mornings and hugs we got from mom, dad always fucked that happy mood up with one evil comment or stare.

I loved my mom's loving attitude every day, I hated his.

This particular morning, though Sher was not as bad as dad, she did seem to have a bit of an attitude, one I was in no hurry to be a part of.

My decision to put Sher's quick temper behind me for the day would prove to be in my favor. It was enough that I hated school, but to hate it because of Sher's behavior, nope I wasn't gonna let it ruin my day.

So Sher rushed out of the house as if she were

three hours late. I looked at the clock, it was seven fifty. I still had fifty minutes to get ready and get to school, because the bell didn't ring till eight forty.

I went in and made me some cereal, and a glass of orange juice. What a fricken simple ass thing to do. I know damn good and well it was not costly because I could see the price tag on the cereal, milk and orange juice.

What a fuckin shame. I thought. Probably the cost of two beers at Sal E's Bar. All dad would have to do was not purchase a few beers or a joint or two and his kids could have had some kind of descent breakfasts.

My poor unfortunate mom, I thought to myself as I finished my breakfast.

Starting my day off remembering what a fuckin jerk my dad was, was not a good beginning to my day. I put my dad out of my mind and realized Sher wasn't being a bitch to me per say, she just didn't want to have a twerpy kid hanging around her and she sure as hell didn't want to wait around on me, when she could spend that extra time where she really wanted to be. .

Sher wasn't following in her daddy's foot steps, she was just being Sher.

I cleaned my dishes, went in to get dressed, then fixed my hair, and got dressed.

While I was making my bed I noticed Sher had left her makeup on her night stand.

Now don't ask me why but like a curious little stupid ass kid, I decided to put a tiny bit of it on.

I had never worn makeup before but I had watched Sher put hers on, not that she needed it, but I did, for sure.

First I put a tiny bit of foundation, Sher was lighter skinned than me so if I put too much on surely I'd look too much like a fricken clown, so I went easy on the foundation. I then applied some lipstick, not a lot, just enough to make my lips glossy, then a touch of blush and some mascara.

Ok, all my life it was a fact that I was always the "Ugly Duckling." Come on my nickname was "Changa" "Monkey." I was flat chested, had hairy arms and hairy legs and I weighed ninety pounds. I was always skinny, and really I never cared about my appearance at all. I wasn't Sher beautiful and built. I was the fricken ugly duckling and I knew it. So, what's the big deal, if, out of curiosity, I put on some of Sher's make-up.

For a second, I really liked what I saw when I looked in the mirror, then I thought of Sher seeing me in the hallway, knowing damn good and well I owned no makeup of my own.

A vision of her drilling me in front of everyone about getting into her personal things, talking shit to me in front of all her friends and my one friend, I would be humiliated beyond words.

Fuck this, I thought.

I got enough problems without my own sister talking smack to me in front of everyone.

So as I went in to the restroom to wash my face, the phone rang.

I answered it. "Hello."

"Hi Malina. Are y'all about ready for school?" It was Matty.

"Yes, I was just about to leave." I said.

"Ok. I just wanted to make sure y'all were awake." Matty said.

"Yes. Sher's already gone." I answered.

"Ok, see you this afternoon." Matty said.

"Ok." My response.

"Bye." Matty said.

"Bye." I said and hung up.

I grabbed my purse and with twenty minutes before the bell, I walked the three blocks to school alone, slowly.

27

I arrived at the school with at least thirteen minutes before the bell would ring. I sat alone on the steps in front of the school near the parking lot, watching the students arrive.

Some would be smiling, happy and excited like this school thing was the happiest time of their lives. Exactly the way I knew Sher felt about school.

I watched one guy get out of the car he was a passenger in, he looked in the mirror and tried to plaster his hair down with his hand, looking like he had just woke up, got in his mom's car without any consideration for his appearance, and arrived at school, hating the fact that he had to be there. He got out of the car and just slammed the car door while, I assume it was his mom, tried to say good-bye to him.

You fucking disrespectful little bastard, I thought to my self. How dare you be so mean to your mom.

He mumbled something hateful about her as he walked past me. If I had been a guy I would have kicked his damn ass for being such a fucking jerk.

I sat there and I sat there, finally the bell rang, and as I entered the school Donna and Greg caught up with me.

"Come on Malina, let's skip school today." Donna said, as we watched a group of kids walking the opposite direction of the school, off to skip for the entire day.

"Heck no, are you crazy?" I asked her.

"Chicken!" Donna laughed.

"Hell yeah." I said. "My sister will kick my ass."

"That a fact." Greg laughed as he walked backwards away from us, yet waiting to hear Donna's answer.

Donna looked at me then looked at Greg, then she smiled a great big smile.

"Naw." She said "I'm gonna be a good girl today."

"Y'all's loss." Greg said.

"Looking good Malina." He said as he turned around and ran to catch up with the group of kids that were running away from the school.

I wondered for a brief second why he said that. I had no love interest in Greg, he seemed kind of sissyish to me.

Donna and I hurried into the school promising to meet at our Home Economics class.

"Love your make-up." Donna yelled as she ran in the direction of her class.

I froze for a second, touched my face, remembering I was about to wash my face when Matty called.

Today, thinking back, I reminded myself of Kevin on "Home Alone," when he applies the after shave, and with both hands on his face, screams as loud as he can because it burns so damn bad...

Well, for a second that was me. Though I didn't scream, I stood there, hands on my face, mouth wide open, fearing for my life, or worse, Sher would approach me as I was standing there.

I looked at the hall clock that hung from the ceiling in the middle of the hallway. Two minutes before the tardy bell would ring. There was no time to go to the girl's restroom and clean my face.

Oh my, I stood frozen undecided as to what to do. Even if I could get to the restroom and wipe some of it off, I ran the risk of smearing the mascara and looking like a bigger dumb ass.

I stood in the hallway for at least ten more seconds, my thoughts not on the make-up but my thoughts on Sher catching me with it on, recognizing her own lipstick and calling me out in front of everyone.

I would be mortified.

What the fuck was I gonna do? Dealing with Sher would be a lot worse on me than any damn tardy bell.

I wondered if I could avoid Sher all day long.

Nope, impossible.

Should I run out of the school and go home.

Why would you do that Malina, it's just make-up?

I needed to make a decision, my class was up one flight of stairs and I had one minuet left.

Tic toc tic toc....

"Oh fuck it," and I ran up the stairs as fast as my legs could carry me to my first class.

Why did I have to be so fricken curious? Why didn't I just leave Sher's shit alone and come to school like a normal nerd?

Who the hell was I trying to impress? I didn't have a boyfriend, no boys were interested in me. And with my tomboyish body I wondered did I look like a skinny boy with make-up on trying to look like a skinny girl with make-up on?

I was frantic.

I walked into my class with my head down, hoping no one would notice me. Of course no one would notice dumbass, no one ever did, why should today be any different?

After all, I wasn't the varsity head cheerleader, I was Malina, the least popular kid in the school.

Why was I so frightened?

I sat at my desk. My teacher Mr. Williams, my English teacher smiled at me.

Why is he smiling? I wondered. He never smiles at me, he never even acknowledges me at all. Hell I bet he doesn't even know if I can speak English or not cause he never talks to me, he has never once asked me any questions in this damn class, now he wants to smile at me.

Bastard, I thought. Damn flirting ass bastard.

No, I didn't mean that at all, he was about the nicest man ever, and actually he was kinda cute for an older guy, I think he was twenty nine or thirty.

Hey! To me he was older.

"Oh Malina calm down, you just have a touch of make-up on, you're not wearing make-up as the silent movie actresses wore."

Calm down.!!!!

Seems I avoided looking at every person in the school as I passed them in the hallway.

Donna met me at my locker during the next passing period.

"Is it too much?" I asked her.

"Too much what?" She asked.

"Make-up." I pointed to my face.

"No crazy, it's perfect. You look great." She smiled.

"Actually it's about time you made your pretty face come alive." She said.

"Are you sure it is not too much?" I sounded too desperate.

"Compared to what?" She said. "Not wearing any at all." She laughed.

"I don't know, I'm just embarrassed."

"What the heck are you embarrassed about. Don't worry, you look great." Donna sounded reassuring.

With seconds before the tardy bell Donna and I walked into our home-ec class together.

I had never noticed Donna's make-up or any of the girls in my classes, or any of my teachers for that matter. Now I completely concentrated on all their faces.

Damn was I the only dumb ass in high school that didn't wear make-up? I mean I wasn't ugly like creepy ugly without make-up, I guess I just looked homely, Carrie homely.

Donna was right, it did look nice, I looked different. I saw myself in a mirror in our home ec class. Not too bad I thought. Not to fricken bad.

Slowly during the morning classes some of the make-up wore off. By lunch I still had some but not like I had at nine in the morning.

Donna and I were enjoying our lunch and as luck, mostly bad luck would have it, Sher walked into the cafeteria. She didn't have lunch at the same time as me, so what the hell was she doing out of her own class, and what was she doing in the cafeteria?

I panicked when I saw her coming toward me, wondering, which of these big mouth bitches went and told Sher I was wearing makeup, and now she was gonna force me to take it all off right there in the cafeteria in front of everyone.

She was just passing through she said, "Mrs. Crow is going to help me find a job." She giggled like a little kid. She was so excited. Her mean pissed off mood from earlier in the morning, now vanished, and turned into smiles and happiness.

"Good." I said. Feeling really happy for Sher knowing darn good and well getting a job is exactly what Sher needed to occupy her free time.

She grabbed at my food, then said "See you twerps later." And took off as fast as she could to get to her class.

Me and Donna laughed at how quickly her long legs got her out of the cafeteria.

I sat there completely relieved that she did not humiliate me in front of my only friend. And not to mention the hundreds of kids all around us that would have been watching to see what Sher was gonna do, and then, the even more humiliated I would have been when they all would have begun laughing at me.

Oh Lordy, thank you Sher for not making me look and feel stupider than I already did.

Another delicious meal in the school cafeteria.

I had often heard kids bitch about how awful the cafeteria food was. I never ate it before because we always had taken sack lunches. But with this free lunch program the government initiated, I really didn't understand all the bitchin about the food. It was pretty damn good. But then it would be good compared to those fucked up bologna sandwiches we were forced to eat.

Hey even Donna scarfed her lunch down, so I knew it wasn't all that bad.

Donna and I sat and talked as we ate, wondering what Greg was doing.

"Probably getting fucked up." She said.

"Whatttt?" I asked.

"Yeah, that's all they do at these skipping parties is smoke weed and drink." Donna said matter-of-factly, as she looked around the cafeteria, then her eyes met mine. "Malina please tell me you have skipped school before?" Donna asked.

I shook my head no.

"You have to be kidding." She smiled.

"No, I'm not." I answered.

"Such a good little girl." She laughed as we both went to drop our lunch trays at the designated counter.

We were about to leave the cafeteria, when we heard a ruckus going on in the corner of the cafeteria near the juke box.

At first I couldn't see anything but a group of kids huddled together.

Then I saw him.

There stood Screwy. Laughing, with all his stupid friends, huddled around a bunch of girls, and of course, Screwy right in the middle of everyone.

I shook my head and laughed.

Still the damn class clown, I thought.

28

When school let out I didn't know whether to wait on Sher, as I had done everyday or, since we lived so close to the school, just go on home and meet up with her there.

I waited and waited, and when I was just about to leave, Sher came running, still in her P.E. clothes.

"You can go on home sista, I'm staying after school. If Matty gets home before I do, tell her I'll talk to her when I get there."

"Ok." I said.

"Will you be ok?" Sher asked.

I know I looked at her kinda funny, because she said. "Ok, I suppose you'll be fine walking alone."

Did she not remember just this morning her hasty departure, and though it had always been dad's golden rule that none of his daughters walk to or from school alone, Sher and I had just seven hours earlier, broke that damn rule.

Well we sure weren't gonna wait on him or Ray to drive us to school. So we did what we had to do. And I sure as hell wasn't gonna snitch on Sher for leaving this morning with out me. It just seemed to work out for both of us.

Oh to hell with dad's rules.

When I got to Matty's I realized she hadn't given me or Sher a key to the front door, so I went to Mary's.

Mary and the kids weren't home either, so I waited on aunt Mary's front porch, which had plenty of shade and lawn chairs to sit and relax.

Within ten minutes Mary arrived with all the kids, looking like an after school daycare unloading from her car. Mary smiled when she saw me on the porch, so did all six of the kids.

Danny and J.J. were the first to reach me and hug me, then came Lori and Katy. Jake and Mark pretty much ignored me, they were just to grown for that huggy stuff.

They were all excited and talking at once as Mary unlocked the door. The kids scrambled to go back inside, only to run straight through the house and exit out the back patio door.

Mary called Katy back in to change her school clothes. Within three minutes she had changed and ran back out the patio door to play with Lori.

Mary's back yard had beautiful grass, a swing set for the kids to play on, a sand box and even a seesaw. It was a child's luxury playground for sure. I could see why the kids preferred to be out doors rather than inside.

Mary made juice and cookies and asked me to take it out to the kids. An afternoon snack she would give them every afternoon, enough to hold them off until supper time.

Danny and J.J. probably thought this was their supper because they ate it as if it was their last meal of the day. So cute, so adorable, I smiled at them as they gobbled down their cookies and juice. All the kids laughing and enjoying being out doors having fun.

My brothers so damn precious, so excited and happier then I had seen them in quite awhile.

I took the plastic cups back in and the crumbs of cookies that were left.

"Would you like some Malina." Aunt Mary asked.

"No thanks Aunt Mary."

"Surely you're hungry?" She asked.

"No, I'm ok." I said.

"Well the juice is in the refrigerator if you change you mind, and the cookies will be in the cookie jar."

I just smiled at her.

Mary went directly to the kitchen to begin, or finish supper she had started earlier in the day.

Aunt Mary went to school two evenings a week. She would leave promptly at six and return at nine fifteen. She was going to school to become a hair dresser.

At first uncle George wasn't happy about it because he wanted her home when he came from work. But eventually gave in if supper was ready and he didn't have to do it himself. After all, he did work ten hours a day and he sure didn't feel like cooking once he got home.

So Mary agreed she would have the kids fed and his supper on the stove two nights a week so she could begin a career.

Uncle earned plenty of money to support his

family.. It wasn't about the money Aunt Mary would say.

"I want to have a career."

"You have one uncle would tease. Raising the kids, taking care of me."

But Mary would insist that she wanted more, and he eventually gave in.

Mary would attend school on Monday and Thursdays. The exact second uncle would walk in the house, she would be leaving, enough time only for a kiss on the cheek, and "I'll see you at nine."

By the time Mary would get home at nine, the kids would already be in bed for school the next day.

It was obvious uncle did his fair share. They pretty much had a routine, they followed and it worked for all of them.

I offered to help Mary with her dinner since after all, she was feeding my two little brothers. She asked me to peel potatoes, I did.

As I was peeling the potatoes Katy came in looking very exhausted.

"Mommy it's too hot." Katy complained.

Mary laughed because she knew Katy wouldn't remain outside too long. She was an indoor type of kid. Yes, she ran out and frolicked around because Lori was out there. But Katy couldn't keep up with all those kids.

Flushed, sweating and thirsty she sat on the sofa as Mary babied her.

Just as I finished the potatoes aunt Matty walked

in.

There was no ringing of the doorbell, or knocking on the door, Matty just walked in Mary's house as Mary would just walk into Matty's house. They were close like that. "My house is your house" was their motto, each feeling completely comfortable at the others house.

As Matty walked in she looked directly at me and said, "I completely forgot to give you this." Waving a house key at me.
I smiled at her.
"Don't loose it." As she handed it to me.
"Lori in the back?" Matty asked Mary.
"Yes." Mary said, reminding Matty Lori was going to grow up a tomboy because Katy would not stay outside but a few moments and Lori refused to come inside and play with Katy's girly things.
Katy liked playing with dishes and dolls, and having tea parties and such. Not Lori, she wanted to be running around and rolling in the dirt. She was literally one of the guys.
We laughed, aunt Matty saying "Then I'm gonna change her name to Larry."
We were laughing as Lori ran in.
"What are you laughing at mommy?" Lori asked.
"Nothing Larry, I mean Lori." We laughed thinking how funny it was that it was Lori that came in instead of any of the boys just as we were making fun of her.
"Where's Sher Malina?" Matty asked.

"She stayed after school, some P.E. thing." I responded.

"Ok, well, I'm going home." Matty said as she grabbed her purse and keys..

"I'll go with you." I told her.

"Lori you coming"? Matty yelled to Lori who was about to go back outside to play with all the boys.

"Nope, I wanna play some more." Lori said.

Matty and I went home, I put my school things away, Matty changing her work clothes, then went directly to the kitchen to prepare supper.

I did everything possible to help her. I couldn't imagine how tough it would be to work all day then come home and have to cook. I wondered if it weren't for me and Sher would Matty and Lori just eat at Mary's rather than cook a complete meal herself. I wasn't sure how they normally did things, I just didn't want Matty any more inconvenienced than necessary.

Just minutes before we finished Sher walked in hot, tired, sweaty, and smiling from ear to ear.

"Almost ready." Matty said.

"Thanks aunt Matty." Sher said still smiling.

"I think I'm gonna take a shower first." Sher said.

"Ok." Matty said.

"Will you go get Lori, Malina, so we can eat." Matty asked me.

Without hesitation I started toward Mary's.

As I walked across the street to get Lori, I could smell Matty and Mary's cooking, combination, which

sent such an exciting aroma through the air.
It sure smells good out here I thought.
Just as I got to Mary's yard, uncle George drove up. He got out of his truck just as I was approaching the stairs to the front door.
"Hello Malina, how's it goin?"
"Good." I said. "How is it for you?" I asked.
He looked at me, laughed and said "real noisy."
We both laughed knowing his two sons were already hyper enough without the extra loudness and hyperness of Danny and J.J..

Uncle had a funny laugh, kinda high pitched, and if you weren't already laughing with him, you would definitely be laughing at him. His laugh was just that funny.

He was a pleasant man, that worked very hard every day to support his family. Once home, he would work around the house doing anything Mary needed done. She never had to ask twice. She just said "George, I need this or that done" and within minutes uncle would get right to it.
If he wasn't working at his day job or working around their house or yard he would sit and watch TV eating his dinner, then sit all alone and watch TV till late at night, never bothering anyone.
Uncle was pretty much a role model husband until he got drunk, which, rumor has it would be occasional, and a bit on the dramatic side.
I myself never saw uncle do anything but take

care of his family and work. But I do remember hearing my mom talking to Mary on the phone occasionally trying to comfort Mary on the nights uncle wouldn't come home directly after work. I remember mom telling her to come to our house if she were frightened, because, as mom said, uncle would not dare go to our house and start trouble knowing he would have my dad on his ass.

Aunt Mary always knew when it was one of those weekends that uncle would be getting drunk because, like clock work he was home every evening at six p.m. sharp, on the dot. If he wasn't home by ten after six then Mary knew he had ran off with his co workers for an afternoon drink.
Only problem, uncle didn't know how to drink one drink and stop. He would continue until he got plastered, then would go home and attempt to torment Mary and his kids.
I never thought of uncle as semi cloned after my own dad, and I especially didn't know uncle ever put his hands on Mary.
I really didn't know exactly what he did wrong only the mixed up stories everyone would say behind his back. But when sober, you couldn't find a kinder man.
Today he was fine.

We walked in together, as Katy ran to him and hugged him. She lit up when she saw her dad, and vice versa.

As I went to the back to get Lori, Mary began serving uncle his dinner. Uncle went directly to the kitchen sink to wash his hands, because as he would say, he hadn't had a bite to eat since he ate his lunch at noon, and by the time he got home, it would be six hours since he ate, and he would be starving by that time.

I could understand why he wanted Mary home, he looked exhausted, but the smell in the air of Mary's food had him smiling as he sat down to eat.

They exchanged compliments, him saying "This sure looks good Mary." And Mary returning the conversation with "How was your day George."

Quite honestly they seemed the perfect happily married couple.

I got sad remembering the only time my dad was nice like that to my mom, it seemed he had to be stoned.

Was uncle stoned? Did he need to be stoned to be so kind to his wife?

As I walked back through the dining room with Lori, an overwhelming urge to sniff the air to see if there was the aroma of marijuana. Actually the only scent in the air was that of Mary's good home cooked food, and with that, my conclusion was... my uncle was not stoned, he was just a nice man.

We walked across the street, as we did I was convinced there would be no dealing with, marijuana, cussing, hitting, ass whoopins, and all the things that had been forced in my life.. Things I did not miss, things I would never miss.

The only thing I did miss was my mom and her love. This could never be replaced by anyone no matter how hard they tried..

29

Once dinner was over, Sher got on the phone, Lori went back to Mary's and Matty was in her room.

I sat looking out the window in the living room, remembering it was Monday night. Mary's car was still in her driveway. It appeared she hadn't gone to school because her car and uncle George's truck were still there.

Actually she should have been gone the second uncle got home, then I remembered she was home serving his food at six o'clock, at the same time I was being nosey and sniffing the air in their dining room for the scent of marijuana.

I wondered if everything was ok because for about six months now she had been going to school regularly. The day she got accepted into this beauty school, so they were called, she went to our house and told mom all about it.

I remember watching them as Mary talked about all her dreams of owning her own place one day. I remember the look in mom's eyes as she listened.

Now I wonder did mom secretly think of having her own career, her own sense of accomplishment.

Sure, being a mom was the highlight of her life, should be for any mom, but then again she didn't have a husband that would encourage her to engage herself in a self accomplished career.

No, I'd bet my fricken life mom never voiced any desire to do anything outside our home. For dad, being his wife was all she needed. Yet a little bit of hope behind those beautiful green eyes, always had me hoping better things for her.

Six months later all her hopes and dreams were buried with her, right along side, were my dreams.

Later that night as we proceeded with our nightly schedule of preparing for school and bath schedule I went to Matty and asked her why aunt Mary hadn't gone to school.

"She's gonna take off a few weeks." Matty said.

"Is it because of Danny and J.J.?" I asked.

She hesitated a few minutes then she said. "Mary wants to give the boys time to adjust."

Well it seemed like a good response to my question, but for some reason I couldn't help but think that wasn't the only reason.

I thought about it a long time. It's a given, Jake and Mark were very hyper and rambunctious I guess you could say. I didn't wanna say loud ass fricken hyper kids but in all seriousness that's exactly what they were. And I'm not saying Danny and J.J. weren't loud and a handful, but they were raised to calm it down when instructed to, mostly because they were so friken afraid of my dad, if he yelled to them to be quiet, they obeyed, mostly out of fear.

Yes, boys will be boys but I have to admit all four boys together, were just too fricken much. They weren't all bad in any way, they were just frickin loud.

Then it hit me. These kids were all a bit much for

Mary and she didn't work all day. So to expect uncle to come home after a long days work and deal with a bunch of loud kids...Naw no way. But surely he would not want aunt Mary to just quit school? She only had about six months before she would graduate.

Matty couldn't watch them, she also worked all day and would be too tired to deal with them. Sher couldn't do it, she had too many after school activities, and they very well couldn't be left alone.

The alternative here was me.

But why hadn't anyone asked me? It was after all only two days a week.

I could do it.

I would do it.

Could it be everyone thought my delicate emotional outbursts had me too stressed already to be able to control four boys.

I thought of aunt Matty and how hard she had worked. I thought of uncles sacrifices, then I thought of my brothers. I didn't want anyone to sacrifice more than they already had just so they could have a place to live. Besides, it's not like I had anything to do seven nights a week. I had no social life as Sher and Matty did. I didn't work as Matty and uncle did. And I hated school, where as Mary loved her school.

So I went in to talk to Matty.

She listened as I asked questions and volunteered my services of babysitting.

After discussing it with me for about thirty

minutes she called Mary and told her we were going over to talk to her.

Mary and uncle were sitting in the living room when we arrived.

I asked Mary why she hadn't gone to school and she confirmed what Matty said, she was taking off to give the boys time to adjust. All of them.

I asked her if she needed me to help out with the kids.

I'm no damn fool, I thought, of course they need help, this is four young hyper boys we're talking about.

"Malina, you see how wild all four of them are?"

That was true, but you don't just quit school and you don't put all this off on your husband that has been working all day.

It's a fact uncle had to watch his own kids while Mary was in school, but he was just too tired to deal with all of them and you couldn't very well tie Danny and J.J. up.

Matty came up with a solution.

On Mondays, I would go to Mary's house and stay there and help out with the kids. It would still be uncle's job to tend to his three but I would help out with keeping the kids quiet if uncle wanted to take a nap or work around the house.

On Thursdays I would take J.J. and Danny with me to Matty's to give uncle a break from them all.

Of course Lori would love it because she would have the boys at her house now to play with.

The plan seemed suitable for everyone.

Matty, Mary and George all agreed I would do my fair share. Mary thanked me and said she was still going take off that week, wanting all the boys to adjust to one another.

When we walked back to Matty's she asked me what made me think of everything.

I told her that I knew Mary left at six and when I noticed she was still home after seven I figured there was a problem.

"I didn't think it would be right for Mary to stop going to school just because of Danny and J.J."

"It really isn't because of them." Matty said.

But it was and we both knew it.

I couldn't just stand by and let Mary's dreams go down the tubes because of my brothers. If they weren't there I know damn good and well she would be at school at that very moment. I just couldn't sit back and not help out.

30

And so our routines began.

Sher with school, Matty with her job. I now had my schedule, helping out with all the kids and hating school, but enjoying my friendship with Donna and Greg.

Monday through Friday I'd get to school only moments before the bell would ring because I never really felt the point of being at school any sooner than absolutely necessary. Usually Donna would be waiting on me, sometimes just Donna, sometimes Donna and Greg.

On several occasions Greg would cut a class or two, other times he wouldn't come to school at all.

Every time he skipped he would ask me and Donna to skip with him, every time I'd decline.

Sometimes Donna would hesitate, then she would say. "Naw, can't let Malina eat lunch alone, then everyone will think she's a nerd."

Bitch, I am a nerd I would think to myself.

We had been at Matty's for a few weeks when Sher finally got the news from Mrs. Crow, the school assistant vice principal, that she was going to help Sher find a job.

School was almost over for the day, when Mrs. Crow called Sher into her office to give her the good news. Sher actually started crying, I know because I was walking past the office and saw her.

Hold on let me reword that, wouldn't want to give the wrong impression of Sher. She was not crying crying, she was teary eyed crying. Can't give the impression Sher was a wimp, could I?

This is the news Sher had been waiting almost a month for. Now the opportunity she would have, not only that she had been a grown up caring for five kids, but now to actually have a grown up job, earn herself her own money, have some real independence.

Yes, this is what she needed. The new chapter in Sher's life. I was excited for her.

Sher was never a greedy stingy person, the heart she possessed I knew she would not be stingy with her earnings. Give a little, take care of her brothers and sister.

Any one could tell she was about to bust with excitement.

We left the office together and walked home. She talked of nothing but her new job, which would be a weekend only job at a department store downtown.

Mrs. Crow didn't want Sher working on school days for fear it would interfere with her school work.

Sher talked of riding the bus to work if aunt Matty couldn't take her. She seemed perfectly fine with it. She would have to dress nicely because she was going to work in the men's department and she couldn't wear just any old thing.

Sher talked of making herself some new clothes

with mom's sewing machine. She talked of buying herself new clothes to wear to work. She talked of going to a store that sold material only, so she would have a large selection to choose from. She bragged so excitedly of all the skirts and dresses she would make for all of us, not just for herself. Now that she would have money of her own she could afford to buy descent material and make all our clothes.

It sounded nice, and exciting, and though I knew if anyone could do it, Sher could, but I wondered when she would find the time. I knew Sher very well, and her mind was made up, she would do it even if it meant she had to stay up late every night.

Sher seemed about to burst with excitement. I had never seen her so happy. Months of stress seemed erased from her face, now a glow of happiness and excitement.

When she told Matty of her news Matty was excited for her, and though Matty never asked anything of us, she told Sher just buy necessities that you need, it will be a great help.

That seemed even better for Sher. Now she really had nothing to worry about but shampoo, deodorant, tooth paste, all the non edible items we would need, Sher would now be responsible for. Seemed it was all gonna work out perfectly for everyone. Sher was happy, Matty was happy.

I would hold down the fort as far as helping out with Lori, which made Lori happy.

Eventually, as we all knew, dad got wind of Sher's job, and of course he had to show up at Matty's, not to offer any moral support or a pat on the back for Sher, but to what else? Bitch about it..

I watched him as he carried on, wondering why is he even here? Why can't he say anything nice?
Sher was his fricken favorite, and yet he was carrying on as if she was doing something wrong. Something immoral. I didn't get it with this fucking guy.. Even Matty seemed scared while he was standing there talking non-stop bullshit..
I knew for a fact Matty wasn't about to ask his ass for any money, yet I wondered what was she afraid of.

Usually by now, I would have already pissed my pants with the first syllable coming out his damn mouth. Perhaps I'm to grown to have that fucking reaction to him anymore.
I tried not to think of the days I pissed myself just because I heard his demanding voice, yet all the memories of me pissing and my mom attempting her best to get me out of the room before he actually saw the puddle of piss, or fear he'd see it running down my legs, hit me then she would have to step in for me and suffer an ass whoopin herself.
Yes, a bit of fear on Matty's face, yet I didn't know why. Perhaps as his youngest sister, she got picked on by him as a child. Perhaps she too as a young girl was frightened of her own brother. Perhaps the sight

of him brought all her own bad childhood memories to the fore front.

Perhaps, Malina perhaps. Oh shut the fuck up Malina. Why do I do this to myself, I wondered? Why do I think of so many different things that have nothing to do with anything?

I knew exactly why I did it.

The site of my dad, still threw my fucked up life into a frenzy. It was best for me to wander with my thoughts than, to look directly at him and pay attention to anything he had to say.

I quickly excused myself to go to the restroom, knowing his loud voice was about to have me pissing.

I left Sher and Matty to deal with him.

His voice could be heard from the restroom insisting that Sher not work on school days, which Sher was all to happy to let dad know it was already a condition of her getting the job, thinking she wasn't gonna let dad take any of the credit for her conditional job.

Sure enough before I got out of the restroom he was gone. I laughed to myself, then sat on my bed as Sher bragged of her job.

More excited than I had ever seen Sher, she couldn't wait to start her new job.

31

It was Friday afternoon, exactly two weeks after Sher was given her job assignment. Her first day would be orientation.

There, she would learn all she needed to know about working in a department store, helping men pick out just the right look, and operating a cash register.

Maybe it was all of our excitement about Sher getting a job, we really hadn't asked Sher what department store downtown she would be working.

The second we pulled in front of the store to drop Sher off Matty said. "Sher this is the same department store your dad used to work."

I wasn't sure if Sher was going to get back in the car and say forget this, or get out of the car and smile with pride.

Yep, this was the same place my dad would go to work five, sometimes six, days a week as a, get this, a store detective.

Back in the day there were no roaming electronic eyes, no video surveillance, it was one on one detective work. Catch a mother fucker shoplifting and haul his ass in, was dad's only objective.

Dad, as all the other store detectives, would not dress as a civilian shopper, nope these guys stood out, black suit, black tie, white shirt. Actually looking like a gangster before he actually was a well known gangster.

He would brag about "Catching that mother fucker trying to steal." He took his store detective job very serious. I guess even a job so simple as store detective he gave it his all.

As Sher exited the car and said good-by, I recalled mom had taken me with her one day to the very same department store. I recognized the store, though I hadn't seen it for possibly ten years. It seems on that day so long ago, mom had some personal business of dad's that I suppose just couldn't wait till he got home.

Hold up, let me back up a moment.

I'm not sure how old I actually was, but I do recall it was just me and my mom. Perhaps I was six years old, I mean I remember it perfectly just as I remembered the baby Jesus incident in kindergarten, so I know I was about that age, a bit older perhaps.

Mom had kept dad's car that day and got all dressed up. She didn't venture outside the house often and never alone. I suppose that was a golden rule of my dad's, "always carry one of the kids with you for "Safety?" Seems I was fortunate more often then the other kids to be with my mom on such outings.

Mom always looked beautiful with every hair in place, not but a touch of makeup. A pinch of perfume. Perfect fitting dress, just below her knee, just enough to show her beautiful legs.

She wasn't dressed seductively, seems with all her

beauty she just looked that way. She turned heads everywhere she went, not deliberately, it just happened.

Even at home with her hair pulled back in a pony tail and her pedal pushers, ha, today they call them Capri, she still looked absolutely beautiful. Just about every man stared at her, women also for that matter.

That particular day she even got me all dressed up in a dress, and put my long hair in a pony tail.

Memory fails me who was watching the other kids that day, perhaps my grandma or one of my aunts. For some reason it was very important that mom take some papers to dad while he was at work.

We drove to a parking lot and mom told me we were gonna get ride in a subway.

Dumb ass fricken little kid, for some stupid ass reason I thought she meant submarine, and that is what I was visualizing, wondering, what the heck are we gonna do underwater. I tell ya I was a stupid fricken kid. No doubt.

So, we left dad's car in the parking lot and me and mom waited with a lot of other people, for not a submarine but a subway, which, as you know is similar to a little train.

After waiting for about ten minutes, I heard what sounded like the whistle of a train. I looked up and a subway pulled up right in front of us. The subway doors opened and people got off the subway, once the passengers that wanted off got off, me, mom and about thirty other people boarded.

There wasn't much seating space available so a man offered me and mom his seat. At first mom said no thank you but the man insisted. I mean really mom was just to beautiful to stand up in high heels, so we sat.

My eyes could not help but stare out the massive windows as we stopped at station after station to pick up other would be subway goers.

As a kid, it felt as if the subway was traveling at the speed of light, you know, similar to the speed of the Orient Express, or so it seemed to me.

But it was actually less then five miles per hour. Within six minutes or so we were no longer picking up passengers, we were headed toward a tunnel. I completely got scared because for a minute the lights on the subway flickered, which was actually the lights coming on automatically, hey I had no idea what was going on.

A few moments later we were traveling in a tunnel which just so happened to be underneath the down town Fort Worth streets.

Closter phobic I felt for a moment as mom explained that we were in fact underneath the streets, but we would be arriving at dad's store in a few seconds. She held my hand knowing I was scared, and her gentle touch was what I needed to comfort me.

Other passengers listened and smiled as mom explained what was happening, where we were going, and how we would get there, so I wouldn't be frightened.

A man sitting in front of us turned around and said, "Don't be afraid Miss, I ride this subway everyday." He smiled at me and mom. A kind friendly smile.

There was an older lady on the aisle seat across from mom said, "Oh yes honey, most of us ride this subway several times a week. You will be fine."

Strangers on a subway ride. Some that took that ride to and from work everyday. Some that rode it to go shopping, others rode it because they had business downtown and it was free to park in the subway parking lot as opposed to paying a parking meter for time parked in front of the countless downtown stores.

Mom thanked them all for their kindness.

All I could see from the massive windows was cement walls that formed the tunnel and dim yellowish lights that were placed approximately every ten or fifteen feet to light the tunnel.

After what seemed like a thirty mile ride, but was in fact only a few blocks, the subway came to a halt.

Seems every one stood up at the exact same time, every one except me mom, and the kind lady sitting on the aisle seat.

Most of the people hurried off, some took their time. Mom deliberately waited for the majority of the people to depart the subway so we wouldn't get in the path of the people that were actually in a hurry. Men tipped their hats at mom showing respect for what I perceived to them, as the most beautiful woman they had ever seen.

The older woman that offered kind words to me, walked behind me and mom as we stepped out of the subway, while dozens of people boarded.

"Thank you for your help." Mom said to the woman. Both exchanging smiles.

"You're very welcome my dear." She said to mom.

" I hope you weren't too frightened?" She asked me.

"No ma'am." I responded.

"We've come a very long way." She said as we entered the department store. "I used to come downtown in a horse and buggy. Times certainly have changed." She smiled one last time as she went her way, me and mom ours.

I turned and watched her walk so slowly, one hand on her walking cane, to support every step she took, and a shopping bag in the other.

Perhaps mom had been to dad's job before because she knew exactly where to find him. We rode an escalator up two flights, once arriving at the very top, there stood my dad. Looking so handsome, almost like a movie star.

It's funny, since I knew he was supposed to be a store detective, for a split second I thought of Elliott Ness, Mr. Untouchable himself, which we watched on TV, every week. The times dad would be home he would watch also, only so he could cuss the shit out of Mr. Ness for capturing the "Bad Guy." He would be so pissed because the good guy always got his man.

He actually smiled when he saw mom.

When we got to him, he kissed mom's cheek and patted me on the head, as one would a dog.

"Did you like the subway baby?" he asked.

I shook my head yes, not wanting to tell him I was scared to death.

Mom opened her purse, took out a paper and pen, and handed them to dad. Dad ushered us to a perfume counter where he took the paper, signed it, and handed it back to mom. She put the paper in her purse, her and dad exchanged a few words, said good-bye to us both and just as quickly as we arrived at the department store, we departed.

The exact same route we took to get there, we took to get back to dad's car.

32

All this was long before his really important gangster days, before he was the established leader of his own crew, and though I'm not sure if the gossip I heard years later was true or not, but some one told me dad got fired from that job, nope not because he himself was a shoplifter, but as family gossip told me, he witnessed a man shoplifting, and though dad was a hard ass and his duties as store detective was to catch a thief and assist in getting the shoplifter arrested.

Only problem, this shoplifter had two little kids with him.

Instead of busting the guys ass, and having him arrested, dad turned the other cheek. He looked away so the man would not have to go through all the arrest crap, get his kids taken to child protective services and have a criminal record.

Dad pretended he didn't see what he was doing. Well gossip says dad approached the guy, said "Get the fuck outta here."

The guy didn't realize dad was a store detective, rather thought dad was just a nosey shopper getting into his business, and told dad mind his own business.

When dad flashed his detective badge at him, he thanked dad and hauled ass with his two kids.

And so it's told the store detectives were being detected, yes the watchers were being watched. Dad was fired, accusations that dad was in on the shop lifting charade.. a fricken blunder for sure.

Dad was called out in front of everyone, I guess trying to make dad an example for the other employees to do their jobs correctly.

"Should your own mother shop lift from our store you are to report her." The vice president of the company would say as he and a couple of the other store detectives escorted dad to the front door.

Gossip says dad didn't go very quietly as he was leaving the building he told the vice president.
"Remember my face.. remember my name." As dad threw his badge in the vice-president's face.

I hear talk, when dad was established as a real hard core gangster, dad and his men ran into the vice president late one night, well if you wanna believe they just ran into him, I say more like they scoped the joint and cornered the mother fucker.
Not to much verbal, I'm sure a lot of threats.
Rumors surfaced that the V.P. retired his position the next day, packed his shit and his family and moved to another state.

Dad lost his job yes, but he was pretty much headed for the gangster life anyway. He had given up two or three careers, all legal, to do the gangster shit. Guess he just loved it more, you know the power of it all.
Yes he lost a fairly good job that day all for

helping out some down on his luck dude that was at the wrong place wrong time, or was he. Turns out the dude he turned the other cheek for would be his long time partner in crime. You bet "Uncle Ray" waited outside for dad that day. You already know the rest.

I'm sure mom had no idea when we left the department store that afternoon that dad was gonna start shit with her when he got home. I heard him arguing with her.
This would be the very first time I would hear them really argue, well he would be the one arguing, she couldn't say too much, he wouldn't let her. ..
I'm not sure what he was pissed about, but I do believe it was the very first time I knew he hit her. I heard the slap from our room, then I heard her cry. He would yell for awhile longer, then stomp out of the house, seemingly pissed at the world.
In all fairness my mom did nothing wrong, other than look beautiful.

Perhaps he thought her dress was too tight, too short, too nice. Who knows? She did nothing to warrant an argument or a slap. But then I suppose he himself noticed her beauty as we left him standing at the perfume counter. Perhaps he watched as other men also admired mom's beauty from a distance. She was his, and so the theory goes. She was his property.
Can't imagine being slapped just because she looked beautiful. Seems to me you would think he would have been proud to have such a beautiful wife.

Nope not him, too fricken jealous.

I would run my mouth against my dad, in my mind; and I would think to myself "Hey dumb ass you're the one that told her to take you the papers." I believe this was the first time I thought to myself, I really don't like my daddy.

I went in mom's room as soon as dad left that night, mom quickly wiped her tears when she saw me. I cried because she looked so sad and confused. She hugged me and said everything will be ok, perhaps she really hoped it would, but as we all know, it never would be.

This, the way I remember it would be the beginning of a terrible life of abuse and pain. Not a very long life, but seems there was enough abuse and pain to last her ten life times.

Perhaps they argued before that day, I just never heard them. Perhaps he hit her before that day, I never knew that either. My memory of that day began as a beautiful one, my beautiful mother, doing as her husband asked of her, resulting in an argument and a slap.

I always paid attention after that day. Yes, I walked on pins and needles from that day forward where my mom was concerned. Hoping every time they argued would be the last, every time he hit her he would never hit her again.

33

And so it seems, now Sher would be working at the very store her precious dad had worked at one time. Would that bother her? Not likely, she loved him too much to worry about tedious things like that.

Would the Guetarro name be remembered by anyone that may still work there that could possibly remember my dad. Highly unlikely, but for Sher's sake I really hoped not.

None of that mattered to Sher now, the only thing that mattered to Sher was that she had a job, she had school, and she had some kind of life that mattered, because after all, her childhood had been robbed from her since mom died.

Even before she got her first paycheck she would already have it spent because of all the things she wanted to buy, the things she wanted to make.

Seems she had it all planned out. I don't think anyone ever looked forward to working as much as Sher did. It was a good thing Mrs. Crow had done by finding Sher a job she would love.

Sher was on top of the world everyday. Already the happiest kid in the school she now topped her self with popularity. She should have won an award at school for being the happiest kid there. She smiled at every one in the hallway, she talked to every teacher as she passed their classrooms. Everyone knew her name. Everyone loved her.

Popularity, was without a doubt for Sher. She came alive knowing practically every kid in the school knew her and loved her.

I, on the other hand, cared less who liked me or who talked to me. I didn't smile at every single person I passed in the hallways. None of the teachers knew my name, even the ones that actually taught me barely knew who the hell I was. I gave a shit less if I had friends, or if anyone liked me, or knew of me or cared for me.
Fuck everyone, I would think.

As committed as Sher was to school and her job, I was now committed to making Matty and Mary's life a little easier, at least I would try.
It's a fact if I didn't have to go to school I sure as hell would not have.
If Sher had her way she would have spent her entire life at the school...day and night and never go home.

Every afternoon when the bell rang I was home in less than ten minutes. I could not get to Matty's quick enough. I didn't hang around in the parking lot loitering like all the other kids did. I didn't stand around and make after school plans, I never had any. I didn't want to do anything. No one I knew owned a car, and even if they had I would have been too afraid to actually get in it with them.

As I saw it, there was no reason at all for me to stay at school. I hated every second I was forced to be there, same as I had hated going in elementary and Junior High.

I also feared seeing my dad and or Ray riding around the school looking for me. I would not want to ride home with them. Can you imagine how I would have felt if they did pick me up after school?

First I'd have to deal with the cloud of smoke that would come out of the car as either dad or Ray would open the car door to let me in.
Second I'd have to listen to my dad and or Ray cuss the shit out of every guy that might pass by, dad or Ray insisting, "What the fuck you looking at?"
Third I'd have to listen to my dad bitch about everything he could and I'd sit defenseless in the back seat, no way out.
Fuck that shit, I did all but run home every afternoon just to avoid being forced to ride home with them.

The only reason I even went to school was because I was to young to drop out.
School, for me was a terrible reminder of all the bad that had happened.
Walking home, usually alone, I would think back on my miserable childhood.

34

This particular afternoon as I walked home I remembered just how much I always hated school. Even more after mom died because I never wanted to be in school anyway, I always wanted to be at home, right there with my mom.

It's not like my mom was able to go anywhere during the day, it's not like she was going to be out shopping or visiting anyone, she just stayed home.

But it didn't matter I wanted to be with her. Have you ever just wanted to be with someone so bad you would do anything to be with them?

What kind of monster whoops their kids ass just because they want to stay home. I could see whoopin me if I were skipping school to go with my friends. I could see whoopin me if I were skipping to go somewhere else. I could see whoopin me if I were skipping to go smoke weed with my friends. Naw take that back, if I were skipping to smoke weed, he would probably have joined me.

Remembering all the times I got whooped by my dad because he could see right through me on the mornings I would wake up to go to school and fake being sick. No I could not fake it every morning, but usually it would be a Monday morning. I couldn't stand the thought of going to school, so yes, I'd do what I had to do.

Sick to my tummy, you bet cha! Well technically

stickin your finger down your throat to make your self throw up isn't really an upset stomach. But it got the job done.

    Then on those cold winter mornings while Danny would be sitting cross legged, in front of the space heater, I'd move him over a few inches, face him away from me so he couldn't see what I was doing.

    Come on now, my dad was a gangster, he always questioned the witnesses before killing them. Hey I never knew if poor lil Danny was gonna have to rat me out. So to keep him from snitchin on me I'd turn him the opposite way of the heater, then get my face real close to the heater so my skin would get red hot.

    Then I'd quickly go tell mom and dad I had a fever, dad of course would have to touch my forehead first and he'd get to feel the best of the heater heat, then by the time mom would touch my forehead my temp would have cooled down, of course she would know I was lying and say,

    "Yes Johnny, she's real hot, she needs to stay home." Mom would then wink at me, obviously where he could not see, because if he thought she was assisting me, then it was a crime, at least in his eyes.

    Rico Statute, two or more involved in an illegal act, considered organized crime. Or so the handbook says, right? Well maybe not, but to him, to have two of us lie to him, a crime punishable by at least an ass whoopin each.

    Unacceptable... Completely unacceptable.

So, once I got the wink from mom I'd crawl back in bed till his ass left, then I'd get up.

One time Sher caught me heating up my face and she rolled her fucking eyes at me.
"Bitch" I thought to myself. You do what you gotta do to kiss your daddy's ass to get you to school, I'll do what I gotta do to stay home with my mom.
I mean realistically, there is no way Sher would ever fake anything to stay home from school.

By the way, it's not like I'd be home alone with mom, remember the jerk usually slept all day, so I'd be forced to walk tippy toed as to not wake his ass.
Hey, I took the chance every time I faked being sick that I'd have to be home with him too. But for me, it was worth being with my mom, having to deal with him.
Yes, he was not a dumb ass, he knew I was faking, but he really couldn't send me to school after whoopin my ass now could he? There was no way I'd stop crying even if he tried to chunk my ass in the car and force me to go.
Ol Ricky Ricardo sure would have a lot of "Splainin" to do had he sent me to school crying my eyes out, and with belt marks on my legs.

It always seemed worth the whoopin though, because the end result for me would be I got what I wanted, and that was to stay home with my mom.
Seems the joke was on him.

Perhaps like my mom, I was immune to the pain of getting hit.

Hey all I wanted was to be with my mom, was that a crime, to want to miss school to be with her, enjoy time with her.

And for that I would get hit.

Perhaps subconsciously my little brain just wanted to spend time with my beautiful mother.

Perhaps my little heart some how knew that it would not last forever.

35

Sher's schedule was full, mine was not. Yes, I enjoyed being with Matty and Lori, though I'd miss my brothers and sisters.

Matty was very kind to me, and always invited me to go places with her, never insisting I baby sit Lori so she could go out. I would offer but in the beginning Matty stayed with us as much as she could.

On the days I would watch Danny and J.J. I would stay in the living room with them, helping them with their homework, if they had any. Or they would color with Lori's coloring books. They would remain in the living room as not to bother Matty if she were to be resting.

Around eight o'clock I'd take them back to Mary's so they could shower and be in bed by the time Mary returned from school. The schedule seemed to be working for everyone.

There was not a single night that I would not cry my self to sleep. I was just so unhappy without my mom.

And so the day's turned into weeks, before I knew it Halloween was rolling around, and I wondered what the kids would do as far as costumes.

For sure, I wasn't going to dress up this year. Just knowing Halloween was approaching had me thinking of all the costumes my mom had made for us over the years. Also I thought of my mom's old trunk, the old chest she kept with all her keep sakes..

Some people call them hope chest, but mom's was more than that. It was big, with a big lock on it. It reminded me of the treasure chest pirates would have full of gold and rubies and diamonds. Yet mom's wasn't filled with such nonsense, hers was filled with all the things she loved, the things she had made for her kids over the years, the letters her and dad had exchanged while he was in the military.

And now, due to the greediness of one aunt, an aunt that crept into our house one afternoon while we kids were gone and took it upon herself to snatch our mom's trunk, and all it's contents. Now left us with just memories of the things mom spent countless hours making for us, especially so our Halloween's could be special..

I never fathomed why the hell that selfish bitch Liz wanted things that did not belong to her. Why in the world would she want years and years of costumes mom had made, love letters between our mom and dad? What the hell could she possibly want with them?

Was she just that cruel of a bitch that she felt the need to destroy us by taking our mom's personal things. Possessions mom intended us kids to have when we got older.

What Liz did made no sense to me, but I guarantee one thing, that bitch would answer for her actions. At one point in my life I would get it out of her if I had to beat it out of her myself.

Well.... not me, I was a chicken, but Sher was not.

One day, mentally and physically Sher and I would catch up with her, and whether she liked it or not, Liz was gonna answer for all the shit she did to us, all the things she took from us.

Halloween was here, and though it was customary to dress up, I really felt a bit too grown to be in a costume. I knew my cousin Marcie was not going to dress in costume either, and since we were about the same age I felt perhaps I shouldn't.

Not that she would have made fun of me if I desired to dress as a pirate, or ghost, or what the hell ever I wanted, because she didn't have a hateful bone in her body. But what if I dressed in costume and she did not? Maybe she would feel left out.

We were all gonna walk the neighborhood together, my aunts, all the cousins, my brothers and sister, me an Marcie. ..

Aunt Mary told Danny and J.J. to decide what they wanted to be for Halloween and she would go to the department store and buy them the costume they chose. That seemed foreign to me. Mom had always taken so much time to make our costumes, being so creative every year.

I suppose Mary just didn't have time to make costumes, or perhaps she didn't possess the talent to sew as mom did and it was just easier and quicker to buy them something.

I talked to Becky and Carrie two days before Halloween and asked them what their plans were.

Becky, only a year younger than me, insisted she wanted to dress up, but when she told Uncle David and Aunt Gloria her plans to dress as a hooker, sending them both into a tail spin, they disciplined her by saying, "You can walk with the kids but you can not dress up." Uncle David was after all, the leader of the church choir.

This idea of Becky's Halloween costume was not appropriate at all, to some, I thought it funny and so typical. Remember Becky was the stand out kid, the attention seeker, and I'm sure she would have drawn a heck of a lot of attention dressed as the proverbial "Street Walker."

Becky laughed when she told me their reaction, not sure if she were serious or just being rebellious for all that had happened to her.

So about 6 p.m. on Halloween, all three of my aunts gathered all the kids, sixteen of us total, minus Sher, she had to work of course, and took us all trick or treating.

It was nothing like our Halloween days and though my dad was a terror of a man most of the time, he did gloat about his kids, the costumes mom had made, and it seemed he enjoyed Halloween as much as we did.

Actually, knowing that he would get stoned, laugh his ass off the entire time we would walk the neighborhood streets Trick or Treating, well it just didn't seem so terrible to have him with us.
Until the weed wore off.
Could not get home quick enough.

Marcie and I would walk at the back of our group so none of the little kids would fall behind. We would laugh at all the kids we saw, even our own brothers and sister.
"I wish you would live with us." Marcie told me as we walked.
"Becky is a nut!" She laughed
Becky did not hear what was being said about her, because she was walking ahead of everyone else.
I laughed. "Why do you say that?" I asked.
"She's always talking back," Marcie said.
"To who?" I asked.
"My mom, all of us, and sometimes my dad."
"Really?" I said.

Now I could see Becky being a smart ass and talking back to all the kids, that's just how Becky was, and I could even see her talking back to aunt Gloria, to a point, but no one talks back to uncle David. No one..
"I'm not going to snitch on her because of what y'all have been through, but one day my dad is gonna hear her and, well it won't be pretty." She said.
"Want me to talk to her?" Like I was some kinda

big shot. Hell Becky would have cussed me out if I tried to tell her anything.

"Naw. Let's just see what happens." Marcie said.

We laughed because we both knew how Becky was, but we both knew just how uncle David was also. He put up with no one. And he didn't have to be abusive to any one to get his point across.

My aunts seemed rushed, perhaps the rush to get home and get the kids in bed, perhaps walking all those blocks wasn't as fun for them as it was for the us. But no matter what, this day was still about the kids, wasn't it?

Danny and J.J. looked so cute, both dressed in cop outfits. Perhaps two cop costumes was all Mary could find, maybe it was just easier, who knows.

Then I thought: If their dad could see them, he might not be a happy camper, witnessing his two sons in costume, representing the opposite side of the law. He may have been tempted to put a contract out on their little lives.

Yes, they looked cute but their costumes were not original, actually we passed a few other Halloween cops as we were walking from neighborhood to neighborhood.

Halloween, just wasn't the same at all for me.

The little kids still seemed excited, and Becky seemed bored. We laughed as we watched Danny arguing with J.J. to walk next to him, and help him with his bag. Any little thing Danny could bitch about, he would.

Yes, my brothers were very cute, even if they were in costumes that would definitely give my dad something to bitch about.

But then it was just a costume, they weren't actually gonna grow up to be cops, arrest his ass for all his illegal bull shit, and have him thrown in prison, now were they?

Would have served dad's ass right if they had though.

Nope, I think they'd probably have a better chance growing up a fricken gangster than they would a cop.

And so we walked and walked, candy then more candy. Seems my aunts were all very tired and though the kids could have walked the entire city of Fort Worth, the streets of North side was just enough for my aunts.

Sixteen kids, sixteen bags of candy, now that's a lot of candy. Also there would be a lot of candy cleaning. You know check every bit of it, make sure some nut case didn't try and poison us or whatever it is authorities warned parents to look for.

The night would end with everyone going home, comparing who got the most candy and anticipating next years trick or treat.

36

Matty went out on a Saturday night with her friend Alley, who was one of those stand out chicks. Not a show off type of girl at all, she was just very loud and enjoyed having fun. She was very cheerful and loved to laugh, actually she loved to make other people laugh.

Matty and Alley had been best friends since their high school days. They hung out just about every where together, every weekend and sometimes during the week.
 Alley was thin, a bit taller than Matty and smiled a lot. She had bucked teeth, not at all bucked like Becky's, though noticeable, it was what made Alley stand out, other than her party animal personality. She was the type of woman you just liked to be around because she made fun, in a good way, of every thing and every one.
 You can bet your life if Alley made fun of you, not only would it be funny, but she was so quick and good with the jokes, she could have you laughing at yourself, no matter what she said.

Any time Matty would be on the phone with Alley they would laugh non stop.
 I couldn't help but over hear their conversations because Matty would be laughing so hard, and by what I gathered they would be laughing about the night before, how drunk they had been, and

especially they would make fun of the men they had danced with and how terrible those guys would dance.

Sometimes I would go with Matty to visit Alley, who, with three kids, still lived at home with her parents. She would insist she could not afford to move out, pay rent and support her kids, so her theory, her parents were stuck with her. I believe her parents loved that Alley lived with them, they were up in age and they loved having their grand kids with them.

Every time we visited Alley, we never went into her house, rather we would remain in the car, while Alley would sit on the curb, right next to Matty's car and they would carry on. Alley such a performer, would even stand up, imitating the men they had danced with. Matty would laugh because watching Alley imitate these men, would be an actual reenactment of their previous nights outing. Watching Matty laugh, you knew for a fact Alley was on point with her dance moves.

Matty and Alley would laugh so much, even I could not help but laugh because, not only were they so damn funny...but Alley would go all out dancing as stupidly as their partners had danced, and she would put on quite an exhibition, not just dancing around for a few seconds, she would damn near dance out the entire song, making Matty cry with laughter. Alley herself crying and holding her side because it was just that funny. At times passing cars would honk, slow down or stop all together to watch Alley perform.

Though I was never with them on their girl's night out, I felt I was, the way Alley reenacted every guy they danced with. Those two women were hilarious, out of the club and sober, I could only imagine how much fun they were when they had a drink or two and surrounded by a club full of people.

It is fair to say I really enjoyed going with Matty to visit Alley. Sometimes we would sit outside Matty's car for hours so they could carry on, laughing and just having a good time.
True friends I would think of their relationship, these two are true friends..

37

Sher was working extra hours now, because of the approaching holidays. Yet, in spite of dad and Mrs. Crow warnings about over working, and her school responsibilities, Sher did what Sher felt she needed to do. I suppose Sher gave her all at work, just as she had school, and in no time she had that department store eating out of her hand, so to speak.

Sher was making a bit of money and was able to buy things like tooth paste, hair spray, clothes soap, dish soap, all the non-food items, which made Matty very happy because now she didn't have to buy them.

Monday evening Sher didn't have to go to work and had no after school activities, so home for once, she began to talk to me about dad and his girlfriend.

Now in all fairness, I really had no idea how Sher knew the things she was about to tell me. As far as I knew dad wasn't coming around and Sher wasn't going to see him, but the fact remains she knew things about dad she could not have guessed, things that had to have been told to her, by her precious dad.

She told me dad had his girlfriend might be moving into my mom's house, mostly because it was rent free.

How the heck, and why the heck, would that woman want to live there was beyond me. Who in their right mind would want to live in that dump just to get out of paying rent somewhere else.

Actually that house had no significance to anyone but me.

According to Sher she was due to have their kid in December, which as I told Sher "I could care less."

I had the feeling Sher was beginning to form a relationship with dad's woman, whose name, by the way was Sharon. She was ten years younger than dad, and had three kids of her own, that according to Sher, had been taken away from her by her own mother.

Sher said Sharon's mom was pissed that Sharon had moved in with dad and even more pissed that she had gotten pregnant by him.

All this Sher was telling me as I lay on my bed watching her fold her clothes and put them away. I wanted to say "I don't give a damn about your dad and his pregnant bitch," but I chose to say nothing.

So as she went on, mostly babbling about dad, Sharon, school, her job, my mind wandered, I did the math.

There were a total of nine kids between dad and Sharon, one on the way, and neither of them were raising their own.

So according to Sher, that was exactly what pissed Sharon's mom off even more, because two damn grown ass adults couldn't take care of their own kids, instead having Sharon's mom raising Sharon's three, and all dad's family raising his six.

"Get your kids and raise them yourself, before you have more kids." Sharon's mom would say.

But Sharon didn't listen to her mom, insisting only that she loved dad and wanted to be with him..

I asked Sher "Did Sharon know about us and mom when she was busy getting pregnant."

Without a doubt, Sher knew the answer to that, but also Sher knew if she said yes and dad and Sharon married, I would never accept her.

Hey I wasn't gonna accept the bitch anyway, so without Sher giving me an answer, I shook my head in disgust because I already knew.

I will always believe mom knew of her, and I will always believe Sharon was what mom was talking about the one time I heard her on the phone insisting to dad she didn't know how much more shit she could take.

Naw, I was in no hurry to know of, or about this Sharon woman. In my eyes she was a home wrecker and she had interfered with my mom's marriage.

I could have cared less about her, I didn't give a shit who she was, and whose kid she was going to have.

I had the feeling Sher was already emotionally involved with dad's bitch, but then Sher still loved him, regardless of what he did or who he mistreated.

After doing some real quick math, nine existing

kids, another on the way, I wondered how much illegal drugs my dad would have to sell to support us all. I wondered how many contracts he would have to take out, and carry through to support his family.

Ten fricken kids all smashed up in that dump. There is no way dad or his bitch would play house and take care of us all.

Dad didn't want his own kids much less Sharon's three. Sharon didn't take care of her own three much less want to play mommy to dad's six kids just so she could be his "woman."

What a fucked up situation.

It would serve them both right, if we had been court ordered to live with them, just so they both got what they deserved. If it weren't so damn fucked up, this shit would really be funny.

38

Sher was working even more now that the holidays were upon us. She was spending the money she earned as quickly as she made it.

It really wasn't a lot of money, it just seemed like a lot because we never had any in the first place, but it was just enough to keep her with the necessities she needed so that Matty didn't have to provide them.

Once a week, usually Friday Sher would take us out to eat, always her treat.. Usually just burgers because it was the cheapest meal for her, but it was in fact still a treat.

She would even give me a small allowance, a few dollars a week, she would say so I could buy myself whatever I might need. Though it was a mere three bucks a week, it made me feel rich, and since I had tried and liked Sher's make-up I now had some spending money to buy my own.

So in return I'd do a load of laundry for her, make up her bed in the mornings if she had to leave in a hurry, or I'd even straighten up her things.

There didn't seem to be enough hours in the day for Sher, always on the go. She would come in after school, get what ever she needed for her after school events, grab a bite to eat and be gone until almost bed time.

Matty was okay with Sher and her independence,

as long as she either called or came home and told her where she would be. Seemed a waste of time to try and control Sher's every move. I mean after all, Sher had done more since mom died than a thousand teens could have done. To try and clip those wings of hers now, naw Matty knew Sher was more adult than she needed to be.
    She let Sher be Sher.

    Actually Matty didn't try and control anything. She wasn't there to nag us and say you can't do this you can't do that. Hell, I probably could have done anything I wanted, I just didn't want to.
    I wasn't about to start doing things that would involve getting my dad in my activities. The less interacting I had with him, the simpler my life just might be, or so I would hope. But I knew my dad, he would want to know everything, and that is just something I would try desperately to keep from happening.

    Days came and went. I really didn't see much of Sher, usually by the time she came home, I'd be getting ready for bed.
    It was like she had to be away, be anywhere but at home. Seemed if she stopped for just one second to breathe, her new life would be over and she would be right back in her nightmare of a life raising her dad's kids and forced to stay home, day after day, night after night.
    It was opposite for me. If I woke from this

nightmare, I would be back where I wanted to be, with my mom.

I would see Sher a lot at school, she was about one of the most popular kids the school had ever had. Even if I didn't want to see her, it would have been impossible. She was everywhere.
One day I could have sworn I saw her go up one flight of stairs and seconds later she was walking into her class room. If I hadn't known better I would have sworn the bitch had a twin.

Her popularity had caught the attention of quite a few of the more popular boys at school.
A senior, named Ray, one of the schools most loved football players had been attracted to Sher, a star athlete that was on the list of the available boys for every senior and junior girl in the school.
A sophomore, Sher had caught his eye. How ironic that her boyfriend's name would be Ray, a senior in high school, the star football player and a very handsome young man, the other Ray, a hired killer.

Ray, Sher's boyfriend, would offer to take Sher home from school, but Sher told him she had to ask her aunt first. I mean, Matty was okay with Sher's independence and all, but now there was a boy involved.
Sher started spending a lot of time with Ray at school. Lunch time, in the hallway during passing

periods, pretty much every where Sher went, Ray was there also. They were "Going together" so it was called. Sher wore his school jacket, she even wore his class ring.

I never understood that concept, about the class ring.

Let's see, a guy buys himself, or his parents buy him a class ring with his or their hard earned money. Then the guy turns around and let's a girl wear it, only to have it thrown in his face when they break up, either because he has found himself a hotter chick, or she found herself a richer guy.

Just seemed wrong to buy a ring and hand it over to a girl. Damn let her get her own ring was my theory.

It was inevitable Ray was gonna want to take Sher home every afternoon from school. It was also inevitable he was gonna want to take her to work, bring her home from work. It was also inevitable he was gonna want to take Sher out on a boyfriend, girlfriend real date.

It was his last year in high school, he couldn't very well spend it alone.

39

One evening, before we ate dinner, Sher asked Matty if she could ride home from school with Ray.

Matty responded "bring him here so I can meet him, but you must ask your dad first."

That was a shoe in, Sher thought. It wasn't likely dad would say no considering dad had already moved on with his life. Matty wasn't gonna actually give Sher permission to do anything without asking dad first. She wasn't stupid. She didn't want the responsibility all on her shoulders.

I wondered why? I mean, dad wasn't supporting anyone, he didn't provide our food, shelter, clothes, or money for our support, so what the fuck business was it of his?

You are stupid Malina. I thought.

Well, I did have my own opinions about every thing, though I rarely voiced them. I learned early on, keep my damn mouth shut unless absolutely necessary.

Thank goodness I wasn't interested in boys yet, or going places with anyone. Hey I was content with a good meal in my belly and a comfy bed to sleep in.

It was the weekend Sher was to bring her boyfriend to meet Matty.

Sher had called the garage looking for dad, I mean there was no sense in trying to go looking for him, we never knew where he might be, assuming he still worked at the garage.

He wasn't there, so she called Sal E's bar and of course he was there.

Sher told, not asked, but told dad she had a friend from school, a boy named Ray and she wanted his permission to have him visit her at Matty's. As Sher was on the phone I sat and watched her talking, and slightly begging her daddy's permission.

To distract her I flipped her off, well really I was flipping dad off. Sher almost burst out laughing, which we both knew would piss dad off, to be laughed at. She covered the receiver of the phone and said. "Stop Malina, before I beat the crap out of you." This time I flipped her off, remembering the horrible ass beating Becky had received for flipping off some jerk kid.

I stopped flipping them both off and blew Sher a kiss, trying to make her laugh so she wouldn't actually beat the shit out of me once she hung up.

"And don't be doing anything you shouldn't." Dad barked at her.

I was disgusted for Sher that he had talk to her that way considering the bastard was fucking around on our mom.

So with permission from her precious daddy, Sher called Ray and within twenty minutes he was at Matty's.

Matty did some small talk with Ray, and told him the rules.

"You can visit her here in the living room, but never in her room, just in case her dad should show up. She must be in by one weekends, and ten on school nights."

Ray agreed to all Matty's rules and thanked her, promising not to ever break the rules, or her trust in him. Spoken like a true gentleman, I thought.

Ray was very nice, saying yes ma'am and no ma'am, and seemed to really like Sher a lot.

With the ground rules in place, Sher had the permission to have just a bit more independence added to her now exciting life. She seemed on top of the world.

Like clock work Ray would pick her up for school and sometimes I'd ride with them. Most times not, I enjoyed walking alone like a nerd. Well not a nerd, it was only three blocks from the school, I didn't need a ride, unless of course it were raining, or cold out.

Every afternoon Ray would take Sher home. They were both in sports so it seems they got home later and later on the nights she didn't have to work. Matty was okay with it as long as she was home by ten. On the nights she worked, Ray brought her home, Matty no longer having to get out at night to get her.

On certain occasions Sher would ask Matty if she could spend the night at her girlfriend's house.

Matty would allow, only if she knew the family.

Now with the new boyfriend, Matty wasn't so sure if it was a good idea to be letting Sher spend the night anywhere.

It was almost every girl's motto, say your spending the night with your girlfriend, then sneak out and go with your boyfriend.

Keep in mind Matty was only nine years older than Sher, she couldn't help but be suspicious when the very next night Sher asked to stay with her best friend, Dede.

Never did Matty refuse Sher when she wanted to stay with Dede, because one of Dede's older sisters was one of Matty's friends.

Some times when Sher would be spending the night at Dede's, Matty would call and ask for Sher and sure enough Sher would be there.

I don't think Matty didn't trust Sher, perhaps Matty would be worried dad would show up and try and do a shake down, find Sher was supposed to be at a friends, then catch her creeping around with her boyfriend.

Seems everyone had to think like dad, think what would he do, how would he react, have a bit of a criminal mind like dad, just to stay one step ahead of him. Seems there were just so many people afraid of just one man.

Matty in her own kind way reminded Sher to be safe, and please don't do anything she shouldn't.

Sher was straight forward when she told Matty her plans one night that she, Ray, Dede and Dede's boyfriend were going to the movies and then to Dede's.

Matty reminded Sher to call her when they returned from the movies. Now keep in mind, this was all so new for Matty. A few months ago it was just her and Lori, now she had the responsibility of two teenage girls, and all the headaches that went with it, not to mention a snake for a brother.

There is no way I would've let Sher go, not with our suspicious jerk father. You just never knew when he would show up and stick his nose in everyone's affairs.

What a terrible responsibility for Matty. What if Sher did sneak off with Ray? What if Sher was irresponsible and wound up pregnant? I cringed at the thought of it.

Couldn't help but think, dad would kill Sher, Ray and Matty. Sher and Ray for doing it, Matty for allowing Sher to go out.

Matty's thought was, she couldn't keep Sher tied up. I mean really now, all the responsibilities Sher had as a fourteen year old teen, and now to try and put restrictions on her.

Sure, no one wanted her to get pregnant, but to try and control her every move, it would have been impossible.

Sher was very excited to go out with Ray, on what I assumed, was her very first real date.

She looked so pretty when she was leaving the house.

"I'll take you some where next week twerp." She said as she left.

Now as you know I was content, I didn't need anything rocking my world. I had just got used to Matty's house, had learned all the rules, and got to see my brothers, daily. I wasn't trying to cause trouble for myself.

40

It was about ten o'clock the night Sher went out with Ray, I was watching TV, Matty in her room. There was a knock on the front door, I looked out the window, it was Mary with all five of the kids, pillows and blankets in hand.

She looked horrible and very scared, telling Matty, George had not come home yet and she was sure he was out drinking.

Mary put Katy in Matty's bed with Lori, and put Mark and Jake on blankets on the floor next to Matty's bed. Danny and J.J. went to Sher's bed.

I remained in the living room, not really realizing what was happening. It was after all only ten o'clock, besides I was very curious what the heck they were doing, because simultaneously Matty and Mary turned off all the lights, closed all the curtains, they even turned the TV off.

We were virtually in the dark.

And so the waiting game began.

Mary smoked cigarette after cigarette, and paced back and forth. She didn't conversate much only saying, "I hope he gets pulled over and goes to jail for the night."

She was scared for some reason. Matty tried to be comforting. I found myself sitting by an open window, waiting, as my two aunts were, but what the

hell were they waiting for?
I was just about to find out!.

Mary put out her cigarette and then we all heard it.
Uncle George came hauling ass down the road slamming his brakes as he passed his own house, reversing even louder than he had when he was driving forward.
Screaming my aunts name "Mary" he yelled as he entered their driveway, honking his horn and gunning his motor the entire time.
"Get out here Mary," he would scream loud enough for us to hear from Matty's.
Me the fuckin dumb ass that I was, not realizing for a second uncle was drunk, I just thought he was screaming for my aunt because maybe something bad had happened and he needed her help?
For a split second I wanted to jump up and yell.
"She's over here uncle" thinking his yelling was because he need her help, not that he wanted to do any harm to her.
Damn Malina, you are fuckin stupid. I thought.
And Sher would have had a field day with this one, if she knew for one second I anticipated letting uncle know where Mary was, Sher would have kicked my ass and sent me out the door to deal with uncle myself.. I'm so glad Sher was not home.
Oh Malina, use your damn brain.

Uncle got out of his car, stumbling all over the driveway, yelling "Mary get out here...Now."

Assuming, I suppose, he thought she was inside their house ignoring him.

"Mary get out here." He yelled like some crazed mad man..

I just stared. I couldn't move. Goodness I had chills all over my body. I had been down this road before, only it was my dad, my mom.

There was a side door on the driveway side of Mary's house which was an entrance to Mary's bedroom. Uncle stumbled up the stairs, almost falling right back down to the bottom, and without even attempting to unlock the door, he just picked up his foot and kicked the door in, yelling "Mary Mary!!!!"

"Damn stupid ass." Mary said, just as we could hear him yelling again, this time from inside Mary's house.

"Where are you Mary?" He screamed over and over.

Mary whispered "Oh he's gonna regret this tomorrow."

Then we could hear things being thrown to the floor, what sounded like mirrors breaking or glasses being broken, also it sounded like he knocked over some furniture.

Strange, when dad terrorized us, he never tore our fucked up house apart, he went straight for mom.

Matty said, "Dammit, here we go again."

Apparently, by the way Matty and Mary were talking, this had happened before.

Then uncle came out and stood in the front yard,

"Mary....Where are yoooou?" he sort of yodeled, looking or appearing to look toward us.

Actually, that sounded kinda funny.

We had every light in the house turned off, it was pitch black, no lights on at all, each of us, Matty, Mary and me peeking out through the curtains, only enough for just one of each of our eyes to see out through our designated area of the curtain.

Fear went through me.

"What if he did see us looking out?

But how could he see us, only our eyes were peeking out through the curtain. He was drunk, he was across the street and we were in a pitch dark house. There was no way he could see us from where he was.

I was scared non the less. What if he did come across the street? What if he banged on the door and no one let him in? What if he kicked the door down and forced aunt Mary to go back home?

What would I do?

Matty did in fact have a phone! We could call the police, but did we dare?

He was not my dad to be in constant fear of, but was he capable of behaving as horrible as my dad?

Was Mary and Matty as afraid of George, as I had been of my own father?

Then, it seemed he got frustrated and tired of yelling Mary's name so, he picked up a brick from the lining of Mary's flower bed and threw it toward us, as if he thought we were here laughing at him. He was so drunk the brick didn't make it to Matty's yard it only went as far as the middle of the street. I don't think he even knew where the brick landed.

I was horrified at what I was witnessing.

Matty seemed worried, but not for us, instead for her sister.

Mary just kept saying "Wait till tomorrow. Just wait till tomorrow."

Uncle carried on for at least fifteen more minutes.

I wondered why the hell all these neighbors would allow this behavior and not call the police.

When my dad carried on like an animal, we had no nearby neighbors to call the police on his ass, we only had a cemetery, but here, the neighbors were fifty feet away. Why would they allow uncle to scream and carry on, and not intervene?

I suppose they figured it was not their business, or perhaps this wasn't the first time the neighbors had to deal with uncle also.

Was he as bad as my own dad?

Did everyone fear him too?

Did every man act like a fucking monster when they were drunk.

I looked at my two aunts standing in the dark waiting to see what he would do.

Seems with mom, dad just pounced on her like a lion against its small prey, with uncle they already knew what he would do, they had apparently been through this before, yet I never knew.

   How could I know?

   And here they stood in the dark, waiting, waiting and wondering. Waiting to see what his next move would be. It was obvious Mary couldn't go home. I knew it could not be safe for her or the kids..

   Then I wondered, did everyone live like this?

   Is this how all or most families lived? Some type of abuse, didn't have to be physical abuse, there was emotional abuse, there was mental abuse. Seems growing up I had become accustomed to all three.

   First off dad fucked us up with all the physical shit he did not only to our mom, but also the random ass whoopins we got, because he would be angry at the world.

   Then there was the mental abuse. That's where my pissing skills came in. Mentally I would know long before he entered the house, I was gonna piss, and no matter how much I told my self don't piss Malina, don't piss Malina, I would piss.

   Mentally, I was one fucked up kid.

   Then there's the emotional abuse he was so damn good at. Beat us, terrorize us, then hug on us and tell us just how much he loved us.

   Yes we lived horribly, but was it possible every one else did too?

   There was no way everyone lived like this. There had to be some good fathers, good mothers out there somewhere. I mean really it's not like you take a head count in school and say, "All you poor kids raise your hand if you father is a low down good for nothing child abusing mother fucker." And who would admit to that shit anyway. Hell, Mary was my aunt, yet I never knew anything bad happened to her or her kids. I just never knew.

And poor Matty, she wasn't even married, yet she stood in the dark right along side her sister.

Was there nothing that could be done?

I wondered if my big bad father knew his sister was being tormented by a man, that when drunk, was quite possibly his equal.

I wondered would my dad beat uncles ass if he knew of his behavior. Would he beat the man because it was his sister being mistreated, yet no one beat his ass when he tortured my mom.

The actions and the looks on my aunts faces, this was going to be a long night, yet it seemed almost routine like for them both.

Now sitting here wondering, this isn't the uncle I knew, this was a drunken monster and now I was sitting here waiting to see what his next move would be, if any..

Why does this sort of thing happen?

Are these men ill?

Do they really think it is ok to abuse their families.?

Yet, this was different, yes, more of an exhibition than any thing else. He wasn't hitting anyone, he wasn't cussing anyone, he was just acting stupid drunk.

But I wondered what would have happened if Mary hadn't come to Matty's when she did, what would uncle have done?

She did show up on Matty's door step literally moments before uncle slammed his brakes in front of his own house.

Would he have hit her, did he hit her and she never told anyone?

Maybe tonight was not as bad as it was for my mom, but it was wrong, and in my eyes it was abuse.

It didn't make it easier for me to know my aunts suffered also, it made me hate the men in my family even more.

41

As I had done with my own mother, I sat right beside my aunts, waiting wondering what do we do next? I wasn't crying like I had for my mom, but I had the same knotted feeling in my stomach. No, I had not witnessed an ass whoopin, and I did not want to, but mentally I was scarred.

Was there any such thing as a happy family? Yes, I knew there was, because I had witnessed it before at my friends house, or was that just a show?

Could it be the alcohol these men drank?

Possibly!

Now having to witness my aunts, being what could only be described as complete stupidity, same as my mom. Stupidity for allowing such behavior from their husbands. But I realized, women don't allow it. It is the man's choice.

What my aunts and my own mom were guilty of was not leaving their asses. But in my mom's case, how could she leave? She knew my dad was an animal and would track her down. Perhaps she always wanted to leave, but was just too afraid that his actions would be far worse if she left, than what she had to put up with just for staying with him.

I wasn't sure what to think about Mary and uncle. Yes his behavior was wrong and it was scary. But as of this second he hadn't touched her, and to tell you the truth, the most he had done was come home drunk and made a fool of him self.

Yet, something caused Mary to leave her house in the middle of the night, with five kids before he got home. The best I could figure, uncle had a problem, and he needed to be stopped..

The three of us sat in the living room, still in the dark, Mary still smoking cigarette after cigarette, Matty still standing by her sisters side. Both my aunts talking, wondering if the coast were clear and Mary could go home.

Go Home? But why would she want to go home?

It had been only an hour since he was throwing bricks at us, now she wanted to go back. But what if he were to wake up and start his shit again?

Conversations between the two sisters continued for about thirty more minutes, at times making fun of uncle the way he behaved. Laughter now, but we all were very scared when he was carrying on.

I was happy when Mary said she would go home in the morning.

Matty got Mary a pillow and blanket so she could sleep on the sofa. I offered Mary my bed, but she insisted on sleeping in the living room.

I finally went to my bed, where, my brothers were asleep in Sher's bed. They looked so cute and peaceful, having no idea of the drama that had been going on around them.

For the moment I did not fear that uncle would

actually come into Matty's house and do anything to Mary or his kids.

I figure uncle knew the boundary line, that's why he threw bricks rather than come to Matty's house and try and force Mary to go home.

When I woke the next day Mary and all the kids were gone, even Danny and J.J.. I wondered how everyone got past me without waking me up?

It was now just me and aunt Matty, even Lori was gone.

Matty was cooking, when I finished getting dressed she asked me to go to Mary's for butter.

Was it safe? I wondered. Yet, I did not ask, rather I did as I was told, though I have to admit I was scared not knowing if, or what I might find when I got to Mary's.

Once at Mary's front door I knocked rather than just walk in.

Uncle said "Come in." I hesitated for a moment then opened the door.

He was sitting on the sofa, same spot he did every evening watching TV, usually alone.

He looked like a child being scolded by his mother. He didn't budge, he just listened as Mary yelled at him.

She did not stop yelling at him just because I entered the room. Hey I was a witness to it all the night before. I suppose Mary wasn't gonna tip toe around the subject just because I was there.

"What the hell is wrong with you?" I'm going to leave you one day... out there throwing bricks and yelling like a damn mad man."

Uncle realizing now, that we for certain were watching him act a fool from behind the curtains.

He said not one word.

The same man that was yelling and cussing and threatening, sat there, like a scared child, too afraid to say a word.

So this is how it was?

Periodically, uncle went off, did his drinking thing, came home, terrorized his family, they would run away from him. Once sober Mary would go home and tear his ass up.

Being the descent man he was sober, he wouldn't dare talk back to her. And so it seems, the same hold he had on her while he was drunk, she had on him while he was sober.

The entire time I was in the kitchen she was yelling at him, almost to the state of complete humiliation, him apologizing every now and then.

I'm supposing the strategy was, humiliate the fuck out of him, make him feel less of a man, hoping the hell he caught from her while sober, was enough to persuade him to never run off and drink again.

So I believe was her intention.

Of course it was the same for her, how humiliating

for her to have to sneak out of her own house, with her kids, and now her brothers kids, just to avoid the humiliating things he would, he could say to her just because he was drunk.

Now he had to take it like a man because when he was drunk there was no reasoning with him. He knew it, Mary knew it.

She did something my own mom never dared to do, she stood up to him, she talked back, she cussed back, she yelled and she was in his face. And unlike my own father, he allowed it. Perhaps realizing he had it coming.
This, for sure was not as bad as what I had lived through, but enough to make me realize I hated living like this.
It seemed yes, it was a man's world, do as they say, blah blah blah, and on rare occasions, give the mother fuckers hell as Mary attempted.
The experience with uncle only made me miss my mom more and hate my dad even more than I already had.

42

A few days later when I went to watch the kids while Mary was at school, uncle was outside with all the little kids playing kick ball.

He would laugh his funny laugh and he would talk kindly to all the kids. I do believe uncle really enjoyed Danny the most. He would pay special attention to him, making sure Danny could kick the ball and run around all the bases and not get caught.

Rarely did my own dad do anything with my brothers, yet uncle seemed to enjoy them.

Things got back to normal, aunt going to school, uncle doing his share with the kids and around the house, me helping out as much as I could. It was just amazing that the same man that was being so kind to all the kids, had behaved as what I perceived as a mad man.

Really, it was just so sad to me.

Finally some peace and quiet.

Everything seemed to calm down a bit, everyone keeping the routine of life flowing again, then barely three weeks later, for some unknown reason, uncle did it again. Yet this time aunt Mary didn't have the fortune to get out of the house before he got home.

Actually me and Lori were at Mary's house when uncle got there.. Matty had gone out with her friends, Sher was spending the night with one of her friends, so me and Lori were visiting when uncle crept up on us.

He parked his car in front of the house rather than pulling into the driveway, and barged in, same as dad had done to mom. Uncle didn't beat Mary, but he cornered her, cussed her and yelled in her face. He threw some things around the house just as all the little kids came in screaming, not really understanding what was happening. Seems they were attempting to protect their mom, something I regret never doing for my own mom..

I couldn't move. I was horrified. Uncle didn't know I was there, he just came in like a mad man, not realizing Lori and I were sitting right there on the sofa..

When he saw me, I think it knocked him into soberness. He had a terrible look on his face, like "Oh shit."

Did he think I would call the police, or worse, call my dad.

Mary and her kids were in Mary's room, Lori Danny and J.J with me in the living room.

Uncle went to the kitchen, I suppose looking for beer, which Mary never allowed in the house.

While uncle was in the kitchen, Mary came running with the kids and told me to come on.

I gathered up Lori, Danny and J.J and we all ran to Matty's and locked the door behind us.

Only this time uncle wasn't outside acting crazy, he wasn't yelling or cussing or throwing bricks, he wasn't even calling out for Mary.

Perhaps he embarrassed himself when he realized I was there. Now I'm not saying I saved Mary from having to fight with uncle. I'm not saying uncle changed his ways because of me, but perhaps he thought, I might just tell my dad, and though my dad was a million times worse to his family than uncle was to his, seems the rule is, "don't fuck with Johnny G's family."

Honestly, what went through my mind at that moment, what right would my dad have to beat up on uncle for what he was doing to Mary? Dad did so much worse to my mom, yet he never even got a slap on the wrist.

Uncle didn't know at the time, but I had no intention of ever telling my dad anything about him.

Uncle's behavior, not that I approved, but as far as I was concerned, that was Mary's place to tell or not tell my dad.. Really how could I possibly tell my dad, knowing dad would probably beat the shit out of him, remembering dad was so abusive to my mom and us kids, and never once did anyone ever intervene for my mom.

Nope, if Mary wanted dad to know, she or Matty would have to tell on uncle themselves.

Mary and the kids stayed with us that night. Perhaps uncle just fell asleep, perhaps uncle wasn't going to do anything wrong, just a lot of yelling.

We will never know his intentions that day,

because the second he saw me sitting on the sofa, he literally stopped in his tracks.

The next day Mary wasn't yelling at uncle, he sat in the same spot, looking like the same lost soul he had only three weeks before.. This time Mary was crying.

I'm sure the stress of uncles behavior, the stress of having to take care of her brother's son's, the fact that she now had two more kids to protect from uncle's behavior beside her own three, was about to take it's toll on her.

Mary was a good wife, a good mother, a good aunt. She went to school in an attempt to help her family one day if she ever got her own place. She cooked, cleaned and took very good care of everyone. She didn't deserve uncles behavior, and possibly he realized it when Mary was crying.

I never understood why men, or women for that matter, drink if they can't control their behavior when they are drunk. Do they not realize the end result of their actions?

I tried to understand people that drink and behave in this manner.

Uncle was not an alcoholic, I mean he did not drink all day, everyday.

He was never mean to anyone especially his family if he was sober.

So then if one isn't an alcoholic that must drink everyday because they are addicted, then getting drunk in this manner is by choice.

You choose to get drunk, put the fear of God in the ones that love you and act a fool.

But why? Why would anyone want to do that to another human being?

Was uncle upset that Mary went to school? Did he not like the fact that two nights a week she was not home when he came from work?

No, it could not be that, because he seemed so proud of her.

I tried so hard to figure why, if life is good for you and you're happy, why would anyone let their drunken behavior ruin perfectly good lives.

People drinking and acting like damn fools would be something I would attempt to avoid all my life, though I would not always accomplish that goal. I thought the days of being around a drunk man were over when I left my mom's home. It was not.

I was very sad for my aunt, my cousins, my own brothers, because I suppose you just never know when someone chooses to drink and go on a rampage is gonna disrupt your life.

I wondered were all families like this? Do all men drink and have such a behavior? I sure hoped not. What a terrible life for anyone, especially the kids.

For as long as I can remember uncle never behaved in this manner again. Actually he worked even harder. Though I'm sure Mary walked on pins and needles for awhile, wondering if and when uncle would do it again. As far as I know, he never did.

43

Dad was coming around now and then, never to give financial help to my aunts, but to let us all know he was still in control of everyone.

Out of no where he would just be there, usually at Mary's, because Matty would still be at work. Of all things, I could smell his cologne as I would turn the corner of our block, walking home from school, sure enough his Cadillac would be parked in front of Mary's house. I'd even choke on the smell, long before I got anywhere near his car. I'd also be tempted to turn around and run back to the school, pretending I had some athletic shit to do, but declined, because that would only be another lie he might catch me in.

Always my stomach in knots at the sight of him, or his car.

Out of fear and the fact he was my father, I would go to Mary's to see him, wondering why would I do that to myself. I fuckin already knew he would be bitching.

This one particular day as I got near his car I noticed, oh of course, Ray was sitting in the car, no doubt, being the look out for dad.

"Hi baby." He said as I walked past the car.
"Hi." I said.
"How was school?" He asked.
"Fine." I lied.

"And your grades?" He asked.

What the hell, I thought. You aren't my daddy, what the hell does it matter about my grades.

"They're good." I said as I laughed to myself. If you call all C's good.

I looked at him as I headed toward Mary's front door, sitting in that Cadi, with his sunglasses on, I'm sure a few joints in his cigarette pack, and it goes without saying, a few guns somewhere stashed in that car.

I wondered, did these two men have nothing better to do. Shouldn't Ray be looking for dad's wanna be killer? Shouldn't he be selling drugs to some drug addict? Shouldn't he be beaten the hell out of someone just for kicks?

"Bye baby." He smiled that killer smile as I waved bye and opened Mary's front door. He was so much like my dad it was sickening. There was a time Ray knew us all by name and called us such. Now he used the exact words his idol used "Baby."

Sickening I tell ya.

Dad's voice would be loud and demanding "If these kids ever act up, call me, I'll take care of it." Sounding like he would take out a contract on his own kids if they misbehaved..

I guess as long as he thought he would be the disciplinarian it would take away from the fact someone else was raising his kids and providing the necessities..

Seemed no matter what, he still called the shots, and that's the shit I heard long before I opened the fucking door.

The second he saw me, he eyeballed me from head to toe, his mouth still yakking about how in control he was, yet he would look me over, never skipping a beat, I'm sure, hoping to find something wrong with my appearance so he could bitch even more.
Mary, in the dining room smiling at me, probably so I wouldn't start crying, dad standing there all dressed up twirling his key chain.

I would attempt no eye contact, but that shit wouldn't work. Had to look a gangster in the eye other wise they think your guilty of something.
Oh I was guilty of something all right. I was guilty of cussing this mother fucker out in my mind.
"Do you hear me?" He looked me right in my eyes.

Damn fucker, I just walked through the door, give me a second to soak all this bullshit in. My evil mind thought.
"Yes sir." I would answer without even knowing what I was yes siring about. Hell I could have been admitting guilt to a crime, even being his would be assassin for all I knew.

And by the way, should I ever meet this worthless

wanna be assassin, I got a few choice words for his dumb ass too. I mean really, the one that got away, that almost had this fucker and fucked up, boy did I wanna meet this dumb ass.

He walked toward me, I wanted to duck down, or cover my head, but even to me that seemed a bit dramatic, he was after all, only bitching, not murdering.

Oh how I wished at that moment I was in sports after school with Sher.

Oh how I wished at that moment I was a fly and could fly the fuck out of there.

Oh how I wished at that moment I had a gun and could bust a cap in his ass, just for bitchin so fuckin much. Give the mother fucker something to really bitch about.

None were true.

He hugged me, mostly as a show, I did the same. Sort of a truce.

I headed straight for Mary, I thought, at least I saved you auntie, now you can save me.

"Do you hear me Mary?" His voice was loud.

"If these kids give you or Matty any trouble I want to know." His fucking evil eyes roaming the both of us.

"Everything is fine." Mary assured him.

"Ok, but I mean it, don't let me find out these kids are acting up and y'all are covering up for them."

Oh shut the fuck up mother fucker, exactly what I wanted to say.

I went out to check on the kids, teary eyed and all and at one point dad left. No good bye's to anyone not his name sake not his youngest son, but did I really expect it.

What a fuckin jerk I would think as I left Mary's and went to the peace and quiet of Matty's. What a mother fuckin jerk.

Though his visits were few and far between, it had me thanking my lucky stars I didn't live under his roof anymore. You have no idea how glad I was I didn't have to see the likes of dad and Ray everyday.

44

Not so quickly!

The next afternoon as I walked home from school peacefully, just before I turned the corner, I smelt dad's cologne.. again.

No fricken way that shit was still lingering from yesterday, no way. Once I turned the corner I did not see his car, relief.. but I smelt him.

There were other kids walking home as I was, but I knew none of those high school boys wore cologne, and if they did, they sure as hell didn't wear as much as my dad.

Now Matty's and Mary's houses were dab smack in the middle of the block, Matty's on one side Mary's across from hers. The closer I got to both houses the more I smelt his over bearing cologne. And just when I got to the house right next to ours, I saw it.

My dad's Cadi pulled up right to Mary's side door, almost as if he didn't want anyone to see it. I wondered if he were wanted, again, and just trying to hide.

Oh my God what now! Prison roll call?

What could he possibly be doing there, again?

Should I go to Matty's before he could see me, lock the door and peek out the curtain as me and Mary and Matty had done, when we were hiding from uncle?

Nope, I guarantee he knew each of our schedules, and where we were at any given moment.

So I took the slow walk across the street to Matty's, dreading a repeat of yesterday, with his bitching and cussing and hell raising.

I could hear all the little kids laughing and playing in Mary's back yard as I approached her house.

I glanced towards dad's car to see if Ray were sitting in the car as he had been only yesterday.

Nope, no Ray.

Not really wanting to, but knew I had no choice, I opened Mary's door. Actually the door was already open, only the glass screen door was closed.

I could see him through the glass door, sitting at the dining room table, laughing.

Dad looked towards me as I entered.

"Hi baby."

Oh fuck, this mother fucker is high.

Mary came out of the kitchen with a plate of home cooked food and served it to dad.

"Damn Mary, that sure smells good."

Definitely high.

Mary smiled a great big smile at her evil brothers praise of her cooking..

"Hi dad." I mumbled.

I walked over to where he was sitting, and as it is customary to do, dead beat killer dad or not, I hugged him.

From the kitchen Mary asked "How's your shoulder Johnny?"

Goodness gracious, that's all it took to open that fricken can of worms.

And so his pathetic pity bull shit started....
"It's doing a lot better." He said as he instantly began rubbing his shoulder.

Now before Mary ever said one word about his damn shoulder, he hadn't even touched it, but, just the mention of it by Mary had him massaging it like he needed morphine.

I watched.

"How bad is it?" Mary asked.

My very first thought, Oh my Mary, did you really have to ask him that, don't you know...

Without warning he unbuttoned his top button to his perfectly starched shirt, and showed Mary!

What was he showing her? There was but a tiny tiny spot on his shoulder. I had to get a bit closer to make sure there was a mark at all.

"Yeah, they got me right there." And he pointed, as if there were a gaping hole in his arm.

Mary looked, hell I even looked a second time.

Goodness dad, I got chigger bite scars worse than that, I thought, just as I envisioned slapping him for his pathetic pity trip he was trying to take Mary on.

I mean what could me and Mary possibly have said to him, I couldn't see anything, I don't think she could either, yet we said nothing negative.

Finally Mary came up with something really really clever.

"Goodness." She said.

I thought of something more clever to say like, "Fuckin sissy." But of course, I said nothing.

Yep, dad buttoned his shirt back up, and continued

to massage his shoulder.
 The fricken power of suggestion I thought.
 He had been sitting there perfectly fine, one wrong word had him on the steps of the emergency room again.

 I truly wanted to shake my head, like, you fuckin fake, but I was in striking distance of one of his boxing arms, I also was not stupid.
 "How was school?' He asked, as he stopped massaging his arm and positioned his plate directly in front of himself, still smiling.
 Nothing better to make you forget your painful wounds than a nice hot plate of Mary's home cooking, huh dad?
 Mary went to the kitchen to get him a glass of tea.
 "Fine." I answered. Picking my words very carefully, knowing how he loved to do a butcher job on our conversations.
 "Good." He said.
 "Where is Sher? he asked, as he took his first bight of food, all while saying "UMMM UMMM."

 The last time I had seen my dad eat was at the hospital, and that was quite a sight, watching him scarf down everything but the fricken plate, even looking closely to make sure he still had all ten of his fingers, that's just how quickly he was eating that day.
 Not wanting to look directly at him, I said. "She's at school."

He was actually taking his time eating Mary's good home cooked food, like a normal person eats. There was no bitching at the moment, no cussing.

I walked past him and went to check on the kids, who were all laughing and playing as they did every day. I wondered if he had even bothered to say hello to his sons.

I was about to open the door and go outside with them, when dad said.

"Do you like living with Matty."

Pause.........silence.

Does a bear shit in tha woods? I thought. Of course, even as a joke, that would not have been an appropriate thing to say, just as he put his second bite of food in his mouth.

And then quickly I thought to myself, "As compared to what dear old dad, living with, no being terrorized every minute of the fricken day by you?

"Yes." In answer to his question..

Now I knew this fucker, he has something up his sleeve. Just yesterday he was all over the fricken place, throwing his weight around, today he was sitting there nice and calm asking normal question.

Hey mean or nice, where my dad was concerned, I always had my guard up.

I waited for a response from him about me living with Matty, but he had none. He was too into his plate of food. Gosh, is that all it takes to make him shut the fuck up, if that were so, when I grow up, I want to be a Chef.

Now, I would have bet my life he was high, he had to be, because he was never nice without smoking a joint or two or three, never.

What did he want? He had to have wanted something from Mary.

Money perhaps?

Well I didn't wait around to find out.

I gave some miserable excuse about having homework and my books were at Matty's which he believed.

I knew my dad had it in him to be nice, I just never knew him to do it without an ulterior motive.

Not sure if it was fear, respect, stupidness or what, but it seems every one of my dad's sisters, though they knew what he did to Becky, and they all knew how badly he treated my mom, and they all knew the sucker abandoned us after my mom died, but all his sisters treated him like he was the best man in the world.

I wondered also, did my aunts have ulterior motives too. I mean really, their husbands were working to support dad's kids, their husbands provided a roof over his kids heads, food for them to eat, and any other necessity, so why, I wondered, why didn't any one speak up to him?

Surely he could not kill off an entire family just because someone asks him questions he does not wish to answer?

There was something. There was a reason they all shied away from putting their foot down and demanding he be a father to his own kids.

But no one would ever say one word to him about it. Ever.

In all fairness to my dear old dad, I never found out what he was up to that day. No one ever mentioned that he needed money, or a favor, or an alibi.

Perhaps just once in his life he wanted nothing from any one?

Yeah right!!!!

45

Thanksgiving it seemed, came and went, spent it at aunt Gloria's as I had all my life, but this year there was no mom.

Dad didn't show up. But really, who thought he would?

The food didn't seem the same to me without having mom's food to select from, but I ate anyway.

Everyone was kind and did their apologies as they did every time I saw them. I felt lost, so out of place, not that anyone was being mean or rude, I just felt alone.

Sher stayed long enough only to eat, said her good byes, then called Ray to pick her up.

I visited with Becky and Carrie, whom I hadn't seen in weeks. I thought I would be able to see them more than I actually did.

Becky and Carrie seemed happy living with aunt Gloria, though Becky did complain that she had a couple of arguments with Cindy aunt Gloria's second oldest daughter. They would argue over stupid things, that would escalate into straight up yelling, but Celia, the equivalent to Sher, would jump in and put them both in their place.

No one ever talked back or smart mouthed Celia, though Becky had done it a few times to Sher right after mom died, it was just unheard of to talk back to Celia, till Becky came along.

I guess Becky and Carrie, being the new kids on the block, wanted shit their way, and I guess Celia always being the boss of her family, said no way.

They would get into it, end result aunt Gloria or Uncle David would be the peace maker.

Though uncle David was strict on his daughters, he was nothing like dad, he never yelled, rather he punished, he took away anything that was of value to you as punishment.

He didn't cuss, not that I ever knew of, and one thing was certain, he never hit anyone, not his wife, or his kids. He ruled, by what I thought was the hand of God.

Each of his seven kids enrolled in catholic school, and in the church choir. It was obvious he didn't have the money to pay to have Becky and Carrie in private school, so they attended public schools.

I mean, no one thought uncle David should have to pay out of his own pocket to put dads two kids in private school. If dad wanted them in private school, then dad needed to pay for it himself, and everyone knew that wasn't likely to ever happen.

Me, Matty and Lori stayed at Gloria's till after midnight, which seemed entirely too long to be there on Thanksgiving anyway.

Sher was home when we got there. Her and Ray were in the living room watching TV. He was polite with his friendly smile and his hellos.

I went directly to bed, feeling sick, not sick like

the flu, just lonely sick, lonely for my mom ..
Though it was a holiday, one to celebrate, to me it just seemed like another day. I really didn't feel like I had to much to be thankful for, though Matty was doing more for me than necessary, my life was so empty.

In two weeks we would be out of school for the Christmas holidays.

Sher was working just enough to get by. Ever so often she would buy things for herself, by putting them in layaway.

Matty was Christmas shopping for Lori and invited me to go.

"What would you like for Christmas?" Matty asked me. Remembering those identical words my own mom had asked me.

"Aunt Matty, you don't have to buy me anything." I told her.

No gift could fix my sadness. No gift could replace the mom I missed so terribly.

It was a nice thought, but getting me a gift was not what I wanted. Matty knew that.

Christmases were always poor for us when mom was alive, me remembering the last Christmas with her and how she was given fifty dollars to spend on her kids, yet mom, being the woman she was, made it a wonderful Christmas.

I just wanted the holidays to be over with so I didn't have to relive it all, so I didn't have to think of what the holidays used to be, and that those loving feelings I'd get from my mom would never be there again.

Christmas, birthdays, any thing that reminded me of mom would be inevitable to roll around every year for the rest of my life, wondering how was I to get through them all.

Finally we were out of school for the holidays. Just about three days before Christmas, Matty came home from work early with some not too good news.

The plant she was working at was closing down for two weeks, and she hadn't been there long enough to get vacation pay, so she was going to go two maybe three weeks with no pay.

"We need to tighten up, it's gonna be tough till I go back to work.

I knew all too well about tough times. I knew to turn off lights we weren't using to bring down the electric bill. I knew to take shorter showers, though I never had one till we moved in with Matty, it was a no-brainer, the longer the shower water runs, the higher the water bill.

I knew to eat only when hungry, not to stuff my face just because there was food in the refrigerator.

Matty even had a talk with Sher about the money she earned.

"I would never ask Sher, but if you have any extra money I sure could use it."

"I only have ten dollars till next week, but I need to get my boots out of layaway." Sher said.
"What boots?" Matty asked.
"I put some boots on layaway and if I don't get them out by Friday I'm going to loose them." Sher explained.
"Well" Matty said, "We really need a little bit of groceries."
Sher and I already knew just how far it was possible to stretch ten dollars because that's what we had been accustomed to spending all those weeks we had been alone.
"Well Sher I'll leave it up to you." Matty said.

I felt bad for Matty, I felt bad for Sher. Both worked hard, but in all fairness Matty had literally supported us all those months, with no help from any one, especially our dear father, and she really never asked anything of either of us.

While I was awake that night, as far as I knew Sher didn't hand over the ten dollars to Matty.
I'm sure it took a lot out of Matty to even ask Sher for her money, but then again she did say it was for food.
For a brief second I wondered why Matty didn't ask dad for help, after all, she was supporting his kids with no help from him.
But then we all knew why! Who would ask his ass for anything, he literally had no shame..

Sher left early the next morning to go to work. Ray picked her up, and would bring her back at two, she had said she was working ten to two.

I was concerned about Sher and Matty's conversation. I really did understand both sides, but there was no way I would voice my opinion to either.

I stayed in my room most of the day, Matty remained at Mary's all day. She never even came home for lunch.

I ate only a bowl of cereal, and skipped lunch, not wanting to stuff my face unnecessarily.

I hoped Matty wasn't avoiding me, though Sher was my sister, I did understand both side of this coin, but in no way shape or form was I gonna pick a side.

46

Matty was at Mary's when Sher came home from work, so when I saw the big bag in her hand I knew what had happened.

She got her boots out of layaway, in spite of Matty's talk with her.

I guess Matty must have been looking out Mary's windows, because within minutes she was at home talking to Sher.

"Sher I just told you we needed food." She seemed very annoyed.

"I'm sorry Matty but I didn't want to loose the money I had already paid on them. I'll give you money next week." Sher explained.

"That's not the point." Matty said.

"Then I won't eat here all week." Sher said, sounding really defensive.

"We'll see what your dad has to say about that." Matty said. And for the first time since we had moved in with Matty, she looked really pissed.

Once Matty left to go back to Mary's Sher argued her point to me over and over.

"We ain't ever had shit our entire lives." She said.

"Matty said we didn't have to pay to be here, she should ask her big brother for help."

I think I knew exactly what Sher was doing. She was preparing herself for the argument she knew she was going to have with dad once he called.

Not one word came out of my mouth as she put her things away and changed her clothes.

I had seen this behavior from Sher before, it was almost like preparing herself for a beating. She got herself all worked up, several times looking as if she wanted to cry. Then she would look like she wanted to beat the shit out of someone.

I figured when dad finally called, he'd scream his head off, Sher would say "yes, and no" and all the bitching would be over. You would think!

Then I heard it, we both heard it, the undeniable sound of my dad slamming his brakes. It was his fucking calling card, the introduction that Johnny G. had arrived. The sound I hated almost as much as I hated my dad's ways.

Unfortunately Matty did not lock the front door on her way out, giving dad what he needed, the opportunity to barge in, like a fricken maniac.

Sher was in our room, I was in the restroom.

"What the fuck is wrong with you?" He yelled at Sher.

"Didn't my sister tell you she needed help?" He was fricken pissed off.

Sher unable to get a word out, because he was already slapping her.

Panicked, I ran out of the rest room and out the front door yelling for Matty. She and Mary came running, a horrible look on both of their faces.

Before the three of us got back in the house we could hear Sher scream and cry and above all that we could hear dad yelling. When we got to our room dad was making Sher pack her things, he was taking her with him.

Sher was crying.

"Johnny leave her alone," Mary screamed.

"This is bull shit Matty, didn't you tell me you asked her for help?"

"Yes, but there is no need to hit her." Matty pleaded.

"The fuck there isn't, I told these mother fuckers to do what ever you tell them." He was bouncing around like he was trying to dodge a bullet. That's just how he reacted when ever he was really mad.

I was crying.. I was back in my old routine of hating the sight of him.

So it seems Matty had gone to Mary's called dad, and told on Sher, expecting dad to call and bitch her out, never thinking he would just show up.

Now Matty and Mary were forced to stand up to him.

Both of my aunts looked horrified, I know Matty never dreamed he would come over here acting like this, but this is what you get when you call the devil himself.

"Where's the fucking boots?" dad yelled.

Sher picked up the box containing her boots, handed it to dad, still never saying a word to him.

Cussing, every other word, mother fucker, yelling and bitching, the same way he had done all my life.

I drowned it all out with my own crying.

He yanked the box out of Sher's hands and threw the box in the trash and told Matty "get rid of those mother fuckers."

Sher was still crying, all her hard earned money was being thrown away.

Dad, still yelling and cussing, went outside to unlock the trunk of his car, stomping his way back in the house, sounding like a fucking kid who would be having a temper tantrum, then getting some of Sher's things and throwing, and I mean throwing them in his car.

Both my aunts literally stood there pretty much their mouths open, but no words coming out.

"I should throw all this shit in the fucking trash." Dad yelled. Mostly because he probably didn't want to haul it all away.

Matty was crying saying "Johnny leave her here, don't take her."

We all knew it was too late. Matty had called and it forced dad out of his comfort zone of the bar or garage, and for that, Sher was gonna pay the price.

"I'm so sorry Sher." Matty cried.

Sher never said a word to any of us. She didn't even say good-bye to me when she left.

Matty and Mary pretty much just stood there, not knowing what to do or what to say, yet I'm pretty sure they both knew Matty had messed up by calling dad.

When Sher got in the car, dad was still yelling at her, still cussing at her. She just stared as if she were hypnotized. I was watching from the window, crying, wishing the hand of God would strike dad dead, because I only imagined what dad would do to her once he got her away from his sisters.

I always thought we were protected by staying with his sisters, I just witnessed that we were not.
This was no different than being at our old house.
He still came and went as he pleased.
He still gave the orders.
He still hit whenever he felt he had the right to.
What was different, his sisters supported us, but not even they could protect us from him.

Dad must have been asking Sher a question, she either didn't hear him, or chose not to hear him, because she wasn't answering him, and as they drove off, he slapped her.
Matty and Mary were crying, terrified in their own right.
Matty knew she fucked up. She had been annoyed with Sher's disregard for us needing food or money, and out of frustration she made the mistake of calling dad.
She got the reaction she did not expect.

Later that day, Matty would come to me and tell me just how sorry she was for what had happened.
It seemed like a kind gesture, but she didn't owe me the apology, I felt she owed it to Sher.
"I swear I'll never do that again. I'll never ever

call him again." She cried.

She was carrying a lot of weight on her shoulders for her hasty judgment call. Mary too.

They had seen dad in action and didn't like it very much. I wondered had they seen this behavior from him before, but never voiced it.

I was again, so afraid of my dad over what had happened, thinking, at least living with Matty I'm free of that horrible man, then witnessing him just waltzing in and hitting Sher, then forcing her to leave, I knew I would never be safe from him.

I went to bed early, not mad at Matty, just scared knowing that by one phone call, one's life could change.

I wondered where he had taken Sher, what had happened to her.

Just as I got in bed, I noticed Sher's boots still in the trash.

I got out of bed, took the boots, box and all out of the trash and hid them under my bed.

Sher had gotten an ass whoopin for the boots at least she deserved to get them back.

47

Matty went back to Mary's, perhaps she knew I was upset and she really didn't know what to say to me. She could say she was sorry, but it would not change the events of that night.

The phone rang.
I wasn't going to answer it because the phone was in the kitchen and one in the living room, and I was already laying down and just didn't feel like getting up.
Whoever it was hung up and called right back, I assumed it was for Matty so again I didn't answer, but when it happened a third time I got up.
"Hello." I said
"Hey Malina." I recognized it was Sher.
"Sher?" I knew it was Sher I just didn't know what else to say.
"Of course it's me stupid ass." She said.
Dad must not have been there for her to be cussing.
"What happened?" I asked
"What the hell you think happened, he kicked my ass." She barked.
I started crying again..
"Don't cry twerp." She tried to comfort me, but I could tell she had been crying herself because her nose sounded stopped up.
"How bad?" I asked.

"Let's just say, the bastard can hit, but I think he held back."

Sher tried to make out like it was no big deal.

"Not the same way he hit mom, did he?" I stupidly asked.

"Naw." she said. I ain't bleeding or nothing, he hit me a few times, but mostly he cussed me out." Sher still trying to sound so tough, or still trying to protect the pathetic father she loved so much.

"He will never change will he?" I asked

"No. I don't think he will, not even getting shot made him change." Sher said sounding annoyed.

"Where are you? " I asked

"I don't know, some apartment in Southside." Sher said.

"Southside?" I asked

"Yep believe it or not, him and his girlfriend live in Southside." Sher said.

I had to think on that awhile. Southside...Now this is the man that lived in North side all his life. He was even fortunate enough to be stationed at the Air Force Base in Fort Worth, so he could still live in North side and not live on the base.

According to dad, "No mother fucking hard core Northsider ever moves to Southside, ever. Eastside or upper Westside for that matter. Hell he disowned a few of his own friends for moving away saying once you move, stay the fuck out of North side. What a fuckin hypocrite he was now.. right.? Well not according to Sher. See his new girlfriend had a fairly nice apartment, I'm sure dad paid for her.

Bullshit, he moved in with her because he knew if he moved her into rat ville, she would pack her shit and be gone.

"Who are you with now?" I asked

"All by myself." She said.

"Where's your daddy? I asked

"Who knows, who cares." She sounded so frustrated.

"Him and Sharon left." Sher said.

"You're not scared?" I asked

"No, why should I be?" She asked.

"I don't know, cause your alone." I said

"And who is with you?" Sher asked me.

"No one." I confessed.

"My point." she said.

"Ok, I get it." I said.

"Where's the boots I got my ass whooped for?" Sher asked, sounding pissed.

"Under my bed." I said.

"What?" Sher asked. "Why under your bed?"

"Cause they were in the trash where your fricken daddy threw them, so I got them and put them under my bed." I bragged.

"Good thinking changa." Sher said.

. "What did Matty say?" Sher asked.

"That she's sorry, she didn't mean to cause all that mess." I said.

"Whatever." Sher said.

"Why did dad make you move out?" I asked.

"Who knows, he was showing off I guess." Sher

said.

"That's what I think." I said.
"What are you going to do about school?" I asked.
"Ray's gonna pick me up." Sher said.
"Which Ray?" I asked.
"Really Malina, for sure not the fucking killer Ray." Sher laughed.
"So you're saying your Ray will drive all the way to Southside just to pick you up?" I asked.
"He better, or I'll break up with him." Sher laughed.
"What a nice boyfriend." I commented.
"Yes he is, and besides it will only be for a week or so, because, I heard dad telling Sharon we're moving.
"Where to?" I asked.
"Guess?" Sher said.
"Where?" I asked again.
"Back to the house." She said
"What house?" I asked.
"Our house dummy." she said.
"Whatttt?" I couldn't believe it.
"Yep right back where we started." Sher said.
"Do you want to go back there?" I asked.
"I could care less." Sher said.
"I thought Ray said for everyone to stay away from there? I asked.
"Who the hell is the boss, Malina?"
"Yeah, but are you going to be safe there Sher?" I really was concerned.
"Hell I won't be there that much." Sher said. "I'll

be with my Ray." She bragged.

It was so damn confusing, her having a boyfriend named Ray, dad having a killer named Ray.

"You, dad and his girlfriend?" I asked.

"Damn your stuuuuupid." Sher said imitating the way dad says stupid with the long u sound, which we all made fun of him for that.

We laughed.

"Damn sista, of course me, dad and Sharon and I know you don't want to hear this but she is gonna have her baby any day, any minute Malina."

"You're right Sher, I don't want to hear it." I said

"Well, I could care less about them. I just want to get back to that part of town so it won't be so hard on my Ray to pick me up and take me wherever I need to go, cause we both know our lazy dad ain't about to haul my ass around."

"Your bossy dad hasn't tried to stop you from seeing Ray?" I asked

"Well actually as he knocked me around, he said no more fucking school for you, no more fucking friends, and no more mother fucking boyfriend. Then he said "if I see that mother fucker around you I'll kill him." Sher said trying to talk with a deep voice as if she were dad..

"Oh my god!" Was all I could say.

"Yep, he threatened to take everything away from me all the way over here, even when we got here he hit me a few more times."

"Damn Sher."

"After he kicked my ass and screamed at me for

an hour, he said Ray could come over here if he wanted to."

"What?" I said

"He told me to tell Ray to bring me something to eat because they have no groceries here." Sher said.

"What the fuck... She don't cook?" I asked referring to dad's woman.

"Hell if I know." Sher said.

"You sure he meant your Ray, maybe he meant his Ray could go over there and make sure your ok." I said without thinking what I was actually saying.

"Ughhh." Sher said.

We both laughed at the thought of loud mouth Ray being Sher's babysitter.

"Sher and Ray sitting in a tree." I began the rhyme.

"Twerp, you better be talking about me and my Ray." Sher said.

"Suuuuure" I lied.

"Ok twerp, I'll come by to get my boots tomorrow." Sher said.

"You sure?" I asked "If you want I can take them to school after the holidays." I offered.

"Are you kidding?" Sher said. "I'm not going to let you wear them for two weeks." she laughed

"I wouldn't dare even try them on." I said.

" Ooohhh they feel so comfy." I tried to make her believe I really was trying them on..

"Now listen here little sista, don't make a damn where I live, or where you live, I'll still beat the crap out you." She tried to sound tough.

But I already knew that was a fact.
"Just kidding." I laughed.
Then I heard a knock on dad's apartment door.
"Gotta go twerp, myyyyy Ray is here." Sher said.
"Better check first." I insisted. "Remember dad likes to trick everyone."
"You're right sista." Sher said.
I could hear her say "Who is it." I could even hear Ray say, "It's me Sher."
"Yep, it's my Ray. See you tomorrow changa." Sher said.
"Ok, bossy." I said to her.
She laughed and hung up.

She seemed to be in a pretty good mood considering she had her ass whooped, but that was Sher always trying to be strong, trying to act tough.
Hell, what was I talking about, she was tough, she was strong. I would of collapsed at the first slap.
It was obvious, dad had over reacted to a situation.
A situation that should never have happened.

Apparently Matty over reacted also, calling to complain, not realizing what he would do.
Sher actions had inconvenienced him for the day, he didn't whip her ass over some damn boots, he whooped her because someone had dared to call him and complain about one of his kids, and with a complaint, came action.
He wasn't the type of father that could pick up the phone, make a phone call and resolve an issue,

calmly. Instead he had to over react to let Matty know he was in control.

Seems to me the simplest solution would have been for dad to simply give his sisters some kind of money for taking care of his kids.

Dad did nothing as any normal man would've done. Everything for him would always be a negative reaction. An over reaction.

Maybe the pressures of not having to be in control all the time was worth the ass whooping for Sher..

I felt very bad for her for what dad had done to her, over some damn boots, yet I felt happy for her because now all she needed to worry about was herself. Living under dad's roof was not going to be easy at all for Sher.

Now, at least she had her boyfriend to get her away as much as possible, and of course, she still had school.

So much she had been through, yet she made the best of it, even if she had to get hit, she still managed to get through it.

She was someone I could never measure up to.

I hoped when I saw her the next day she would have no bruises or cuts on her face as mom had.

There was no way I could imagine seeing all that again.

48

When I woke the next day, Matty had made breakfast. She must've told me over a dozen times how sorry she was. I couldn't disrespect her and say,
"Matty stop, it's not me you need to apologize to." But really, wouldn't she already know that?
Maybe she felt she owed me and Sher an apology.
I told her of Sher calling the night before. I also told her that Sher said dad continued hitting her even when they got to dad's apartment.. Matty cried, even though I assured her Sher said she was ok.

"Malina, I really didn't think your dad would come over here and carry on like that." Matty said through all her tears.
"No matter what, I will never call him again and complain about anything." She sounded so convincing.

But we all knew not telling things to dad was as bad as telling him, because if he finds something out and you knew, and you didn't tell him, then he had your ass too, just for not speaking up.
With dad, it was always a loose-loose situation.

Matty said she was taking Lori to spend time with her dad, if I wanted to go with her to drop Lori off.
She was visibly shaken.

Did she really not know dad would freak out the way he did.

I told her Sher was going to come pick up the boots.

"Is it ok?" I asked, wondering, the second I asked, why am I asking? Surely Matty wouldn't want to keep the boots from her.

Sher paid twice for those fucking boots. Once with her hard earned money, once with an ass whoopin. By all rights they were Sher's boots, no question about that. She deserved them back. Surely Matty would not want to honor dad's demand and throw them away. They were brand new, they had never been worn.

"It's fine." Matty answered almost as if she didn't want to even see the boots, for fear they would remind her of what one phone call to her brother had caused.

I figured then, just how afraid these two sisters really had been of dad. They knew dad hit Sher and yet they stood by, doing nothing.

They heard him cussing Sher, again doing nothing. I wondered if he had been a monster of a brother growing up? Did he hit them when they were kids, did he cuss them, did he have them so afraid of him that they didn't dare speak up now as adults?

Apparently so.

What a horrible hold he had on all the people that loved him.

It was such a sad confusing world to me.

Matty had no objections to Sher getting her boots back. I mean really, the entire thing was not over the boots, it was actually all over ten dollars. Does it go toward food or does it go to Sher's boots?

Sher chose the boots. In Sher's mind she wasn't spending ten dollars on boots, she was saving the other fifty five she had worked so hard for and paid a little every week towards, until they were almost paid off.

It was Sher's choice and she made the choice that made more sense to her.

Regardless, boots or no boots, we still didn't have the ten dollars for food anyway, so when you think of it, this was all for absolutely nothing.

Matty left to take Lori to her dad's. I cleaned and did some laundry. It was a very lonely feeling to be all alone, no one there but me.

Kinda creepy feeling.

Being at Matty's wasn't a bad thing, it just seemed there was not a lot to do. Her house stayed clean, mostly because there was no one there to dirty it. It had nice decent furnishings, something for Matty at such a young age to be very proud of, and I'm sure she was.

She never had any of her girl friends over, rather she went to their homes.

Lori spent ninety percent of her time at Mary's so there were never toys thrown about, and when Lori did play with toys, she always put them away, never being told to, she just did it.

Once Matty cooked, the kitchen was always promptly cleaned, shower was cleaned by each of us after we used it, just seemed the place stayed nice.

I wasn't complaining.

I have to admit I sure missed all the arguments between Becky and Carrie over their jacks tournaments. I missed Danny crying to J.J. just so he could have his way. I even missed Sher being so bossy. How would I ever have known all her bossiness would come in handy when she had to take over as head of our house when mom died and our dad abandoned us within twenty-four hours of her death.

Yes, I missed everyone, yet I knew there would be no going back.

Dad was just too violent. Six kids would never be any kind of match for his brutality. That shit I did not miss, I would never miss.

Being alone did in fact give me plenty of time to think and remember.

Such a mixed up mind of thoughts in my head. I lay on the sofa and was gonna watch TV instead I just lay there, and I thought.

49

I closed my eyes for a second remembering things from my life. After witnessing my dad in action, it was a sure thing I would remember something violent my dad was involved in, not necessarily something he caused, but something he "Took care of" none the less.

Of all things to cross my mind I thought of a time we were at home and mom got a phone call, she was so upset and crying. When mom hung up the phone she called dad, at the bar of course, and told him Helena's brother Henry had been drinking in a bar and he had gotten into a fight. He had been beaten so severely he was taken to the hospital in an ambulance.

Helena's phone number was found in Henry's wallet by one of the paramedics because even the paramedics didn't think Henry would survive. A very horrified Helena immediately called mom after learning her brother was on his way to the hospital.

Helena was crying so much because she thought her brother was going to die, which had my mom so upset because Helena was in fact mom's dear friend.

Henry was Helena's younger brother. He was only fifteen when Helena and Ray were married. Henry lived with Helena all his life so it was definite when Helena and Ray married, Henry remained with them.

So over the next eight years Ray was like an older brother to Henry. A father figure.

Ray never involved Henry in any of dad's bullshit, but he did take Henry under his wing, help him find a job, and he even helped him get his first car.
Yes, in a house full of females, Ray loved Henry as if Henry were his son.

Sometimes Ray would take Henry with him to run family errands, when he wasn't up my dad's ass doing the gangster bullshit. Periodically Ray and Henry would stop by the local bar so Ray could have a cold beer..
While there, they would play a game or two of pool, eventually Ray teaching Henry trick shots and shit, things Ray had spent learning from being in bars with my dad. Henry was a fast learner, caught on very quickly and before you knew it Henry was beating Ray at every single game they played.

Ray didn't have much leisure time, what little time he had away from dad, he spent with Helena and his daughters. But Ray also knew Henry needed a father figure, considering Helena and Henry had neither mother nor father.
So it was Ray that introduced Henry to the game of pool and Henry loved it.

Henry began playing pool with Ray when Henry was about seventeen years old, and now at twenty-three Henry was about the best there was. He was no pro, but perhaps given the opportunity, he could have been.

Henry got into a scuffle once at the pool hall with a few other pool players. They accused Henry of hustling them for money, luckily for Henry, Ray was there with him. Ray was in the restroom when the scuffle began, so when he came out of the restroom and saw Henry in trouble, well let's just say Ray was not known as a "Killer" for nothing, though he didn't kill anyone that night, it was told he almost did.

Ray always told Henry, "You're good, you're damn good, but don't ever hustle anyone, beat them fair and square and you will have no problems." Ray knew for a fact Henry hadn't hustled those three idiots, but Ray also knew just how stupid some drunks act, and he always voiced his concern over Henry's safety.
It was a given Henry was to always call Ray if he were to ever get in shit at a bar or pool hall. "But if I find out you were hustling, I'll kick your fucking ass brother-in-law or no brother-in-law," Ray would tell Henry, then hug him. Tough love, I guess.
Henry knew Ray's ground rules and as far as Ray knew, Henry kept his word and always played a clean game.

So when dad got the call from mom that Henry was in the hospital, every one feared he got beat because someone was accusing him of hustling, which Ray knew was not true.

Ray had murder in his eyes when he and dad got to the hospital.

They say Ray punched a hole in the wall, when him and dad left Henry's hospital room. Hanging on by a thread, literally unrecognizable.

Dad by his friends side, went to get the name of the bar, where Henry had been beat. He cared not who beat Henry or why he was beat, only wanting the name of the bar because Helena couldn't remember the name when she got the call, because she was so frightened.

See the way dad saw it, if an establishment allows one of their customers to get beat and they don't help, or even, though he hated police, if they don't at least call the police to break up the unfair five on one fight, then in dad's eye, it's an eye for an eye.

Dad and Ray believed whole heartedly Henry hustled no one. Some drunk ass idiots, perhaps jealous that Henry was such a good pool player, perhaps just some drunks that fucked up.

Reasons were not dad's or Ray's concern when they drove twenty minutes to get to the bar on the outskirts of town.

Armed and dangerous, dad and eight of his men, as it was told, went to the bar Helena's little brother said he had been, though he could barely speak, he was in fact able to say one word that Ray recognized, and within minutes, dad, Ray and the crew were on their way.

Upon entering the bar, dad, his eight men, and Ray, who incidentally locked the door as soon as all dad's men were in the bar.
Dad ordered the few women that were there, to go to the restroom and shut the door behind them.
Then dad and all eight of his hired killers proceeded to beat the hell out of every man in that bar, whether they had anything to do with beating Henry or not.
Each of the badly beaten men was guilty by neglect, dad would insist, justifying his actions against the men that didn't put one hand on Henry, saying "You low life mother fuckers, wanna just sit there and do nothing."
So for that, everyone was guilty just for being in the bar..

Dad and his fleet of hired hands tore everything up in that bar, every bottle of beer, every glass, every chair, every table, juke box, everything.
Every man in that bar was beat within an inch of their own life. Every man lay on the floor badly beaten, unable to move.

Who knows if their inability to move was from the pain of being beat, or their fear of dad and his men. None the less, they all, unlucky eleven of them, even the bartender, lay on the floor and when dad and his men were finished destroying everything, they brought the women out of the restroom, who were already hysterical from all the sounds they could hear from the restroom and warned every mother fucker in there.

"If any one so much as thinks about calling the cops, I got every mother fucking license plate out there. I will find you mother fuckers and I will kill every one of you sons of bitches, your wives and your mother fucking kids."

"And, should my man die, you mother fuckers better leave this mutha fuckin planet." and.....he went on ... "You bitches" he said to the women that had been forced into the restroom, "this is what will happen to you bitches if you ever say one word." He yelled and pointed to all the men lying on the floor, each in their own puddle of blood.

Each woman was crying hysterically, when dad said "Shut the fuck up bitches, where were your fucking tears when my man was being beat? Did any of you whores cry for him? That could be one of your sons one day." He was screaming at the top of his lungs as he pointed to all the men on the floor.

As horrible as it was, as terrible as the scene was, it seemed to every gangster there that night, every action taken on Henry's behalf was, logical, and justifiable..

The destruction dad and his men had done, all the damage to the bar, all the ass whoopins and all the terror that reigned over every one there that night. All twenty minutes of destruction was done swiftly and violently with Ray standing at the locked front door of the bar.

Once Ray had locked the door, and as dad and his henchmen literally beat the fuck out of everyone, Ray not once moved from his spot near the front door..

He stood as he had been instructed, with a machine gun in hand, the one the F.B.I. had tried so desperately to find years before.

Dad would not allow Ray to lay one hand on any of the men that night, because as dad said. If Ray hit just one of them, Ray, without a doubt, from anger, would have killed them.

While following out dad's orders, Ray was also instructed, "If one of these mother fuckers so much as attempts to leave, or moves even an inch for that matter, kill um. Empty that fucking gun on um and kill them mother fuckers, all of them." Dad had said.

No it probably was not right what dad and his men did to the people in the bar that night. Well it wasn't right for young innocent Henry to get beat for what dad said was, "no fucking reason at all."

Henry recovered from the physical aspect of the ass whoopin he received from five drunk men. He recovered from the pain, but a tiny bit of his brain was not right after that. Perhaps from the physical beating, perhaps he was just so afraid that night when five angry drunk bastards beat and kicked him almost to death.

Henry was not a street educated kid, he really didn't do many things unless they included Helena, Ray or his nieces. Only a handful of times had he ventured off on his own to play pool, this being one of the few, almost cost him his life.

50

Why was I thinking of such terrible things? Why did my mind have to always go back to the terrible things in my life?

I convinced myself, I was thinking all the bad things I could remember, because, again in my life, I had been traumatized by this horrible excuse of a father and though I wasn't the one that suffered the blows, Sher was, I was again a witness to it all.

I was thinking what dad did, in retaliation for his friend Ray, as dad justified his actions defending Henry, yet he was the same man that beat my mom, for some fucked up bull shit. He was the same man that had slapped my sister.

I was sick, I didn't want to think anymore, I wanted to laugh, to smile to be happy, but for me that wasn't going to happen.

My mind wouldn't stop thinking back on all the horrible events from my past.

Startled when I heard the sound of someone honking outside which distracted me from my thoughts. Thoughts that at the time seemed so real, as if I had been there and witnessed it all myself.

It was Sher and her boyfriend Ray honking outside. She came as she promised, though she didn't call first, she didn't try and sneak around so no one would see her, she just showed up.

She didn't go into the house, she just honked and I went out, with her boots in hand.

Matty was across the street at Mary's by then and I knew they must have heard Sher honk, but no one came out, not even Danny or J.J..

"Here Ray, these are the damn boots I got my ass whooped for." Sher said, as she handed Ray the boots.

He looked at them and shook his head in disgust.

"Let me see your face." I told Sher

"Why what you gonna do? She said like a real smart ass.

"Nothing I guess, just like everyone else." I said. Not really meaning to sound like I was throwing Ray under the bus for not getting a gun and blowing dad's head off for slapping his girlfriend around.

Sher showed me the marks on her face. I could see a hand print and some redness, shaking my head as Ray had done only a few seconds before me.

"It's s ok Malina, dad did his little act in front of everyone, I'm ok."

Sher tried to make it seem less important than it actually was.

Ray said nothing, what could he say? He was a mere 17 year old boy, he was no match for dad, and he wasn't stupid enough to make us think he was. The only way he could protect Sher was to marry her, and there was no way that would happen.

Sher was too young and I'm sure after living how we lived, she had no intention of marrying anytime

soon, not even to save her own ass from an occasional ass whoopin she might receive from her precious father, anytime he felt it was warranted.
"You gonna be ok here sista?" She asked me as I stood by Ray's car.
"Better here, then with dad." I said.
"I agree." Ray finally said something.
"I know he's y'all's dad and all, but that shit ain't right." He said looking at Sher with so much sadness in his eyes.

I wondered how much of our lives Sher had told him. He was her boyfriend yes, but I didn't want him blabbing all over school what a monster dad was.
The people that were of concern in our school, the principal, the counselors, the vice principals and all our teachers, already knew what they needed to know, but to have everyone else know, was something I wasn't ready to deal with.

I worried Ray would tell his parents and it snowball from there, not worried anything would happen to dad, more worried what would happen to Ray's parents for trying to help.
"Ok sista, we gonna leave, before anyone does come out." Sher said referring to our aunts.
"You gotta face them one day." I said.
"No they gotta face me." Sher said, which in it's own way was true. Sher did nothing wrong. Why should she feel like she had to avoid anyone?
We hugged good by.

I watched as her and Ray drive off in the same direction she and dad had driven off only yesterday, difference is, she wasn't getting hit upside her head as she drove away, she was smiling and she was sitting near her boyfriend, and in spite of the marks on her face, she still looked happy.

Ray was the bit of sunshine Sher needed to be able to deal with all she had been through.

Maybe there was a guardian angel named mom looking over Sher to get her through everything.

For once, after all the hitting and cussing she had taken, plus trying to be a mom, Sher finally looked happy. She had a boyfriend, someone that didn't depend on Sher for everything, but someone that Sher could depend on..

She was allowed to be a little lady, not a mother and father. She had a tiny bit of happiness and she had them damn boots and yes, Sher was happy.

In case you're wondering, Sher has long since thrown those boots out. But she does posses a photo, a full length photo of herself wearing those damn boots, a reminder of a very bad day.

I think Sher gets teary eyed when she looks at the photo. A reminder of just how easily she got whooped, but also a reminder of her strength, she stood up for what she believed, ass whoopin or not.

51

It was the day before Christmas, Christmas eve, Sher called.
"What you doin?" She asked.
"Nothing, laying around." I said.
"Where's Matty"? Sher asked.
"At Mary's wrapping gifts for Lori." I said.
"Got some news." Sher said.
Everything evil and mean went through my brain. Someone shot dad and this time they didn't miss. Dad's woman left him.
Dad was in jail. If only, if only, I thought.
I remained quiet only wondering, what now?
Just as she said it, I was already thinking it.
"Sharon had the baby." Sher said.
Was I really wanting to be a straight up bitch, to a woman I never met and a baby, a baby by all rights was now my baby whatever.. even my hate for the monster father of ours, had me questioning myself, if I could actually hate a little newborn baby.

I hated Sharon, she was cheating with my dad behind my mom's back. Possibly mom knew, maybe she didn't, but it was hard for me to have any kind words for her. I tried to think of something nice to say, knowing Sher was still my sister and I still had to respect her.
"What is it?" I asked.
"A boy." Sher said.

Well...... I froze.

"Yep a little boy." Sher said. Trying to make an awkward conversation not so awkward.

What was there to say, at the moment I really didn't care. Now dad had himself a third son, but would he even take care of this one, he damn sure hadn't taken care of the other two.

And how would my brothers feel about this news?

Would they be happy or sad?

"Are you going to Gloria's tonight." I asked, only so I could change the subject.

It was the yearly Christmas get together at Gloria's.

"I don't know yet." Sher said.

"Look Malina, I know it's very hard for you, and I know nothing is fair, but we can't blame this little baby."

"No Sher we can't, but we do have a little brother barely five years old and dad doesn't do shit for him. How can I be happy for one he has now with another woman, not our mom, and the fact he has always been so fucking mean to all of us?"

I started crying thinking of dad being nice to some kid and the whoopins I witnessed my self that he gave to my brothers.

"Yes I know Malina, I just wanted you to hear it from me, not anyone else." She said.

"Thanks." I said. Not that hearing it from her made it any easier.

What I figured, Sher had been forced to live with dad and Sharon, and even though Sher knew how dad was, she still had to put up with him.

"Sher." I said.
"Yeah twerp."
"Can I ask you something?".
"What's that?" She asked.
"Aren't you worried? I asked.
"Worried about what?"
"That he might beat you like he did Becky."
She paused for a long time, then she answered.
"Yes sometimes I do worry because he does come in real drunk, and I really don't know how, or if Sharon can control him."
"I stay away as much as I can, because I don't want to listen to his shit or deal with his drunk ass. But until I turn seventeen I have to live somewhere. I'm not going to live in the streets, even if I were to run away to Ray, or one of my friends, dad will find me and beat the shit out of me."
"The only advantage I have that Becky didn't have, not only could I not protect Becky, but all this beating shit I don't think Sharon knows about or is used to any of it. For now I don't think dad wants to show his bad side to her. She did just have a baby."
"Ok. I get it I do understand, but I would be so afraid." I said.
"I mean he did whip your ass over some damn boots, aren't you afraid he will do worse just because he can?" I asked.

"Don't worry Malina, I may have taken his shit for a long time, and he may have gotten away with what he did to Becky, and I know I was unable to protect her, but I'm not gonna be his punching bag. I'm not gonna spend the rest of my life there, I'm just stuck till I turn seventeen, then adios amigos."

I laughed when she said that. It seemed a strange thing for her to say.

"Well you know how I feel, I'm just so sick of every thing he does." I said.

We all know one day he will have to pay for everything he has done." Sher said.

"Soon I hope." I said.

"Did you know he has to go to court in January?" Sher asked

"For what now, I thought he had a year for that." I said.

"This is an entirely different charge." Sher said.

"What?" I asked "Now what?"

"Something about drugs." Sher said.

"I'm not surprised." I said.

"You know we gotta go." Sher said.

"Why?" I asked.

"His lawyer wants all his kids there." Sher said.

"You gotta be kidding." I said.

"Nope, not kidding at all." Sher said.

"Please Sher don't tell me anymore right now, it's ruining my Christmas." I said.

"Ok sorry, didn't mean to throw a bunch of bad news on you all at once." Sher said.

"It's ok, seems I'm so used to it now." I said

"Well. I'll tell you what, how about me and Ray pick you up in a couple of days and take you to the movies with us." Sher sounded happy.

It was a nice thought.

"Yeah sure, I'll ask Matty." I said.

"Ask, no…you tell her." Sher laughed.

"Well, if I go to Gloria's tonight I'll see you there." Sher said. "What time y'all goin?"

"Matty said around eight." I said.

"Don't worry Malina, I don't think dad's going to Gloria's, he's at the hospital with Sharon." Sher said.

"Good...... ok I'll see you when I see you." I tried to sound cheerful.

"Bye little sista." Sher said. "And Malina. I'm wearing my boots." We laughed.

"Bye boss." I said and hung up.

Oh please dear lord don't let dad be at Gloria's. please. I really don't want to see him.

Matty came home with gifts all wrapped up and put them under the tree.

"You ready to go?" Matty asked.

"Yes let me get my shoes on." I told her.

Matty locked up the house and we went to Gloria's.

52

There were so many people there, again as there had been every year. Every where I looked I saw memories of last Christmas when mom was there.

We ate, as we did every year, everyone sang Christmas songs, as they did every year, it was all the same routine, only this year my mom's beautiful smile was not any where to be found.

How different things seemed without her. Not just for me but it always seemed my mom was the one laughing and talking to all the women and all the kids. Seems everyone always smiled, now it just seemed the motions were being done, but there seemed to be a lot of happiness missing.

Perhaps it was just me.

Perhaps it wasn't me, and it was the toll of watching dad's kids that it was taken on everyone.

I mean, here my aunts and uncles were raising all dad's kids with no help from dad what so ever and yet he had just had another kid. Perhaps my aunts and uncles felt as Sharon's mom did.

Take care of what you already have, now it was too late. Dad had his new baby and I'm sure everyone thought the same thing, dad's family and Sharon's family,

"Was dad and Sharon actually gonna take care of this one?"

Perhaps these were just thoughts I was passing through my mind, as I sat and watched everyone coming and going, wishing with all my heart my mom was sitting right beside me.

I must have been staring out in space when my cousin Marcie sat beside me.
"You ok?" she asked.
"What does ok mean?" I asked, Marcie laughed.
"Yeah, I know what you mean." Marcie said.
"Wanna talk? Marcie asked, seems she had asked these same questions when mom died.
"What's there to talk about. You know my dad had his baby, right?"
"Yeah, I heard."
"Well Malina, it's done, all the bullshit he put y'all through, he already did it." Marcie said.
"You know Marcie, I have a lot of hate in me for my dad, but I know I can't hate that little baby."
"No you sure can't."
"But damn he's a... and I looked around to make sure Gloria or uncle David or any other adult wasn't around to hear me cuss, especially uncle David, you know church choir leader and all.
"My dad is a no good rotten mother fucker."
Marcie, I suppose, did not expect such language from me, because she laughed out loud, so loud everyone in the house turned and looked at us. And with her laugh came my laugh, then she laughed louder then I laughed even more. Before I knew it half the people there were laughing also and they didn't even know what they were laughing at. A few moments more of laughter, Marcie and I were almost

crying.

"Girl you are so funny." She was finally able to say.

"It's the fucking truth." She began to laugh again.

I mean it was funny, but I personally didn't think it all that funny, then I realized Marcie and her brothers and sisters were never allowed to say not one cuss word. So to hear me freely cuss just kinda threw her for a loop. She thought it very funny and courageous.

Marcie and I sat back for about thirty minutes comparing notes about every one and every thing.

We started in on, who in the family had gained the most weight, what couples were splitting up, who lost their job, who in the family had gotten uglier since last Christmas, well in our opinion, really just needed something to point out and laugh about.

Of course Marcie and I knew we had not gotten uglier, because she too had begun wearing just a touch of makeup. Not enough for aunt Gloria or uncle David to complain about, but just enough to change our appearance some what, just enough to make us feel good about ourselves.

Always talking and carrying on with Marcie made me happy. She was never fake in any way, she never was unkind, always nice to me.

No one knew what we were laughing about, no one knew who we were laughing about. Everyone just knew we were two young girls making the most of a Christmas party where it was obvious neither of us wanted to be.

At the customary just before midnight giveaway Gloria gave out her yearly Christmas gifts. Everyone ooohhh and aaaawwwwing everything.

It all seemed so robotic to me now. No one was really in the Christmas spirit. Maybe it was just me. Maybe I was the scrooge, maybe I was bringing the entire Christmas party down.

Except for mine and Marcie's outburst of laughter, everyone seemed to be, just there.

Even all the little kids seemed so bored. I realized, dad the magician story teller was not there to excite them all with the same fricken stories he told over and over year after year.

I suppose all the kids would rather have that then have no entertainment at all.

Then the evening got worse, as I suspected it would. Dad showed up, with his cigars and smile. Everyone congratulated him, and patted him on the back.

Goodness, did no one here respect my mom's memory. But it was dad that was related to every one there, he was their relative, their brother, they had to be happy for him, didn't they?

When dad approached me he hugged me then just moved on to the next relative. I was so relieved he didn't try to conversate with me.

I was not his focus. He was the focus there now,

and much to my surprise Sher and Ray walked in.
Apparently Sher and Ray drove dad to Gloria's.
Sher hugged and kissed all the kids, they were all so happy to see her.

Ray was sort of overwhelmed with all the people, and all the commotion around him. It was like wall to wall people, even out on the front porch and in Gloria's back yard. It was a lot for him to absorb all at once considering he was an only child.
He asked if I were ok.
"Look around." I told him
"Yes, I see what you mean." He laughed.

Sher, Ray and dad sat at the table where Gloria waited on them hand and foot as if they were the Royal family.
Me, forced to watch dad act as if he was the happiest man alive. I was nauseated.
Matty saw me and asked if I wanted to leave. She had to have been reading my mind.
Matty and I said our goodbyes to everyone, lastly dad.
"Want to come with us Malina?" Dad asked, looking at me through the corner of his eye.
Was this mother fucker kidding? I thought.
Please someone intervene.

No sooner than I thought that, and before I could answer him, the phone rang.
It was the hospital.

Dad jumped up to answer the phone.

"Ok. ok I'll be there in thirty minutes." He told the nurse.

"Let's go Sher." Dad ordered her like he always ordered killer Ray around..

"What happened Johnny?" Gloria asked.

"The baby is having some respiratory problems, I need to be there." Dad said.

He didn't say goodbye to his own sons, just rushed out.

It was expected....dad's behavior.

Sher hugged us all as dad rushed to Ray's car, having to stand there and wait till Sher came out of Gloria's house to unlock the car doors.

I could hear dad telling Ray as they drove off,

"Hurry man. I need to be there."

I didn't wish anything bad to happen to dad's baby, I really didn't.

As I watched them speed off I thought to myself,

"Talk about needing an intervention."

53

Once dad left, as Matty was gathering Lori and her things I sat with J.J. and Danny. They were so cute, really not knowing exactly what had happened in their young lives. All they really knew was, one day they had a mom and a family, next we were all separated.

But they were just babies really. They did as they were told. They never asked questions and no one offered any information to them.

It was like moving pawns on a chess board, they don't talk, they are just moved where you want them, they have no say in the matter, win or loose.

Me, Matty and Lori left Aunt Gloria's, another family tradition behind us.

I admired all the Christmas lights on all the houses between Matty and Gloria's house, even Lori was saying "Oh Malina look at those." Her excitement of all the beautiful decorations and lights.

It was a very cold night, the sort of bitter coldness that would have me sleeping in a sweater and possibly a jacket if I were going home to sleep. The bitter kind of cold, no matter what mom attempted to do to get our old house warm, she would not be successful. Even four to a bed our bodies would still be cold and shivering. .

Things I hated so much when I was there, wishing with all my heart I was going there tonight with my brothers, sisters' and especially my mom.

Only last year we had spent Christmas and Thanksgiving with both dad's family then mom's family. Now as far as I knew mom's family hadn't contacted anyone to find out how we were, where we were, or what our lives were like. For the moment I did not wish to think of any of them, as I felt none of them thought of us.

When we got home Lori saw all the gifts that Matty had already placed under the tree, thinking Santa came while we were at Gloria's.
 She was so excited, laughing and screaming, then flopped herself down on the floor and began ripping the presents open. Screaming louder with each passing gift.
 I remembered then Lori's excitement the day, about two weeks ago, when Matty brought the artificial Christmas tree from her storage in aunt Mary's garage.
 It was a small tree, which had no smell of pines and no icicles as we always had at home, but it was in fact a tree, and it excited the heck out of Lori.

I smiled as I listened to Lori, thinking it just seemed so different. At our home, though there were not an elaborate amount of gifts, the excitement from all of us was almost overwhelming.
 All of us would be so excited, and it seemed our Christmas's took hours to open every gift, each of us

admiring what the other received.

Six loud kids laughing and having a good time, always about the happiest days of our lives, with so much love from our mom.

But I suppose for Lori it was the best for her. She had no brothers or sisters to share the occasion with, but she did have her mom, aunt Matty, and in that aspect she was very blessed.

I was in awe of a little kid like Lori, knowing what a blessing she had by having her mom. Yes, it was exciting to see Lori's expressions on her face as she opened gift after gift. The look of pride aunt Matty had on her face knowing her hard work paid off to be able to provide a descent Christmas for her child.

Then Matty handed me five gifts, which I hadn't expected any thing at all.

I knew she had no money to buy things for me, then she produced two gifts for Sher.

Matty, like Sher, had put things in layaway.

It seemed so ironic to me that they had both put things in layaway, yet Sher's turned against her.

I was happy that Matty thought of me, I was sad Sher wasn't there to enjoy the moment.

Matty got me two pair of pants, two shirts, a purse, a bracelet and some shoes. She also got me a camera, an instant camera, which was something I really liked.

I hugged her and thanked her.

"If you want, we'll go tomorrow and take pictures ok?" She said.

I was excited, yet I felt guilty for being excited.

Matty and Lori remained in the living room, Lori enjoying her toys, Matty enjoying her child. By the time I lay my head down the excitement had run its course, I was sad thinking of a Christmas without my mommy.

This would be my first one without her, knowing now I would have a lifetime of them to get through.

I lay in my bed, looking at the camera Matty gave me, realizing at that moment, I had no pictures of my brothers and sisters, none of me or Sher and believe it or not there were no pictures of my beautiful mom.

Christmas or not, I cried myself to sleep.

54

Christmas, was over as was the new year, the holidays were behind us. This year was a quiet New Year, without dad and Ray blasting the skies with all their "HOT" pistols and rifles and shot guns, and... whatever weapons they used to scare the shit out of us and the entire neighborhood.

I often wondered if anyone ever got hit from all those stray bullets they sprayed into the air.
.
Along with a new year, came a round-up by the local police department.

Seems for a few years now, once the holiday's were over, the police department would schedule a yearly round-up of all the hoodlums in town and yes, even the top notch gangsters would be taken in for "questioning."

Dad was not exempt from this either. He had his ass hauled in same as everyone else.

Best I could figure, every year some dumb ass head of the police department ordered to "bring in" a bunch of the cities bad asses and try to coerce what ever illegal crimes, or murders or drug dealings they thought they could get these criminals to confess to.

Now you got to be one big dumb ass, or one scared mother fucker to talk to these idiot detectives, because if for some reason you told them anything you knew, well you would, with out a doubt be the next crime the detectives would be trying to solve.

As all gangsters do, they keep their moths shut, and demand an attorney. It was all really just a show of force from the cops, all the gangsters made their grand appearances, refused to say anything, and would be released.

All the things dads men knew, and all the things they had actually done as an order from dad would go with them to their graves, so dad never had to worry that his own men might rat him out.
That, and his men were scared for their lives, and their families lives. Talking to popo about anything dad and or Ray ever did, was kept strictly between dad, Ray and his men.

This year was no different, dad, Ray and perhaps twenty of dad's men were inconveniently hauled in, questioned for about ten hours, then released.
Now you would wonder how the hell did they take dad, Ray and any of their men in, without catching them with their illegal drugs, or stolen weapons, especially dad and Ray.
Common sense, dad had a friend in the P.D. One that let dad know exactly when they were coming for them, and, as good, clean, hard working citizens, nothing was ever found on them.

Every year, once released, dad, Ray and a few of his men would stupidly sit out on our front porch and boast.
I remember one year so clearly.

Dad with his loud talking mouth would brag, "Stuuuuupid mother fuckers, they think I'll ever snitch on a mother fucker?"

Seems that year the police had found a body floating in the river. They had no clues and no identity of that person. They attempted to strong arm everyone, but got no where.

I assumed dad knew who did it, but it wasn't his problem so he stayed out of it.

"I ain't no mother fuckin snitch, but I'll tell you mother fuckers right now, if I have to take the rap for that son of a bitch, he damn sure better be sending me commissary money, he damn fuckin sure better take care of my family, and Ray, make sure you beat the mother fuckers ass every time you see him just for being so fucking stupid."

So it seems, a gangster would rather go to prison, for God knows how long, leave his family behind, leave his organization behind, just so no one would call him a rat?

Made no sense to me at all, yet made all the sense in the world to me.

I suppose when you hear your entire life, "Never rat a mother fucker out," you understand the concept. Seems kinda crazy to me, but then if you're a rat you pretty much can't ever hold your head up with pride. And if you're a rat, you will sure spend the rest of your life looking over your shoulder. Guess dad would have rather been in prison then hide like a snake.

Being the daughter of a fricken gangster was not anything to brag about ever, but there sure was a lot that went on, day and night it seemed. I guess growing up I never really understood just how dangerous living that life was, especially for the kids.

I mean think about it, an arsenal of guns and bullets everywhere. Drugs everywhere, in our house, in dad's car, damn if I remember correctly my poor mom had to carry some of the illegal drugs in Danny's diaper bag anytime they went somewhere together.
I really wonder how the hell my dad got away with all the shit he did. Even if he never killed anyone himself, I mean like pull the trigger himself, how did he get away with all the drug dealing. Were cops that stupid and blind?
Couldn't they smell that shit anytime they pulled him over? Seems the more ruthless the gangster, the more feared, and the more feared, the less likely anyone was to fuck with him.

55

It was now time to return to school from the holidays, with that came new drama with dad, and the beginning of another year without my mom.

Me and Matty had a long sit down talk about everything, I think she beat her self up over what had happened between her and Sher and all.

I knew she messed up, hell even she knew she fucked up, but I wasn't gonna rub it in her face. I didn't want to relive it anymore, seeing Sher get hit by dad only made my hate that much stronger.

Sher was threatened by dad she would have to give up school, that she loved, her friends, that she loved, her boyfriend, whom she apparently loved. But in all reality, other than hitting Sher and cussing her, dad wasn't going to waste his time driving her to school and back, to work and back.

All Sher's hard work of raising dad's kids was over, the responsibility of dad's other fiver kids no longer was Sher's responsibility, it was dads sisters, and like it or not, they did it.

I was preparing for school while Matty was also getting Lori's things ready. I watched as Matty and Lori interacted, what a really good obedient kid Lori was. She pretty much did everything Matty told her to do. Matty raised her very well. I believe the only time Matty really had any trouble with Lori, was when Lori insisted on staying at Mary's to play with all the kids.

   I suppose Lori just got lonely being an only child, and wanted to have some one to play with, some one to hang out with.
   Sometimes Lori would talk to herself, almost like having an invisible friend I guess, which reminded me of Becky when she would conversate with the Angels. I wondered now, was Becky talking to the angels at aunt Gloria's house.

   At home we all just got accustomed to Becky's angel conversations, but I could not help but laugh to myself thinking of Marcie's reaction the very first time Becky would talk to the angels there at aunt Gloria's house. I had a vision of Becky staring at the ceiling, talking, carrying on as she customarily did, and Marcie completely freaking out yelling for uncle David saying "Dad come here quick, get this crazy girl out of here."

   I missed my sisters, I missed Sher, I mostly missed my mom.

   I completely dreaded the walk to school now. It was cold and I hurried to get there quicker than usual. I knew if I asked Sher and Ray to give me a ride so I wouldn't have to walk, they would, but damn they just loved getting to school so damn early.

As I approached the parking lot I saw them sitting in Ray's car, for a moment, I thought they were arguing, and I wanted to turn around and walk away from them.

"Not them too," I thought as I approached Ray's car and Sher turned to look at me.

"Hey sista." Sher said smiling.

"Hey." I said to Sher then to Ray.

"How's everything?" She asked.

"Ok." I said. "Why"?

"Nothing!" Sher said.

"Ok ladies, I gotta go." Ray interrupted.

"What no school?" I asked.

Sher reached over and kissed him goodbye. "See you after school?" Sher asked him.

"Of course baby." He smiled as Sher got out of the car and shut the door.

I walked a little ahead of Sher as to give them time together.

Sher came running up behind me.

"What are y'all up to?" I asked

"Why do you ask that?" Sher asked.

"I don't know," I said "Y'all just seem different."

"I'll tell you later." Sher said, and walked as fast as she could past me, as if she were running away. She seemed very pre occupied.

Just as she vanished into her classroom Donna crept up behind me.

"Hey Malina." Donna said.

"Here I got you something." As she handed me a small box, beautifully wrapped in silver wrapping paper.
"What?" I was so surprised.
"Yeah I got you a little gift for Christmas." She was smiling ear to ear.
"Gosh Donna, I.." She interrupted.
"Don't worry my friend, it's better to give and I gave, besides I don't like anyone else in this entire school except you and your sister."
We stopped walking so I could open it, and saw that it was a very beautiful charm bracelet. It had all kinds of charms hanging on it and it jingled when I moved my hand.
"Gee thanks Donna." I said as I hugged her.
"No need to thank me." She smiled, "Now let's get to class." She said just as the bell rang.

Since it was now a new semester at school, we had all new classes, new teachers, possibly new friends. I was so excited to learn me and Donna had four of our classes together.
Donna was a lot like Sher, she loved to talk. So during one of our new classes together, we did just that. We talked and talked and laughed. Our teacher was busy doing the new student bull shit so as Donna talked about her life, I listened.

She told me she had one sister and two brothers all a lot older than herself, whom had all moved away from Fort Worth for various reasons, leaving Donna and her parents alone. She looked kinda sad as she mentioned her sister, and she seemed to not even remember her two brothers names.

Listening to her describe her life, it was obvious she was babied by her parents, and she was spoiled rotten, but toward me she was a good friend, and I enjoyed any chance we had to talk or hang out.

And as Donna pointed out about her cousin Greg, he was an only child and was as spoiled of a brat as she was. At school they didn't act like what I considered spoiled brats, they seemed normal, and I got along very well with both of them.

Each of the classes we shared, Donna and I sat next to one another so we could talk whenever possible. We also would still have lunch together, even Greg would still sit with us.

Donna didn't really ask me questions about my life, actually I didn't ask her either, she just volunteered information to me. She knew Sher was my older sister, she knew we had other siblings. Other than that she never really asked, and I never volunteered anything. The least anyone knew of the bullshit life I had, the better for me, better for them also.

56

It was nice to have a new friend. Someone that accepted me the way I was.

Donna knew I had days I'd be very sad and other days I'd be happy. Donna never really questioned or pried in my life, nor I in her or Greg's for that matter. Things about my life, things about her life just never seemed to matter. Unless either of us felt like talking about them.

That's why, on this one particular day, when we were having lunch together, I was completely shocked when she asked,

"Malina can I ask you a question?"

"Sure" I said.

She hesitated for what seemed an hour, well, she paused long enough for me to stop eating my delicious lunch and look up at her.

"Your mom and dad, where are they?" She looked too serious.

I looked at her, trying not to cry. Just hearing the word mom, and knowing how lucky she was to still have hers.

"Why?" I asked

"Well, you never talk about them, I just wondered." She said.

My eyes filled with tears, I couldn't hold them back.

"I'm not trying to hurt you Malina, I promise," She

sounded so sad.

"My mom died last year." I said. "My dad. I'd rather not talk about him."

"I understand." she said. "Can I ask you something else? She asked, yet she sounded almost afraid to ask.

"Look Donna." I began, She interrupted….

"I know you probably don't want to talk about it Malina, but there's a reason I'm asking." She tried explaining.

"What, why?" I almost sounded pissed.

"Would you tell me first how your mom died?" She was insistent.

Again my eyes filled with tears.

I couldn't help but wonder why, why after four months of being friends was Donna asking such questions.

"She died in her sleep, some kind of pneumonia the doctor said, and I miss her and I hate my life without her," I was deliberately being mean to my friend, that looked almost as horrified as me.

Now I was flat out crying, right there in the school cafeteria, where everyone could see me.

I didn't care who saw or who heard me.

"I'm not trying to hurt you Malina, I just wanted to know, and I want to be the one that tells you what all these immature kids are saying around here before you hear it from someone else."

"What?" Now I yelled at my only friend.

When I yelled, she shook, a bit the way we kids shook when dad would bitch at us or hit us.

For a second I felt very sorry for her.

"Now keep in mind I don't believe it for one minute, and I want you to know you are my very best friend, and..." she got teary eyed.

"What?" I yelled again.

"Everyone is saying your dad suffocated your mom, killed her and got away with it." Donna's voiced seemed to get more of a high pitched tone as she got near the end of her sentence.

She blurted it out without realizing the impact that statement would have on me.

You talk about getting hit in the face by a Mack truck, by my dear friend, in the school cafeteria, in front of what seemed like millions of students.

For me to think of my mom dying peacefully in her sleep was one thing, but to think my dad killed her, suffocated her, the actual words coming from anyone outside of our family, just sounded so horrible, so cruel.

I couldn't even look at her, not because she told me the school gossip, but because I was so ashamed that still, my monster fathers actions were haunting me, and maybe just maybe she and all the school gossips were right.

Perhaps the mother fucker did kill her, I mean he did have a fucking kid born six months after my mom died.

Was I ever gonna be free of this evil man?

Was there no ending to all the bullshit havoc his fucked up life would have on mine?

I stood up and ran, and I mean ran out of the cafeteria. I wanted to run home, to my mom's house, but that's where dad lived now.

I wanted to go to Matty's but no one was there, so I ran to the office, crying all the way, to Mrs. Crow the assistant principal, but she wasn't there.

Then through all my confusion I ran to the nurses office where I remembered the quiet room Mrs. Crow had showed me when I first got to school.

I burst into the nurses office, who about jumped out of her seat when she saw me, not realizing at first what the heck I was doing. How fortunate for me no one was in her office at that time.

She saw who I was through all my tears and said,

"Come on sweetie!" She stood up, opened the door to the tranquil room and said "Everything will be ok."

I'm not really sure, but I think that's what she said, because I was just so upset. Coming to the nurse was exactly as Mrs. Crow had told me it would be, "No questions asked, no pressures."

I threw myself on the bed and cried and cried and cried, eventually I fell asleep, not quite sure for how long.

I heard the door open, but closed my eyes so whoever it was would think I was still asleep and leave. Maybe it was the nurse, maybe it was Mrs. Crow, whoever it was, left the room and shut the door behind them.

I lay there staring at the ceiling. I wondered if

there was any way in the world I could just live in this room, alone, never have to talk to or see another living being ever again.

I was in the restroom, which was connected to this very private room, when I heard someone enter the room again. Who ever it was, was waiting on me to come out of the restroom because I never heard the door reopen.

I washed my face, and when I came out of the rest room Mrs. Crow was sitting on one of the chairs. She looked up at me as I came out of the rest room and smiled.
"Are you ok Malina?" she asked in the kindest voice I had ever heard.
"Yes." I answered.
"Do you feel like talking about it?" She asked.
It was just me and her, no principals, no office clerks interrupting, no students coming into her office being nuisances.
"Yes." I said, to my own surprise.
"What happened today?" She asked.
I told her of mine and Donna's conversation.
"Was Donna deliberately being mean to you?" She asked.
"No." I said. "Donna is my friend, she gave me this." And I showed her my charm bracelet.
"That's very pretty, and that was very nice of Donna." She said.
"Oh Mrs. Crow, Donna is my friend, I know she

didn't ask those questions to be mean." I was crying.

"I understand Malina, and I agree, I think it was better you heard that gossip from a friend, rather than idle gossip in the hallways."

I hadn't even thought of that. Yes, it would have been horrible for me to have heard kids talking shit in the hallways.

"Ok Malina, I'm going to explain something to you. People, especially kids, can be very cruel at times. They don't think before they speak. Sometimes kids can be bullies and sometimes some kids like to hurt other kids feelings just for the fun of it. I believe what Donna overheard was just that, idle gossip, and being that she is your friend, she didn't want to see you get hurt." She explained.

That may have been true, if this had been anyone else these little school gossips were talking shit about, but what Mrs. Crow didn't realize, my mom's family thought the same as these mean gossiping kids at school did .

Should I tell her? Should I confide in her? Or should I just let the gossip run its course? Knowing if I let these damn kids get the best of me, Mrs. Crow may just have to let me move into the quiet room for life, because I'm pretty damn sure with my state of mind, I'd be in that room everyday, more than I'd be in my classes.

As cruel as all the gossip was I didn't want anyone to know what half my own family suspected of my dad. Can you imagine the shit they would have said if it were confirmed how mom's family felt?

Mrs. Crow was nice and I knew she cared, but I also knew if I confided in her every last detail from mom being beat, to Becky's horrible ass whoopin with the belt, it would force her hand legally, and she might be obligated to contact the authorities.

Not only would dad find his ass locked up, but it was quite possible Matty, Mary and Gloria would also find themselves answering such questions as "Why did you not report the abuse Johnny Guetarro bestowed upon his kids." And I'm pretty sure an answer like, "Cause he's our brother, or, because we're afraid of him," may have just had my three aunts in a little hotter water than they wanted to be.

So… I kept my damn mouth shut.
I wasn't gonna be the one to cause my dad to be locked up. If and when that fucker ever saw the inside of a prison cell, it would be by his own doings, not mine.

Then and there I decided, fuck it, I'd just let Mrs. Crow think it was school gossip, nothing more.
How could I possibly let her know that in spite of any doctors report, I myself thought it quite possible he did kill her?

57

Mrs. Crow instructed me to ignore any of the students that might say something concerning my mom or dad.

Are you kidding? I thought. How the hell do I just "Ignore" all three thousand of these mother fuckers?

Mrs. Crow had been with the school system long enough to know, these type of rumors don't just die down, at least not till there's a badly beaten victim, even if the beating isn't physical rather emotional.

Besides, emotional shit in my life, hurt a hell of a lot more than physical shit ever did. Physically the bruises heal, emotionally not so damn easily.

Damn I'm still suffering over all the fucked up crap I had seen and heard in my life. I'd rather be hit any time of the day.

Furthermore, Mrs. Crow knew she had a wimp on her hands. There was no way to protect me, and she knew it.

She couldn't very well get on stage during one of the pep rally's and announce.

"Ok, all you muther fuckin gossiping bitches, or bastards, what ever the case may be. I do not, repeat, do not want any of you to talk shit about Malina and Sher's mom and or their low life mother fuckin daddy, if you do I'll expel your sorry little asses."

Not likely she would use that type of language but then again this is my story, right?....

Sure I would have liked that to happen, getting embarrassed by her would surely have been easier then dealing with each gossiping mother fuckin kid one by one.

Emotionally, at school, my life was fucked. I had no protection from anyone, not that I knew of..

Mrs. Crow sat with me for what seemed like a week, then when she believed I was comfortable, she sent me back to class. I was scared at first, scared to look at any of the students in the hall, or that I passed on the stairways. Each student I passed I wondered, does she know, does he know that it's quite possible my dad killed my mom.

I was so upset, so stressed over everything Donna had told me at lunch.

Donna panicked, found me in the hall, she couldn't have apologized more. She was crying and was very upset, not only because she thought she ruined our friendship with school gossip, but also she said that Sher sought her out, and had her cornered in the girl's restroom about to beat the shit out of her.

"She really was gonna hit me!" Donna cried.

"I really didn't mean to cause so much trouble."

"It's ok Donna. Everything is ok." I said.

"Yeah, well, you tell that to Sher before I see her again, or should I say, before she finds me again." Donna was terrified.

Apparently when I was having lunch with Donna,

someone saw me jump up and run out of the cafeteria. Without really knowing the facts about why I was upset, someone told Sher "Donna did it." Nothing more.

According to Donna, Sher charged at her like a mad bull. Sher didn't even give Donna a chance to explain.

As Donna said, with tears in her eyes, "Malina your sister had me cornered and was yelling in my face.. "bitch, what the fuck did you do to my sister?"

Honestly I couldn't help but feel sorry for poor ol Donna, she was like me, she wasn't a fighter, she probably would have been knocked out with one punch from Sher, if Sher had actually hit her.

Donna always said she didn't like anyone at school but me and Sher, and now, one of only two people she did like, was trying to kick her ass.

I knew that feeling of being scared of someone, I knew that terrible feeling of getting an ass whoopin. One thing was certain, I did not want my friend getting her ass whooped by my sister.

Donna was no match for Sher, it would have been the comparison of us kids getting our asses whooped by my dad.

No comparison at all.

Sher came at her full force. Donna had no idea how to talk her way out of that one. Luckily for Donna, the person Sher was with talked Sher out of really hurting Donna.

I knew I had to find Sher before Sher found Donna again.

After I talked with Donna in the hall, I went looking for Sher in her last class of the day, but she wasn't there. Dede said she had gotten an early dismissal.

Strange? She didn't tell me she was going home early, and why? Why would she want to go home early anyway?

Well at least I knew Donna was safe for the remainder of the day.

To be perfectly honest I don't think Sher was ever going to hit Donna. If Sher had any intention of hurting Donna, she would have just done it, ask questions later. Maybe it was the fear in Donna's eyes that kept Sher from hitting her, maybe Sher's real intention was just to scare Donna.

Sher knew Donna was my friend, my one real friend. I don't think she would have hit her knowing if she did, then I'd have no friends at all.

I felt really bad for Donna because at this point she did not know Sher had left school for the day. There was no way to let her know, she was already in her last class, and I couldn't very well barge in and say, "Hey friend, you're safe for the rest of the day."

So I went to my last class.

I thought of Donna as I ignored my teacher, well actually everyone ignored her, only difference everyone else was up out of their seats, talking and throwing things. It was an art class, and I suppose she thought all this behavior was an expression of art.

My thoughts on Donna and how scared she had been, noticing that horribly sad look on her face as she pleaded with me to get to Sher before Sher beat her ass. It was sad for me to look into the eyes of a really scared person. I did not like that at all.

Once the bell rang and school was out for the day Donna and I caught up with one another. Usually I walked home alone, sometimes I walked with Donna to the near by convenience store that was one block from the school.

Once at the store I would continue to walk home, Donna would hang out at the store, wait on her mom to pick her up, or her and Gregg would catch a ride with other friends.

Donna had said Greg lived two blocks from her, so might as well both get a ride together, rather than one walk one ride.

As we walked toward the store Donna asked me if I had talked to Sher about the incident in the girls restroom.

"No, I think she got an early dismissal." I told her.

Donna looked concerned but not scared like she had earlier.

"You will talk to her, right Malina?"

"I sure will." I told her. "Don't worry Donna, Sher knows you're my friend."

"I really hope that's enough to keep her from

tearing my ass up the next time she sees me."

"I'm sure Sher just thought, actually I have no idea what she thought, but I will talk to her tonight, ok?"

"'Ok." Donna sounded so relieved.

We continued walking toward the store.

"I'll tell you what Malina, if I'm ever ever ever in shit here at school with anyone, will you please tell Sher to have my back. She is one scary ass bitch." And the second she said bitch, Donna quickly covered her mouth, and looked at me like, oh hell no, I fucked up again.

"Donna."

"I'm so sorry Malina, I'm so sorry…

"Donna it's ok. I know what you meant."

"What I was trying to say is, if I ever get in shit here, I want Sher to be on my side,"

I laughed." I know exactly how you feel." I said.

"Oh, I'm so relived to hear you say that, and please don't tell Sher I called her a … well you know what I said, because I know just saying that b word about her is enough to really get my ass whooped."

We both laughed because it was a fact.

Finally my friend was laughing again and it made me happy. I hoped Donna could forget about the fact that she came inches from getting her ass beat, yet it would have been ashamed had Sher actually hit her. Donna was in fact only trying to help me, but Sher had no idea of the details yet.

We continued walking to the store, I glanced at Donna, thinking, how sad I felt for her. I remembered all the times in my life I had been so afraid of my dad, so afraid to get hit, and now to think my friend was afraid, and she actually hadn't done anything wrong.

I believe it was a power trip my dad was always on, you know having everyone terrified of him. A feeling, apparently he enjoyed.

On the other hand, I hated the feeling, knowing someone was frightened because of something concerning me.

Power…bullshit. This type of control was just not for me..

I knew that night I would have to talk to Sher about the incident with Donna. I hated the thought of my friend being so frightened, and it would be up to me to straighten it all out.

58

I was saying good bye to Donna, when her mom drove up.

I hadn't met her mom yet, so as soon as her mom pulled the car over to the curb to pick her up, Donna pulled me by my arm to her car.

"Come on Malina, I want you to meet my mom." She smiled so proudly.

"Mommy" Donna began, just that one word brought tears to my eyes. I wiped them away before Donna could see what I was doing.

"This is my dear dear Malina, Malina this is my mo"...and she stopped. She looked frightened to say the words.

"Donna I know you have a mom, don't worry." I said.

I wanted her to know, to me it was a blessing to have a mom, I didn't want her to be ashamed that she had a mom and I didn't. I knew after all we had just been through with Sher and all, Donna was trying to be careful with my feelings, and that, I thought, was exactly why I didn't want anyone at school to know my business.

"Malina, you are all Donna talks about at home, I'm so very happy to finally meet you." Donna's mom said.

"Me too." I said, all while thinking, oh no I don't remember Donna's last name, I can't call her Mrs.

whatever, so I said "me to, Miss."

She smiled, a kind warm smile.

She looked kinda old compared to what my mom looked like, but then again, she did have three kids older than Donna.

She had light blond hair and she wore it up, like my mom used too. She was cheerful and happy just like Donna.

"Come on girl's, get in, we can drive Malina home."

"Oh yes Malina, come on." Donna said, as she opened the back seat door for me to get in.

"No that's ok." I said.

"Get in Malina." Donna kinda tugged at my shirt so I would.

Once in the car, I couldn't believe how damn clean her car was. Not that Matty's car was dirty or anything, but Matty's car had the obvious signs that a young child had been in it, a doll, a toy, candy wrappings, but this car looked and smelled like a brand new car.

"Where would you girls like to go to get a bite to eat? You both must be starved, I know for a fact Donna always is." Her mom joked.

"Yes Malina, where ever you would like to go." Donna said.

"I'm so sorry, I can't." I said.

"Why not?" Donna insisted, and she looked like she wanted to cry again.

"I really have to go home. I have to ask my aunt first."

I remember Matty insisting Sher let her know anytime she was going to go somewhere. It was in fact a respect thing. Just in case something happened, she needed to know where we were at all times.

"Is your aunt home so you can ask her?" Donna's mom asked.

"No ma'am, she works till after five." I said.

"Tell you what Malina, unless you just love walking home from school, I do pick Donna up on Wednesday's and Friday's, we always go grab a bite to eat. If you would like to go with us, and if it's okay with your aunt, we would love to have you with us."

She smiled the entire time she talked.

"Yes ma'am, I'd like that."

Donna and her mom both smiled.

"I'll ask my aunt." I said.

By the time the conversation ended we were driving up to Matty's.

"Ok, thank you for the ride, and I'll ask my aunt." I said.

"Bye Donna, see you tomorrow." I said as I got out of the car.

"Bye Malina, I really hope you can join us." Donna's mother said.

"Bye Malina. See you tomorrow." Donna said as she waved.

I watched them drive off wishing that could be me with my own mom.

How I wished Donna and her mom had been driving me to my old house. I would have no shame in them seeing our old fucked up house, just to go back, back where I wanted to be.. At that very second I remembered what my mom always told us.

"Don't be sad for what you don't have, be happy for what you do have."

I don't think that statement held any truth to it anymore.

What I don't have? I don't have my mom, and no I really can't be happy for what I do have now, because what I have now, does not include my mom.

I would have traded all the embarrassment in the world for Donna to see that old rat trap house, just so her and her mom could've had the pleasure of meeting my beautiful mom.

Watching Donna and her mom drive off was sad for me, watching a mother and daughter having that special mother daughter time together.

I didn't go inside right away, instead I sat on the porch, though it was very cold out, thinking, not a few months ago, I was surrounded by my brothers and sisters, wondering what the heck was going to happen to us all. Now I sat alone, with my thoughts, with my memories.

How ironic, my dad was told we were going to live with our aunts so we didn't have to go home to an empty house, yet that's exactly what I was doing. I knew it wasn't Matty's fault, I mean she did have to work, and admit it or not, we all knew the real reason we left our house.

It's just the way it had to be.

59

Finally Sher called me that night. I didn't want to call her knowing dad might just be there and answer the phone. As frightened as I know I would have been, I'm sure I would have hung up on him, and knowing his ass, he would have had the operator trace the call, find out it was me, then drive to Matty's just to kick my ass.

"What's this shit Donna made you cry twerp?"

First words out of her mouth.

"What did that little bitch do to you?"

"She didn't do anything." I defended Donna.

"Bull shit, my spies said that little bitch made you cry, I told you anyone fucks with you, they gotta answer to me."

I wanted to laugh but I already knew Sher was pissed, so I didn't.

For the hell of it I changed the subject.

"I assume daddyyyyy isn't home, the way you're cussing." I tried to laugh.

"Fuck that mother fucker too." Sher growled.

"WHATTTTTT?" I asked.

"You heard me, fuck that mother fucker too." Then she started to laugh her ass off.

Oh my goodness, Sher sure was taking a chance that dad would walk in while she was talking shit, or better yet that he may have a tape recorder hidden somewhere on the premises.

"Don't worry lil sista, I'm home alone, no dad, no

Sharon, no one, just me.

"So what did your friend do to you?" Sher asked, very kindly this time.

I told Sher everything, and without any interruptions at all, she listened.

A very long long pause from the last word I said, to the first word Sher spoke.

"Well I'm not gonna apologize to her because she shouldn't have made you cry, and I do not, repeat lil sista, do not apologize to noooo one, but I will talk to her, and I will thank her for telling you the gossip before you heard it."

"But... I do want to know who told her."

"Why?' I asked.

"Just because I want to know who the gossiping bitch is."

"What if it ain't gossip?" I asked.

"Well if it ain't ...She stopped in her tracks, not really knowing what to say at that point.

I reminded her Donna was my only friend, and I really hated that Donna was so afraid of her."

"Well too bad." Sher laughed

"Don't worry Malina. I wasn't ever gonna hit her."

"Good." I said.

"Not at school, anyway." She laughed.

"Calm down Malina. I ain't dad, hit first."

That was exactly what I had thought not a few hours before. I was so glad to hear her say that.

"So, why did you get an early dismissal?' I asked.

"Bye twerp, gotta go, dad just drove up." And

with that Sher hung up.

Some how Sher managed to avoid letting me know why she had left school early and honestly it wasn't my business. I had no idea what her and Ray were up to.

After we finished dinner that night, I talked to Matty about going to eat with Donna and her mom. Matty was okay with it.

Though Matty never complained again about needing money for food or anything else for that matter, it always stuck in my mind. Not that she went to dad with the conflict between her and Sher, but just how quickly things can change, and I knew I never wanted Matty to fell like she had to allow me to do things.

I knew for a fact I was not an adult yet, and for what ever reasons, if Matty had told me no, then I would not have joined Donna and her mother on Wednesday's and Friday's.

Perhaps like me, Matty knew I was coming home everyday alone, though I could very easily go to Mary's if I wanted. Maybe she wanted me to have a bit of a social life and this was my opportunity.

I thanked her because going with Donna and her mom was just what I needed.

One Wednesday after we ate burgers, Donna asked if Matty would let me spend the night with her on Friday.

"I'm pretty sure she will, but I still have to ask." I said.

"We're planning on taking Donna to the Drive Inn theatre this Friday, and we would like for you to go with us." Her mom said. It sounded like fun.

"If you like I can talk with your aunt first, to give her our address and phone number and so we can meet. And by the way Malina, you can call me Elizabeth. My name is Elizabeth." She smiled as she said it.

"Thank you." I said.

When Matty got home that afternoon I asked her if I could spend the night with Donna and go to the Drive Inn with her family.

Matty said yes, and she seemed really excited that I had been invited.

Though Matty worked long hours and actually came home every day and cooked supper, relaxed awhile and spent time with Lori, she really didn't have time for much else. I suppose in her eyes, it would be good for me to socialize and spend time with my friend.

After I called Donna and told her Matty said I could spend the night, I then packed a bag and had it ready so when I got out of school Friday I would already have my things prepared to go directly to Donna's.

Thursday all day at school, that is all Donna could talk about, going to the Drive Inn theatre.

Once in the hallway as Donna and I were going to class, we passed Sher and Ray. Sher looked at us and gave Donna the "Evil Guetarro Eye" and sort of did her famous, "Elvis eyebrow" the indication to me she was just fucking with Donna, but Donna did not know that.

Donna stopped talking altogether, when she saw Sher, fearful Sher would approach her right there in the hallway, and hit and or embarrass her. But I knew the lift of Sher's eyebrow told me she had no intention of approaching Donna, but rather it was Sher's way of making me laugh.

Once in class Donna asked, "Did you talk to Sher."

"Yes I did, don't worry Donna, Sher is not gonna do anything to you."

"Malina, did you see the way she looked at me."

I had in fact, that's how I knew Donna was safe.

During lunch, just as poor ol Donna feared, Sher came in and stood right beside Donna.

I thought Donna was gonna sprint right out of the lunch room.

"Ok Donna you wanna tell me who's spreading gossip?"

Donna was frozen.

"Only because you did a good thing for my lil sista, am I gonna drop this, but you tell whoever told you the gossip, they need to stop talking shit before I send my dad after them.

Donna's eyes filled with tears, hell my eyes filled with tears.

Donna was teary eyed over her fear of Sher, my eyes were filled with tears over the thought of my dad going after some dumb high school kid and fuckin them up, and the fear everything Donna tried to protect me from, wasn't all gossip.

Sher stood right in front of us, for all of ten seconds, raised her eyebrow one last time then hauled ass out of the cafeteria as she did every time she came in to the cafeteria and knew she wasn't supposed to be there.

Simultaneously me and Donna wiped our tears, all the loser kids just staring at us, wondering if Sher had been there to beat up Donna and me.

Donna and I looked at each other for a second, then we started to laugh. You know that laugh you get when you cry, and laugh at the same time. She was crying for one reason, me for another.

What a sight me and Donna must have been, sitting there, cry laughing, unable to cry one hundred percent, or laugh one hundred percent.

Relief I suppose for Donna she hadn't got smacked by Sher.

Relief for me, my evil father wasn't really there to harm anyone.

Just the threat of him was enough for me.

60

Donna and her mom showed up right after dinner Thursday night so Matty and Elizabeth could meet, and as I hoped they would, they hit it off very well.

Matty agreed that I could go with them but assured Elizabeth that if she said she was going to be with us, then she must be with us, not let us wander off.

"Malina's dad is very very strict and though she lives with me, he still keeps an eye on her.

Not too fricken close of an eye, I thought. I hadn't seen him since Christmas.

It really was of no concern to me, we weren't planning on sneaking out with any boys, at least I wasn't.

"So if you say you and your husband will be with them at all times, then I'm okay with it." Matty said.

"I'd just hate for her father to show up and get upset, if for some reason you aren't with her."

"I assure you Matty, we will be with them every single moment." Elizabeth said. "And I do understand about Malina's dad being strict. You have nothing to be worried about."

Matty and Elizabeth exchanged phone numbers and Elizabeth gave Matty their address, suggesting to Matty she was more than welcome to stop by their house anytime.

Yes, they got along very well, and for that I was grateful.

I was a bit excited because I hadn't spent the night with any friends since before mom died.
It would be different, and a Drive Inn movie.

An evening at the Drive Inn theatre with Donna and her family would not exactly be my very first time to experience such an outing.
Let's see if I can remember details just as they happened? How I wished I could forget.

My little brain ventured back a few years. Who knows why in the hell my father would want to take six young, and I mean very young kids, to a Drive Inn movie..

First off, it was hotter then hell, or what I figured hell may feel like, of course with my daddy dearest acting as the devil himself. I had a quick glimpse of what hell would be like, you know we had all the fixings that night, all that was missing was the pitchfork.

Anyway, you cram six kids, the devil, and my poor mom, who had no desire to be at such a place with Lucifer himself either, and it could only spell disaster, but then again, that's is just how life with dad was.
Pure Hell.

Before we ever got to the Drive Inn, my dad suggests cramming me, Sher and Becky in the trunk of the car so his cheap ass didn't have to pay the additional admission fee. For some reason I thought the Drive Inn price back then was by the car load.

Anyway, he wants us in the trunk, my mom, though she rarely had any say so over any of us when he was around said.

"No, take us home if your gonna stuff my kids in the trunk." Perhaps she was fearful his hateful ass wouldn't let us out of the trunk, once he crammed us in there.

Ok, so the bastard had to pay an extra fifty cents each. First fight of the night.

So it's just getting dark, well only an idiot would expect all six of us kids to remain in the car, really idiot, Danny was barely one year old, he still wore diapers.

Second fight of the night.

Okay Danny is a baby, he does not alert you when he has to poop. Did my gangster father really expect him not to poop for four hours?

Now, my dad was very comfy sitting in the front seat cause he pushed his fricken drivers seat all the way back, thus crushing Becky and Carrie's legs. Yet no one complained.

The little speaker thing that was placed on the window for all of us to hear the movie, well of course it was on dad's side of the car, and he wasn't about to turn the volume up so we all could hear the movie, it was in fact right by his ear, so he had the volume comfortable enough for his damn ears only.

The only sounds we could actually hear were guns being shot, and our dad's big mouth talking back to the screen. Again, with volume only he could hear, it seemed we were watching a silent movie. Just a bunch of mouths moving, because I couldn't make out what any of the people were saying.

I did in fact know there were a lot of cuss words because I could tell, from habit, exactly when one of the men on screen would say "Mother fucker" just by reading their lips.

In a house with every other word being such, you damn well know those words without actually hearing them. Hell we all knew when dad was gonna say a cuss word long before he actually even said it. Just the way he formed his mouth, we could have bet, mutha or fucker was the next words we would hear..

This particular evening was not exactly Drive Inn Theatre weather because it was somewhere in the vicinity of 110 degrees and humid as hell, and of course, his old jalopy had no air conditioner, and even if it did, ol stingy was not about to run his car for four or five hours and waste all his gambling and dice money on gas.

Obviously we have to roll the windows down to breathe, and of course every mosquito from the nearby Trinity River, and as far away as Lake Worth chose that particular night to attack all six of us.

Here all five of us sat in the back seat, because of course princess Sher is up front between mom and dad, that to me didn't seem like an honor, but to ol kiss ass Sher, sitting by her daddy was her choice, her privilege, and an honor for her.

Five kids in the back seat scratching somewhat like a dog with zillions and zillions of fleas.

Dad, annoyed by our continuous scratching, because it interfered with him hearing a ridiculous movie about gangsters, orders all of us to stop scratching, and just like the game Simon says stop, we stopped.

But not because Simon said, but because this here mother fuckin father of ours demanded it of us.

I wondered at that moment why the fuckin mosquitoes weren't eating him alive?

I visualized one mosquito biting him and spitting out dad's blood, warning all the other mosquitoes "POISON" thus causing all the mosquitoes to flock to us kids.

So here we sit, scratching like drug fiend's and of course, one of the kids gotta go potty.

Third fight of the night.

"Didn't I tell you kids to use the fuckin bathroom before we left the house." He evil eyed each of us as he bitched.

Ah, yes you did father you certainly did instruct us

to empty our bladders before we left our house, but believe it or not, our fricken bladders don't understand gangster lingo.

   It was such a blessing when he sent me and Sher and... well all five of us went to potty.

   The second I rolled out of the car, literally, I stretched my legs as if I had been on a coast to coast road trip and hadn't been allowed once to rest my weary legs from sunny California to the beautiful east coast state of Florida.

   Once out of the car, and stretched, and away from our dad's big fricken mouth, we were able to enjoy the peace and tranquility of being away from him.

   Of course we took our sweet time in the restroom, I mean what a fuckin luxury to flush a friken toilet without filling a bucket from the bathtub. Besides, there was nothing exciting at all about getting back to our car, and our big mouth dad.

   Really, who the fuck wanted to see some damn gangster movie anyway, we lived a gangster movie, and then to have to listen to my dad chant, "Kill that muther fucker, kill his ass." As fucking loud as he possibly could.

   Nope not one of us were in any type of hurry at all.

   So once we all used the potty, we slowly walked past the concession stand. What a fricken sight we five kids must have been, with our tongues hanging out our damn mouths as we eyeballed all the fricken sweets.

Oh my! Sodas and hot dogs and pop corn and candy.... keep on truckin kids, cause you ain't getting none of that for sure.
Unfortunately, when we got back to the car, which was so fricken easy to find cause you could hear my dad's big mouth from the restrooms, he was still running his mouth.

I dreaded getting in the car, I mean the mosquitoes had damn near drained all my blood from my body even though they had seven other people in the car in which to choose from, they went directly to me.
Shit, why even bother getting in the damn car, why not sit outside the car, give the pesky little mother fuckers open range on me.

Mom gave us a blanket to sit on, she probably didn't realize just how uncomfortable sitting on a hot, wooly, sweaty blanket would be for us, especially on a bunch of rocks and hot cement. Yes, the cement was still hot from the 120 degree day we had just had.

So me and Sher then Becky then Carrie, just as we had all slept, that miserable four to a bed, sat on a hot scratchy sweaty blanket, to stare at a fucking movie we had absolutely no interest in.

Yes, as expected, dad is yakking non stop, then out of no where, some poor dumb ass a few cars over decides, number one, he either got tired of hearing dad's loud mouth over the actual movie, or he had just arrived at the Drive Inn and he too was a loud dumb ass like my dad. I'm assuming he was talking shit to the movie screen, same as my dad, and my dad's mouth was aggravating him.

   Well, of course some one louder than the great Johnny G caught the great Johnny G's attention.
   Dad, afraid of no one, yells, "shut the fuck up." The other guy say's, "No, you shut the fuck up." It seemed to echo, "No you shut the fuck up, shut the fuck up, shut the fuck up."

61

Gunfight at the Ok corral, was what went through my weary mind, of course my mind was weary, I had no blood left, the fuckin mosquitoes sucked it all out of me.

Though dad was not afraid of anyone, and he sure as hell didn't ever back down from anything or anyone, he gets out of his car and went directly to that other big mouth guys car. I could see the bulk of his pistol in his back waist band as he walked away from us, just like a real wise guy wears it.
Usually there is some type of back-up some where lurking in the shadow's, just to be able to "Have dad's back" so to speak, but who thought dad might need back up at a Drive Inn movie, his wife and kids with him.
Dad rushes out of our car and goes straight to the passenger window of who ever car, which was rolled down, and we watched and we waited a few seconds knowing for sure we were gonna hear, bang bang bang, ready to cover our ears, and lay flat on the ground.
Then all of a sudden my dad disappears in the car, windows roll up.
I mean it literally looked as if dad had been yanked into that car, snatched without warning, that's just how quick it happened.
Standing there one second, vanished the next,

though we all knew where he was, we never saw the door open for him to get in.

Did this mother fucker jump in through the window, and we missed it.

It all happened so damn quick, like BAM... gone!

Did someone just kidnap my damn dad?

No way it could have been a kidnapping, the car would have sped off, then they would have demanded a ransom, which we could never have paid.

So here we kids and mom are sitting, sitting, waiting and wondering if our mom was gonna be a widow, and we wait and we wait and we wait. Eventually we kids climb back into the car which was a bit comfy, without dad yakking non stop, though we paid no attention to the movie, more or less we just sat and stared at the car dad had disappeared into. All of our heads turned to the left, waiting and wondering .

Within thirty minutes, it seemed, dad opens the passenger side car door, and a great big cloud of smoke came out of the car, with no regard for other people in the vicinity what so ever, or the fact everyone at the drive inn could get a whiff of the illegal drug dad and whomever had been smoking.

Dad came back to the car high as hell, mom disgusted by his behavior, and we kids just sat there, waiting, and waiting for the movies to be over so we could go home.

Now it's a fact you would have thought, all that "High" he would have gone straight to the concession stand and brought back some goodies, cause I knew he just had to have the munchies, but then buying snacks for eight people probably would have broke the illegal bank, so to speak.

Dad, now so high he really couldn't shut the fuck up even if he wanted to. And he went on and on and on talking non stop so no one else could enjoy the movie either.

At this point I'm hungry, I'm tired and I'm disgusted wondering, why the hell did he bring us here anyway. None of us were enjoying any thing about being there, so why were we even there? Why the fuck didn't he come alone, or take Ray instead of cramming us all in the car for four miserable hours.

Control I tell ya! It's all about control.

The end of the second movie was near, and I looked over to the car dad had gone and smoked a joint in, as the car door opened and out came the biggest man I had ever seen in my life.

He was well over six feet tall, he must have weighed four hundred pounds, he was bald, he was dressed very nicely, and he was a black man.

He walked over to dad's car window, kinda leaned his head in, handed him, I'm sure a joint or two, and said "Here's my number, call me."

Dad shook the man's hand assuring him he would call.

"Hey there lil ones." He said to all of us as he smiled, showing off one very shiny gold tooth.

His name "Tiny." Obvious reasons.

I would have bet my miserable little life Tiny was also carrying his weapon that night, I'm sure right in the front seat of his car, where he could reach it at a moments notice.

Dad, hot headed as he was, not thinking what the effect it would have on his kids watching him kill a man, or he himself getting killed.

A complete stranger had pushed dad's buttons, forcing him to play his hand, out of anger and feeling disrespected.

Two men, testosterone flying high, by all indications would never have been friends, had they met under different circumstances.

The love of an illegal drug, without a doubt, saved one of, or both of their lives that night.

I called it right that night, "Gunfight at the OK Corral." How right I would have been, if it weren't for the love of that damn drug.

Dad would have a long and very good relationship with Tiny, not quite sure if it was because Tiny had some kick ass weed and dad liked that, or because as dad later said, "I respect the shit out that mother fucker, he didn't back down, he reminded me of me."

That, and I'm sure dad would have had to shoot Tiny with the gun he always carried in his back belt, because if it had come down to kicking Tiny's ass, dad would have lost that match, hands down.

I don't give a shit how many boxing matches dad won in the Air Force, he could never have whopped Tiny's ass. Never.

Dad, Ray and a few other henchmen combined could never have taken Tiny down.

Tiny didn't go to work for dad, he had his own thing going, but he was a good friend, and dad welcomed him to our house on many occasions because I always figured dad could get two things from Tiny he would never get from anyone else.

Killer weed, number one in dad's book, and number two, anyone that didn't fear Johnny G was someone dad needed to keep close. And he did.

Yes, I had one Drive Inn theatre experience in my life, which was more than enough to last me a life time. Some how I figured going with Donna and her family could not possibly compare to going with my father.

62

I saw Sher at school on Friday and told her of my plans to stay with Donna and go to the Drive Inn.
"How exciting for you Malina." Sher said.
"You're gonna love it."
"You've been before?" I asked.
"Sure." She said. "Me and Ray go all the time."
What? And she never told me, goodness I felt disappointed in her keeping a secret from me.
"You'll have a lot of fun, but you better not be sneaking off with no damn boys." She said in a stern voice.
What is wrong with everyone, I wondered. I didn't even like a boy, or know any for that matter.
Maybe I was just stupid and slow. Perhaps of my new interest in make-up everyone assumed I was trying to fix my self up for a boy. Ha-ha, what a joke!

I was excited about watching a movie on a big screen, eating popcorn, and having fun. Hoping, no knowing there was no way being at the drive inn with Donna and her parents could be any where near as bad as being there with my damn dad. Boys were the furthest thing from my mind.

As soon as we got out of school Friday Elizabeth was waiting for me and Donna. She greeted us with a big smile and asked where we wanted to go eat.
"How about spaghetti?" Donna said to her mom.
"Sounds very good to me, how about you

Malina?" Elizabeth asked.
. "I'd love spaghetti." I said.
Elizabeth drove me to Matty's to get my overnight bag then we drove to the nearest pizza place, that also had spaghetti on the menu. Elizabeth ordered us all spaghetti and me and Donna ate till we could hardly move.
Elizabeth ordered a plate of Spaghetti to go, for Donna's dad. Then we drove to Donna's house.

I hadn't been to Donna's yet, heck I had absolutely no idea where she lived.
I was shocked, I actually thought it would be a little tiny house big enough only for Donna, her mom and her dad. It was the exact opposite.

A large two story frame house with the same kind of wrap around porch we had, but theirs wrapped all the way around, without the terribly constructed add on room.
Her house was painted a dark shade of gray, with a bit lighter shade of gray painted around the windows and door frames. I saw no holes in the siding, no broken down old stairs, no signs of destruction and neglect.
A nicely varnished porch swing, just as aunt Gloria had at her house.

My first impression was the house looked similar to a beautiful castle from the outside, with the oval shaped windows.

Their front screen door wasn't like ours, theirs was made of glass as aunt Mary's, and they had a big wooden door with a metal knocker to knock on the door, rather than ring a door bell.

The second Elizabeth opened the front door, I immediately saw a beautiful staircase, which went up about ten steps, then made a turn to the right then it looked like ten more steps. It was beautiful, with beautiful shiny varnished steps.

The foyer, Elizabeth called it, had a coat rack in one corner and a tall potted plant in the other.
To the right of the foyer was the living room with big bay windows, sending lots of light in the room. Two beautiful dark burgundy sofas and a big fireplace, with lamps and a coffee table and a beautiful rug in front of the fireplace.

Just beyond the living room was another room, which had many shelves filled with books, I believe it was a library at one time, but it was now converted into Donna's parent's room, with a very large bed, a white bed spread, can you believe a white bed spread, with lots and lots of different colored throw pillows, covering the entire pillow area of the bed.
The room had one massive picture window with very thick dark blue drapes hanging to block all the sunlight that seemed desperately trying to get into the room.
There was a desk right in front of the window, the

kind of desk you might see in an attorney's office, dark cherry wood, with a dark blue leather, high back chair. A telephone on the desk and an ashtray full of cigarette butts, apparently someone in the family was a heavy smoker.

Quite an impressive room, especially knowing the type of beat down old home I was raised in.

We walked back through the living room, back through the foyer and to the kitchen which was at the very end of a long hallway.

I did not expect what I saw when we entered the kitchen. Seemed like such a nice warm home, except for that kitchen. It was just one step above our kitchen in our old house. This kitchen had no business being in such an elaborate home.

First thing I noticed, it was old and smelled of mildew. The faucet in the sink dripped, making me realize some one didn't take as good care of the kitchen as they did the rest of the house.

The cabinets were tall like ours were, and they had old tarnished brass handles. The refrigerator was old, like ours, not a modern convenience I would've expected such a grand house would have.

An old, very old antique looking gas stove was at the very far left of the kitchen, though it was old, it was shiny and very clean.

There was a small table set off to one side of the room, enough for four people. There were also lots of windows in the kitchen, with no curtains on the windows at all, which made it bright, and gave just enough light for you to see the neglect and wear and tear of the room.

Perhaps upgrading this old kitchen was on the to-do list for Donna's parents. It wasn't a dirty kitchen at all, it just didn't stand up to the standard of the rest of the house, so far.

Donna said "Come on let's go to my room." So we hauled ass up the stairs where there were four bedrooms, Donna's being the grandest of them all.

When she opened her door I saw the biggest bed I had ever seen in my life, with a massive headboard that had lots of carvings and designs on it. Definitely a bed fit for a queen and Donna, to her parents, was definitely the queen.

Her bed was placed right in front of the massive windows, thus blocking any view of the outside. Seems the bed should've been on another side of the room, giving one the opportunity to admire the windows, the view, and the sunlight.

Just my opinion.

Donna had clothes thrown every where, which made the room look dirty.

She showed me the restroom and the other three bedrooms that were stuffed with years of personal things from her brothers and sister, whom hadn't lived there in years, yet left all their belongings for her parents to store for them. It wasn't easy to see the rooms with all the stuff stacked to the ceiling in each room, impossible to tell if the rooms were nice or beaten down like the kitchen.

Three great big bedrooms of nothing but storage.

Now, I understood why her parents slept in the library, they couldn't get all that crap out of there if they tried.

The restroom was enormous, with what I believe was the equivalent to a sunken tub, something I'm sure Donna took bubble baths in. There was a double vanity sink, and a large walk in closet that stored what seemed like hundreds and hundreds of towels and wash cloths.

The restroom was immaculately cleaned, and it smelled of potpourri, not that I knew what the fuck potpourri was really. I had seen and smelt it in my Home-Ec class so I vaguely knew what the hell it was.

Thinking back on our restroom at home that had a sink that flooded and rotted the floor, an old tub, no shower and a toilet we had to use a bucket to flush. Come on now, my old home smelled of funky mildew, dead rats and just plain funk. All the pine sol in the world would never have made that house smell anywhere near as nice as Donna's bathroom. None the less, hers was a restroom fit for a princess, king and queen.

It was definitely a fact, Donna and I came from two entirely different worlds for sure.

63

We were in Donnas room because she was attempting to show me her elaborate collection of shoes, her overstuffed closet of clothes, and sort through the piles of crap she had thrown about everywhere.

I thought of all the hours me, mom, and Sher spent trying to make our house look nice, and here Donna had shit thrown everywhere, and her room still looked better than our old house did five seconds after we cleaned it.

It was a lot to absorb, looking at all those shoes and clothes and stuff everywhere. Though I wasn't impressed by it all, I just thought what a mess. What a deliberate funky mess, yet it didn't seem to bother or embarrass Donna at all.

It was apparent Donna's room was not cleaned daily, perhaps on rare occasion she, or her mom would put the clothes and shoes away, but in all fairness, I would have bet Donna was just used to it.

We were, or she rather, was rummaging through her mess and out of no where Donna screamed, for a second I wondered if she saw a rat or something, then she flew past me, screaming "Daddy, Daddy."

She flung open her door and screamed "Come on Malina."

It all happened so quickly I felt the urge to run like a mother fucker to see what the hell had Donna

so damn excited.
I followed, but walked rather than ran.

As we got downstairs her dad was just walking into the house.

"Daddy Daddy." Donna yelled, sounding so much like Sher I wanted to laugh. I had never in my life heard anyone get so excited to see their dad.

Well, I guess some kids do that now don't they?

As soon as Donna saw her dad she ran to him and hugged him, another foreign thing for me. His eyes lit up the second he saw Donna.

"Donna my baby girl." He hugged her as if he hadn't seen her in years.

"Daddy daddy, this is Malina, my dear dear friend Malina from school."

He looked at me, smiled, and reached out his hand to shake mine. I will always remember the look on his face when Donna told him my name. He looked directly in my eyes, such a kind warm look, almost as if he wanted to cry. He literally stared at me as if he had seen a ghost.

"Well well, this is Malina? Malina it is a pleasure to finally meet you." He shook my hand but he also hugged me, something I was not used to at all. Hell my own dad rarely hugged me, but then I think Donna's parents were a lot like my mom, not at all like my dad.

He appeared so much older than Elizabeth. If I hadn't just met him as Donna's dad, I would've

thought he was her grandfather.
I really didn't know what I expected.

Donna turned into a completely different person when her dad came home, almost babyish, which, after the hellish life I lived, I wasn't used to at all.

At school she seemed so mature, so smart, like she knew so much... that is until Sher got a hold of her.
"Daddy we are still going to the movies right?" Donna wanted to be assured.
"Yes yes Donna, I just need to change clothes and get a bite to eat, and we'll be off." He said. Smiling at Donna and Elizabeth and me.
"Have y'all eaten yet honey?" He asked of Elizabeth as he reached over and kissed her on the cheek.
"Yes dear, we ate spaghetti. I brought you a plate." Elizabeth said, then went directly to the kitchen, I suppose to prepare his plate for him.

Goodness this was one cheerful family, I thought.
But honestly I bet this was how families were supposed to interact, wasn't it?

Donna's mom packed a little picnic basket and took some blankets in case we got cold. It was the middle of winter after all.
All the way to the Drive Inn Donna carried on, daddy this, daddy that, which I suppose if I had that type of relationship with my own father I probably

would act the same.

Naw... not me. Even if I liked the mother fucker I don't think I would have behaved that way.

Donna chatted all the fricken way to the Drive-Inn, she chatted as we parked, she chatted even as the movie began, her parents actually listened and responded to every fricken thing she said, and they even included me in all the conversations.

Seemed like a bunch of energizer bunnies on speed, all yakking at the same damn time. But no cuss words, no yelling, no abuse.

The movie was exciting, which I was actually able to hear, cause no one was yakking non stop throughout it. Surprisingly Donna shut up and actually watched the movie.

We ate hamburgers, popcorn, candy, anything we wanted, Donna's dad bought us. He was the absolute most patient man in the world, smiling and calling us honey, and saying "whatever you girls want from the concession stand, just get it."

An entirely different family an entirely different Drive-Inn theatre experience. It was nice and Donna's parents were very nice, but if I had my way, I'd prefer to be a the Drive Inn with my brothers and sisters all crammed in the car, my dad, ugh, bitchin and cussing about every one and every thing, just to be with my mom. Nothing compared to being with my mom.

Nothing.....

64

It was after eleven when we got back to Donna's.

I called Matty to let her know we were back, it wasn't a condition that I call Matty, I just did out of respect, she did in fact have the right to know where I was.

I could hear Lori laughing and carrying on in the background, which at the moment reminded me of Donna. I thought to myself, damn Lori sounds more mature than Donna.

We said good night to Donna's parents and went to Donna's room.

I half expected her to pull out a baby bed, or a play pen and crawl her ass in it and fall asleep. I couldn't help but laugh.

We talked and talked and laughed. We talked a bit about mom and Sher and all the kids. We stayed up all night it seemed. We never ran out of things to talk about or laugh about.

Right before I went to sleep, I thought of my mom, and the kids and Sher, I cried as quietly as I could. I didn't know if Donna was already asleep, or she just didn't say anything so I could have the moment to myself. She was a good friend, I think she really understood me. I hoped she realized just how good her life was.

It was after noon when we woke and her parents fixed us a great meal, actually all sitting down together at once to eat. Donna's dad actually helped Elizabeth with the dishes as Donna sat there doing nothing. I got up to help them but Elizabeth insisted I was a guest and guests don't do housework.

Once the kitchen was cleaned, Donna and I went to her room to get dressed. She had a hard time finding something to wear, not knowin if the pile of clothes on the floor was clean or dirty. Elizabeth showed up with yet another pile of clothes, these she had just removed from the dryer. I was amazed that Elizabeth would give her more clothes, knowing they would probably wind up on the junk pile on the floor.

Donna put on some jeans and a sweater, then just left the pile of clothes on her bed. If they had been my clothes I would have hung them the second Elizabeth handed them to me.

Once dressed Donna and I went downstairs. Her dad was reading the newspaper, sitting on the sofa, smoking a pipe, Elizabeth was in her room brushing her hair.

"You girl's ready?" Her dad asked..

Then, almost as if they had it all planned out, they took us downtown to see all the sights.

I had a really good time with Donna and her family. It was nice being around people that reminded me so much of my mom and her loving manner.

When they dropped me off, Matty was just

coming from Mary's.
"Sher's been calling for you." She said.
"Is anything wrong?" I asked.
"I'm not sure." Matty said.

I had a bad feeling in the pit of my stomach, but I really didn't want to call the house and ask for Sher, so I asked Matty to. Apparently Sharon answered so Matty asked for Sher.

Sharon told her Sher was not there, but she would have Sher call the minute she got home.

Couldn't have been to important I thought, if it were an emergency Sharon surely would have said something to Matty.

As I was getting ready for bed Sher called.
"Hello." I said.
"Hey twerp, how was the movies?" She asked.
"Good." I said.
"Gotta talk." She insisted
"What now?" I asked.
"Dad's going to court Wednesday." Sher said.
"And…" I said.
"Well Malina, dad's lawyer wants all of us there."
"Why?" I asked.
"Just does." Sher said.
"Okay." I said. There was no sense in arguing about going, I was still a minor, and dad was still my legal guardian, I knew I had to do it.
"We have another problem." Sher said.
What now, I thought.

"We have to go with Sharon."
"What... and why?" I asked.
"Dad said so that's why." Sher said.
I laughed to myself, "Really?"
"Malina you need to meet her."
"Sher just because you gotta live with them, doesn't mean I gotta put up with them." I was so damn annoyed.
"Malina it ain't looking too good for dad." Sher said.
Like I give a shit, I thought.
"It won't look good for dad, if his own kids haven't even met her, besides, like it or not, this is our little brother." She said.
I didn't say one word.
"You can't be mad at a baby Malina." Sher said.

Seems me and Sher had this conversation before. I was no closer to accepting dad's woman than I was months ago. A little baby I would consider, I said consider, but the woman that cheated with my dad behind mom's back, naw, I wasn't eager for that to happen one bit.
"Come on Malina, no one says you gotta like her, just be nice, meet her." Sher seemed to beg.
"When and where." I finally said.
"Tomorrow, your house, I'm taking her to meet all the kids tomorrow afternoon."
"Okay." I said.
"See you when I see you." And with that Sher hung up.

This is one introduction I was not happy about at all.

The woman that had an affair with my dad, which more than likely is what broke my mom's heart, was coming to my house, almost as if I really had no say so in the matter. In other words like it or not, which I did not.

Again something for dear old dad, always do this or that for dad, what the fuck did he ever do for any of us.

Then my mom flashed in my mind.

Goodness, I thought on this long and hard and I do believe my mom was not gonna be happy with me at all.

65

Just as she said, Sher and Sharon showed up the very next day, no courtesy phone call, no warnings, just a quick toot of her horn and there they were.

Screw them, I'm not going out in the cold to greet them, I thought to myself. So I opened the door and waved for them to come inside.

I was not crazy about this meeting, but I knew what Sher was trying to do, she wanted her dad to look good in court, and unless I planned on simply falling off the face of the earth, I wasn't going to be able to avoid Sharon forever.

It just seemed too much too soon, I really wasn't prepared. I get a phone call saying daddy is going to court and by the way you gotta meet the home wrecker, because it's what dad wanted.

Bigger was the shock when I saw them carrying dad's little baby with them.

What the hell did I think she would do with her newborn baby, leave it with the monster.

"Oh my!" I thought.

At that moment I sure wished Matty was there to help me with this situation, even though Sher and Matty hadn't talked since the whole, Sher, get a beaten by your dad, boot situation.

I wondered what was going to be tougher on me, do this with Matty and risk Sher going off on her, or do this alone and get so emotional that I would run everybody off.

Too late, they were at the door.
Once inside Sher hugged me as Sharon walked in carrying her baby in a carrier.
Sher took Sharon to the sofa and they both took off their coats.
The baby was covered with a blanket, I couldn't see him at all.
"Malina, this is Sharon, Sharon this is Malina." Sher tried to make the introductions simple.
Sharon reached out her hand to shake mine, I froze for a second then I obliged.
As Sharon shook my hand she said "Malina I'm very pleased to meet you, Thomas sure has some beautiful sisters." She added.
I didn't know whether to hug the bitch, or slap the shit out of her.
It was intended as a compliment, I know, but I didn't want her to be nice to me. I wanted her to hate me as I hated her.
Quit being so damn hateful Malina. I said to myself.
"Thank you." Was all I could say.

Sher, Sharon and Thomas, on one sofa, I sat in the chair across from them.
She is a blonde. The woman I saw at the garage twice, was a brunette. The woman I saw at the hospital was a brunette.
Did my sneaky, conniving, low life dad have more

then one pregnant girlfriend?
No fricken way. I thought.
Surely this was the same woman. It had to be. Though I wasn't about to ask, besides, Sher was sitting right there, eye balling me, like "Twerp you better not say anything wrong."

Thank my lucky stars dad wasn't there, cause I knew for sure if he were, there would be no way he wouldn't be bitching about something.

"Ok Malina, here's the plan." Sher began.
"Tomorrow me and Ray will pick you up, then we'll go with dad and Sharon to the courthouse"
I really didn't know what to say, we had already done this charade almost a year ago, now we were required to do it all again.
Ok, I got the plan.

Then the little baby started to cry. Sharon took him out of his car seat thingy, and he opened his eyes.
He was absolutely the cutest baby I had ever seen.
"Wanna hold him Malina?" Sher asked.
I was horrified at the thought.
"Can she?" Sher asked Sharon.
"Of course she can." Said Sharon.
Sharon stood up to bring him to the chair I was sitting on. I had never held a baby before, if I ever held Danny or J.J. when they were this little, I sure didn't remember it. I had no idea what to say, what to

do.

At that very second my mind went back to the time I was in the kindergarten play and dropped baby Jesus, though it was just a doll I will always remember looking all over the place for my dad, in that crowded school, to see if he was smiling or frowning.

Now, I thought, I'm so damn nervous, if I drop this kid, my dad ain't gonna be smiling at all, in fact he may just send Killa Ray after me, should I be that fucking clumsy with his little newborn baby.

Sharon put him in my arms, pulled the covers away from his face and said," Thomas, this is one of your sisters, Malina."

I was overwhelmed with so many different emotions clouding my brain at once. Here I was, with the woman I hated, the baby I probably was about to fall madly in love with, my sister Sher, whom at that very moment reminded me too damn much of the dad I couldn't stand, and mostly a vision of my mom.

Thomas looked directly in my eyes.

Hey, little babies can't see yet can they?

I didn't want him to look into the eyes of the sister that hated his mother almost as much as she hated his father. I kept my mouth shut, thinking, Thomas you are so cute, I really don't want to hate you.

This time, in my mind, I said," I'm so sorry mommy, I don't want to dislike a little baby."

My mind was all over the place, trying to be loyal to my mommy's memory, trying to hold and adore

my new little brother, and hating the blonde headed woman that sat across from me.
I felt weak. I felt sick. I felt sad.

Then Sharon spoke, "Malina I know all this is very difficult for you and I won't try to say I know how you feel, but I want you to know, you too Sher, I'm not now, nor will I ever try to take your mom's place." "I'm very sorry for what has happened to her and all of you, and maybe bringing a baby into the world at this time was not a very good idea. But it has happened, and I hope someday we can all be friends."

I myself, had no idea what to say. If I didn't hate the bitch so damn much, it might have been a heart felt speech.
A few seconds of silence, then Sher said.
"We will have plenty of time to talk bout that later, right now we need to concentrate on dad's court thing tomorrow."
"Yes." Sharon agreed.
I was still holding the baby, horrified as I was, I looked at him and he was asleep.
Did this kid have to actually be so damn adorable?
"We'll pick you up at eight, ok Malina?" Sher asked.
"That's fine." I said.

I wondered then, if Sharon knew about dad. I don't mean about him being a gangster and all, just curious if she knew what kind of monster he was. One that beat his kids, that abandoned us, that damn near starved us.

Also I wondered if he ever hit Sharon, did she know about Becky, did she have any idea what kind of father he was to his kids, did it cross her mind if he would be a good father to Thomas? So many questions were going thru my mind.

My conclusion on that subject, there was no way she could possibly know all those horrible things about that monster and still give birth to a baby, and still stay with him. Unless she was a fuckin nut herself.

Then I remembered, damn, she didn't even have custody of her own kids, her mom was raising them.

This was all too much for me.

Where was Matty, why wasn't she home yet helping me survive this very uncomfortable situation?

Sher knew me very well, so I believe Sher knew I had enough.

"Ok, we need to go." Sher said.

Sharon took Thomas out of my arms and began wrapping him in his covers.

"Ok sista, I'll see you in the morning." She tried to smile that happy smile she gets when she's at school.

"Ok." I was at a loss for words.

"Goodbye Malina, I'm very very happy I got to meet you." Sharon said.

Just in a nick of time huh Sharon?

Couldn't have you go into the court room tomorrow and put your hand on the Bible and lie to the judge if he should ask how or if you spend any time with Johnny G's kids, now could we?

"Me too." I lied.

I walked to the door and opened it, them saying bye over and over.

When they got in the car I shut the living room door.

I watched them drive off, quite the sight I thought, my sister I loved, my dad's bitch I hated.

66

I sat in the living room all alone, still able to smell Sharon's cheap perfume. It was nothing like my mom's.

A blonde, I kept thinking. What happened? She didn't look like a cheap trashy blonde, she just looked like a completely different person.

While I waited on Matty's return I decided to call Donna, she was my friend, I knew I could talk to her.
"Hello." Donna said.
"Hey Donna, it's me." I said.
"Hey Malina, what's up." She said.

I started crying as I told her what had happened. She listened.
"I can't imagine having to meet his new girlfriend and sit in a court room with her, all in twenty four hours. I honestly don't know what to say." She said.
"Wanna run away?" She laughed.

I laughed, but I had no reason to run anywhere, I hadn't done anything wrong. Everyone else had.
"As tough as it is my friend, I think you have to go through with it. Look doesn't your dad still have custody of you?" She asked.
"Yes." I said.
"Then, to tell you the truth, I'm no Einstein, but I think he still has the right to snatch you out of your aunt's house anytime he damn well pleases. So if it

were me, I'd just do it and get it over with. Besides in a court room he really can't do any harm to anyone, can he?" She laughed

She didn't know this father of mine, she was unaware of his monstrous capabilities. Maybe he would shoot the judge, shoot me, shoot everyone in the courtroom for that matter.

"Hey, just go make the appearance you need to make, if that's all they want, do it and thank your lucky stars you can go home to your aunt's house and not go home to his house, like Sher does."

Damn Donna sounded so smart.
What excellent advice I was getting from my friend.
"Thanks Donna." I said.
"And about the baby, really Malina, you can't blame that little baby. No one says you gotta love the mama, just don't be mean towards a baby."
She was right, I knew she was right.
"Can you spend the night Friday and we'll go to the Drive Inn again to celebrate." Donna said.
"Celebrate what?" I asked.
"For starters, that you have a nice place to live now, I mean, I really don't know anything about your dad, but I do know you're my friend, and I do know some of the things you've told me about your childhood, and I also know you're very hurt, so let's just call it a celebration that you live with a nice aunt and ...well we are friends.."

We laughed.

"Ok Donna, thanks for all your advice. I really do appreciate everything you said."

And we hung up.

I went to my room to prepare for the horrible day ahead of me, thinking of everything I had just been through. Thinking of my mom, my jerk dad and his ways, my brothers and sisters. How can my brain cope with all this?

Matty came in and I told her of Sher and Sharon's visit.

"Are you ok?" She asked.

"Not really." I started crying.

"I just feel like I'm doing something bad against my mom." I cried.

"Malina, your mom knows you love her. There are some things you may have to do in your life, you may think she may not agree with, but sometimes you just have to do them anyway. You're not being disloyal to your mom by caring for that baby, or being kind to Sharon. Your mom raised you the right way, she wouldn't want you to hate everyone. Let's just take this a step at a time, and if you want I'll go with you Wednesday." She said.

"Would you?" I asked almost too excitedly.

"Of course I will." She said. "Besides, I owe Sher a big apology."

I was so glad to hear her say that.

So it was agreed, Matty would go with me to the

dreaded bull shit I knew I would have to encounter at the court house. Now, I just had to let Sher know Matty would be taking me.

Sher had no reason to be angry if Matty went, Sher was living with the monster, and by the looks of things, getting along very well with dad's bitch, surely she wouldn't still be upset that Matty had called dad that day.

Things were looking up for Sher finally, she had her job, her school, her boyfriend, her new brother, and very few responsibilities, or so it seemed.

As we all knew, living with an off the wall, over hyped up, pot smoking snake would always have it's twists and turns, it was one thing we kids all learned early in life.

Always expect the unexpected.

If dad were in a good mood, something sure as hell would change that mood right fricken quick. And if he were in a bad mood, well too fucking bad, he would remain in a bad mood, until he smoked several joints.

We just had to take this evil man as he was. Couldn't make him a better person if we tried.

Hey some kids have nice dad's some don't. We unfortunately got dealt the hand with the fucked up dad.

I may be wrong, but I'll just bet my ass some of you had a fucked up dad, or fucked up life or fucked up something...But then some of you probably didn't.

67

The dreaded court date was upon us.

I called Sher and reminded her Matty was going with me and she suggested we take J.J. and Danny with us.

Dad was already in the court room when we all arrived, talking with his attorney, all dressed up, as he always was.

Matty pulled Sher aside, I'm sure to apologize, but I could tell Sher only half listened to her. Sher was just too concerned about dad.

Once the bailiff came in the courtroom he told Sharon "Should the baby cry, you will have to leave the court room miss."

We, meaning all seven of dad's kids, his sister, Matty and his... well Sharon, in the courtroom and there sat my dad, waiting now, staring into space.

Not sure why, but I felt he was looking around for mom. I guess he figured she would be there somehow, as she always was.

In a strange way he looked like a frightened child.

Always so handsome, he just didn't seem such an evil person, you would never think it to look at him.

So deceiving...

I didn't want to feel sorry for him. I knew what he was, handsome or not.

"All rise." The bailiff said as the judge entered the

courtroom. We all stood up as we had the previous time we were forced to show support for our father.

I glance over at Danny and J.J., still so cute still so young, yet they didn't look as frightened as they had the first time we were there. Perhaps they already knew what to expect. Such perfect little kids. I mostly watched Danny, wondering what was going through his little mind.
Then I saw Danny punch J.J.'s leg, and J.J. punch him back.
Hey, they were little boys, what can I say. Sher also saw them and whispered for them to stop. On command they listened to her and stopped.
Becky and Carrie could very well have been asleep, they paid no attention to anything.
Baby Thomas, he slept, not making a sound.

As we were standing, in walked the judge, the same one we had seen the last time we were there.
The judge sat, we all sat, same as last time.
"Good morning." The judge said.
A bunch of muffled "Good morning's" from people throughout the court room could be heard. Even Danny said good morning, yet he was about three seconds behind everyone else, with his deep voice, causing a few giggles, as people looked toward him. The judge looked over the rim of his eyeglasses to smile at Danny, Danny getting a bit shy, and sitting back to avoid the stares.
"Mr. Guetarro is this your family?" He asked

pointing to all of us.

"Yes sir." Dad said.

"Is this newborn yours also?"

"Yes sir." Again dad said.

"Very nice, very nice." The judge smiled at each of us, then said "Now to the business at hand."

"In the case... blah blah blah" was all I heard the court lady say.

Dad and his attorney instinctively stood up.

"In the matter of John Vincent Guetarro vs. the state of Texas, sir your case is dismissed."

Could have heard a frickin pin drop.

And just like that, the attempted murder charge was dropped, he was free to go. No nights in jail, no slap on the wrist, nothing.

Well well, well… Fort Worth Texas had it's very own "Teflon Don." Or so it would seem.

Now wait a minute, Sher said there was another case something about drugs. What the hell happened? And who the hell did he attempt to kill and why was it dismissed?

Oh Malina, shut the fuck up, what do you care?

Slimy bastard!

No I did not wish my father to get a life sentence, though it seemed I myself had one.

No I did not wish him to fry in the electric chair like the fucking rat he was, but a few nights in jail couldn't' have hurt that damn much. Besides, a little

discipline in his life might be just what he needed.
Lucky bastard, I thought. Lucky fuckin bastard.

Dad shook his lawyers hand, turned and smiled at all of us, even posing for a second as if he expected movie cameras to be there filming him.
Show off mutha fucker, I thought.
I thought he had another case, but I suppose they don't cram two cases at once, especially one that has nothing to do with the other.

I did not give a shit at this point, I merely wanted to get the hell out of the court room and away from my dad, the judge, the bailiff, the... all the fricken people in the court room. I just wanted out of there. I looked around for a window to jump out of, but figured I'd get my ass beat for embarrassing good ol' Johnny G, no matter how bad I got hurt.

Dad was excited as we left the court room, hugging each of us as he and Sharon and Sher went one way, me Matty and all the kids, the other.

For the moment he had his life back. He was given a second, third, fourth...oh who the hell was counting. He had another chance now, a chance to be with his new baby, possibly to spend time with his other kids, though that seemed highly unlikely.
Dad's focus when leaving the courtroom was Sharon and Thomas, poor Danny and J.J., his namesake, was pushed to the side, once again. I guess

they were pretty much used to that shit by now.

It was still early so Matty offered to take the kids to school if they wanted to go.
Dad had been set free and it wasn't even lunch time yet, of course they wanted to go to school. They were a lot like Sher, they loved school.
We dropped them off, then Matty asked if I wanted to go to school.
As much as I hated it, I really wanted to be somewhere that had a lot of people so I wouldn't have to think about the court room I had just left. Before she dropped me off at school, I asked her if I could spend the night with Donna and go to the movies with Donna and her family on Friday because I knew the second I saw Donna, she was going to want to know if I would be going with them or not.
She agreed.

I was pretty much disappointed in the judicial system. All the bad I knew my dad did, to his family mostly.... Just seemed there should have been a way for him to be punished without actually ratting the mother fucker out.
But as unfair as life had been, it would never be my place to pull the switch on him, if he ever landed his ass in the electric chair.
Another court date behind us, I just wanted the memories of this day to vanish.. for good.

68

Once at school Donna ran up to me.
"Are you still gonna spend the night Friday?" Donna asked.
"Of course I am." I said.
At that moment the bell rang for lunch and I went with Donna to eat. I hadn't checked into school yet, so I really wasn't concerned about being late for anything.

Sher was back at school also, smiling and having a good time with all her friends as she always did. She approached me right before me and Donna got to the cafeteria.
"You okay sista?" She asked, Ray by her side.
"Yes, I'm okay." I said.
Ray looked as if he himself wanted to cry, thinking if dad had gone to jail, perhaps he would never have to worry about dad hitting his girlfriend.
"Okay, I'll call you tonight." Sher said. Possibly just making small talk so I wouldn't cry. Sher knew I was more upset about Sharon than I was about our dad at the moment.
"Okay." And with that Sher and Ray went on their way, me and Donna to eat lunch.

As Donna and I sat and ate I told her some of the courtroom events. She listened as I talked, but I was careful not to say too much, or talk to loud. I remembered these gossiping bitches sitting around us, and I knew if they overheard just too much, they might start running their mouths again.

Once we ate, Donna went to class, I went to the office to check in. I really considered just going home, but what would I do there but think of my bullshit father, his bitch, and their kid.

I got through the day, thanks to Donna, actually I got through the entire week thanks to Donna.

Several nights during the week Donna would call right before I'd go to bed just to check on me. Several times Sher did the same knowing meeting Sharon and Thomas all at once was a lot for me to absorb.

Dad got what he needed again, a show of hands. In other words his kids saved his ass one more time. Puts a lot of sympathy toward a court, to see a bunch of sad kids sitting there, looking worried to death their father would be sent to prison for life for trying to kill someone.

What a judge may have interpreted as sad for dad, was actually sad because of the way we had been abandoned.

All that mattered was dad got his kids to appear in a courtroom just when he needed them. You would think he would say "Thank you" huh?

It was finally Friday. I was a bit excited that I would be spending the night with Donna again, and going to the movies.

We were having lunch together, just me and Donna. Greg again, at a damn skipping party.

I asked Donna if she liked going to skipping parties.

"Not really," She said.

"Well sometimes I do, it really just depends who is having them and where they are."

I personally couldn't imagine skipping school, knowing Sher would be looking all over the place for me, not to mention, if I should be so damn unlucky to go to one and it be the day dad and Ray show up at my school.

Nope...No party in the world was worth that ass whooping.

I looked at Donna as she talked about Greg and the numerous parties he attended.

Damn he was only sixteen, yet it seemed he had been to more parties than most people go to in a lifetime.

Donna was a lot like me she was thin yet very light skinned like Sher. Her hair was really short almost like a boy's and she always had on big round earrings. She wore short skirts, but not too short. Her hair was almost blonde and her eyes were blue as the sky. She was a very pretty girl.

As she was talking about Greg, she said "Malina have you ever noticed the way I walk on my tippy toes.?"

I wondered where that question came from. Last I recall, she was discussing Greg.

"No." I lied.

"Damn liar!" She laughed.

"Hey, I hear all these damn jealous bitches talking shit about me behind my back." She laughed.

It was a fact Donna had a strange walk, it seemed every fifth or sixth step she took, she took it on her tip toes.

When I first met her I noticed it right away, yet of course I never said anything to her about it.

"I have taken ballet lessons since I was seven years old." Donna explained.

At first I didn't want to acknowledge that I had in fact noticed, but come on she was my friend, what was the point in lying?

"Ok, I have noticed a time or two." I confessed.

"Of course you have, and thanks for not staring or talking crap, but I do it out of sheer habit, because all the damn hours I have spent on my toes during ballet class, it's just seems I can't stop doing it.

"That makes sense." I said.

"Not only that," she said with the biggest smile on her face, "Who do you know that has legs this beautiful." And with that she stuck her leg in the aisle for everyone to see.

We could not help but laugh, she simply did not care who talked shit about her, she did it for attention, and she got it.

69

Donna's parents picked us up right after school Friday afternoon, as Donna said they would and drove me by Matty's to get my things.

Matty was home early, on the phone laughing with Alley. I laughed remembering just how crazy and funny Alley always was, as I got my bag and said bye to Matty.

"Have fun, and be careful." Matty said as I closed the door behind me, then got into Donna's parents car.

We went to Donna's dad's favorite restaurant. He was so much like Donna, always smiling. As a matter of fact, all three of them were always in a good mood.

Were they on some kind of drug? I wondered. An entire family of happy people, just didn't seem normal. What was I talking about, I seriously doubt too many people lived in the kind of household I had been raised in. If it weren't for the love of my mom, who knows how twisted each of us kids would have turned out.

We, meaning Donna, me, and her parents enjoyed about the best meal of chicken fried steak and mashed potatoes I had ever eaten. Come to think of it, that was the only chicken fried steak I had ever eaten. No wonder I loved it so much.

Now I understood why it was her dad's favorite.

Donna's parents took us to the Drive Inn, and just as the previous time her dad insisted we get what ever we wanted from the concession stand.

Before the movie began I watched as Donna's dad held on to every word Donna and Elizabeth said. He actually looked in their eyes when he spoke to them. I was always too afraid to look my dad in his eyes, yet Donna's dad did just that. He answered every question they asked, he smiled when he talked, he said thank you and yes honey, and he touched Elizabeth's hand at times. He seemed like a very kind loving man.

It was amazing the patience this man had. As much as Donna talked, at times asking her dad the stupidest question in the world, he still answered her, smiled at her, and never seemed frustrated.

As I sat in the back seat and listened to them, I realized Donna talks a lot, just like my dear old dad. I had a vision of being trapped in a vehicle with Donna and my dad at the Drive Inn, both of them yakking non stop, each louder than the other, both wanting to get the last word in. Only difference my dad always carried his gun, and in this vision I could see my dad bustin a cap in her ass just to shut her up.

Just thoughts.

The movie was a comedy and we laughed the entire time. I do believe Donna's dad laughed so hard, he cried.

Once the movie was over we went back to Donna's and up to her room to chat. After about an hour Elizabeth came up and asked if we wanted a snack before bed.

Donna didn't give her a chance to finish what she was saying. She damn near threw her mom out of her room, and slammed the door almost in her face.

I was completely shocked over Donna's behavior.

It seemed every time I saw Donna and her parents, especially her mom, they always got along so well.

Yes, I craved the attention of my own mom, but I never saw that Elizabeth did anything wrong at all, so I couldn't imagine why the hell Donna was mistreating her. Was she so damn spoiled that she thought it was okay to be so rude, so mean, especially in front of a friend.

She had just thrown her mom out of her room, yet within fifteen minutes Donna was yelling down stairs to her mom to bring us some snacks. And just like a good mom, or a frightened mom, she did as Donna instructed her.

I felt bad for Elizabeth, being ordered around by a fricken kid. Only yesterday Donna was giving me the advice of a lifetime, speaking to me like she was all grown up and shit, now she was acting like a damn spoiled brat. This was rubbing me very very wrong.

If that had been me around my parents my dad would have been knockin some teeth out my fricken mouth if I had ever been so ballsy.

We ate the snacks, listened to the radio and talked awhile, yet the look on Elizabeth's face as Donna slammed the door on her remained in my thoughts.

I told Donna more of the ordeal in the court room, though I didn't go into details about the attempted murder part of it, how could I, I didn't know any details myself.

"Why are you so mean to your mom?" I wanted so badly to cry when I asked Donna.

She looked at me like she had no idea what I was talking about.

"I'm not mean to her." She defended herself.

"Donna yes you are."

"Oh Malina, she knows I don't mean it."

"It still isn't right." I said.

A blank look on her face when she said that, indicated to me, this little bitch really didn't realize how badly she treated her mom.

We would talk about my mom. I'd tell Donna just how much I missed her, and I'd tell her that I missed my sisters that lived with Aunt Gloria. I would never tell her details about my dad. The less an innocent girl knew of a low life gangster, the better off she would be.

My dad was nothing to brag about. Had he remained in the Air Force, remained a fireman or a boxer, sure I'd brag like hell, but how do you tell your very best friend, your father is a killer, a drug dealer, a child beater, and well, everything bad under the sun.

I was concerned if her parents knew anything about my dad's lifestyle they would not care too much for me, rather worry about Donna's safety when we were together. I always told Donna "I'd rather not talk about him." Being the great friend that she was, she always left the subject alone.

Yes, I knew I had me a very good friend in Donna. It wasn't easy for me to make friends, I wasn't one of those real personable people. If I had it my way, I probably would have remained friendless, but then I guess it was just luck and fate when Donna and Greg approached me that first day of school in the cafeteria.

I woke once during the night thinking of Donna's mom, seeming almost like she was afraid of Donna.
Ok I get it, Donna was the baby, her parents spoiled her, they gave her everything she wanted, and for that, Donna should be the most grateful kid in the world. Yet she was treating her parents like they owed her something.

Never ever in my life would I dare speak to my dad like that. Sure I was horrified of him and I talked shit behind his back, and of course all the cussing and shit I did about him in my mind, but never ever would I disrespect him to his damn face, even though he was a low life gangster. Hey if he were anything but a fuckin gangster I'd of had so much more respect..

Then there was her mom, her mom of all people. To yell at her and slam the door as she was talking, ordering her mom out of her room. I had never seen such behavior.

I would never dare even think of speaking like that to my mom, ever. And, though my mom did not have a mean bone in her body, if any of her kids had ever dared to talk to her in such a manner, I would've hoped my own mom would have slapped the shit out of us, though I would have bet my own life she never would have.

70

The next morning Donna and I woke, then ran downstairs to the smell of Elizabeth's breakfast aroma.

Elizabeth was pouring orange juice for me and Donna as we sat down to eat. Donna's dad was, heck I really don't know where he was at that moment.

Now, I do not believe it to have been intentional, and perhaps had Donna's dad not walked into the kitchen wearing his shoulder holster, I may never have learned his occupation. But I can bet the look on my face, a moment of pure shock, and the silence in the room, pretty much sealed the deal.

Someone was gonna have to explain the gun, the shoulder holster, the handcuffs.

A cop? Was Donna's dad a damn cop?

Nope.....Get this, he was a fricken detective.

Not a store detective, but a real detective, with a gun, badge, the entire works. That explains why he was always so nicely dressed, why he would go out of town a lot.

Can you believe, a fricken detective?

Possibly he may never have intended me to learn of his career, or perhaps he did it on purpose, I'll never know. But neither Donna nor Elizabeth had ever mentioned it to me, but again it was none of my business.

I suppose, after a few moments he thought he should explain the holster thingy and all, fearing maybe I might think he was a straight up ol gangster or something.

Okay him and Johnny G did dress alike, and they both carried weapons. Yet, we had machine guns in our house, but then I guess he would never have known that, how could he.

It wasn't an entire fleet of detectives that raided our house years ago looking for dad's machine gun, it was the F.B.I.. I knew that because they had the words F.B.I. on the backs of their jackets.

My dad and Donna's dad opposite sides of the law.
Oh Oh! Now that was a scary thought. I had a queasy feeling in my stomach.

I'm sure somewhere along the line he had to know my last name, my dad's name. Surely he did a background check before he ever allowed me into his house, surely he knew whose daughter was sleeping under his roof.

Surely?

And what about my dad?

I knew for a fact if dad found out whose house I had been staying on the weekends, in his eyes, I'd be the trader giving out top secret information to the enemy.

Hey, I didn't even know any top secret information.

I'm innocent, I didn't know names of people dad killed or that he even, for a fact, killed anyone.
Why should he? He had Ray for that.

The only information I knew about my dad as fact, was that he beat my mom, and that, I never told anyone.
So really, my dad would have nothing to worry about where I was concerned.
But I'm sure he would stick his nose in my business if he knew my very best friend's dad was a detective. He would, no doubt about it, put an end to my friendship with Donna.
He couldn't very well have his daughter in the presence of who he considered the enemy; anyone with a badge.

And Donna's dad, whose name was Jim.
Jim...this was the first time I heard Elizabeth call him by his name. She always said, "honey" or "sweetie," and Donna always said "daddy" so until that very moment I never knew his name.

I wondered why, Jim, not once in all the time I spent with them, he never mentioned my dad, ask me my dad's name or ask any questions about my family.
Why?
Wouldn't he be curious who I was, who my family was, what my family was?
Well, dumb ass Malina, because he probably already knew the answer to any questions he might

have.

Seriously, we all lived in North side, less than a mile apart.

There is no way Jim didn't know who my dad was, or what he was.

There was no way my dad would not know Jim.

So, Jim sat down, buttered his toast, looked me directly in my eyes and said. "Does the fact I'm wearing a gun scare you Malina?"

What kind of question is that? I wondered

"No." I said.

"Do you know what a detective is?" He asked.

"Yes sir." I said very politely.

Now for just a split second I wondered was he serious? I mean not all men come to the breakfast table wearing a gun, other than good guys... bad guys. Right?

Though, to be perfectly honest, I don't remember dear old dad ever having his on while he ate dinner.

Definitely he kept one or two in the car, in his waist band, in Danny's diaper bag, yes, but never just there at the table.

I was kinda confused. But guns were common in my life, so shocked I was not.

Jim went on to explain that years ago he was indeed a police officer, spent a lot of time working the streets and then, after many years and a lot of hard work, he was promoted to detective.

This wasn't looking to good for mine and Donna's

friendship at all.

Yet, I knew this was not a subject I dared share with anyone. Not Matty, not Sher, not anyone.

I decided then and there to pretend I had no idea of Jim's occupation. If anyone ever asked I would lie and say "I don't know, probably a traveling salesman or something."

And if Jim ever asked me about my dad, I would lie and say "Johnny who," and try and laugh it off.

Goodness, did there always have to be something in life to go wrong.

I liked Jim, he was kind to me. I always felt welcome in their home, never uncomfortable at all. He was pretty much what I thought to be the perfect dad.

So knowing he was a detective did not sway my decision about my friendship with Donna one bit. That entire family was just too good to me, for me to worry about minor details, like cops and robbers.

Yes, Jim told his story quick and easy. No long drug out bullshit story, just told me the truth.

However, there was one truth I felt he did not tell me.

Was Jim the good guy, trying to catch the bad guy?...The bad guy... my dad?

71

Time was slowly passing.

Sometimes I'd look over at Sher's bed and wonder where she was or what she was doing. I wondered if she were getting along with Sharon, I wondered if she were happy. Of course I would see her at school and all, but my room seemed very empty without her and all her belongings. Sometimes Lori would sleep in Sher's bed, but mostly Lori stayed with Matty.

Several times a week I'd call Becky and Carrie just to see how they were doing. They would take turns telling me of the things they did at aunt Gloria's, they'd tell me of the chores uncle David assigned to them, and they'd tell me of the arguments they got into with aunt Gloria's daughters. Mostly stupid little arguments, no fighting, just a lot of talking crap to one another. They informed me for spring break Uncle David was going to take them all camping for two days, which Carrie seemed very excited about, Becky did not.

"I don't want to go lay in a nasty old tent all night." Becky complained.

"I do." Carrie said. Probably the very first time Carrie ever sided against Becky.

"Shut up Carrie." Becky growled.

"It'll be fun Becky." I lied.

"Liar." Becky laughed.

"I think I'll pretend to get lost while we're there, just to scare everyone." Becky laughed.

"Becky!" I said.

"I'm just kidding, I wouldn't want to scare aunt Gloria." Becky laughed.

Well like it or not Becky was just gonna have to go and make the best of it.

Dad hadn't been around since the bullshit with Sher, I guess having a new baby was taking up all his time. I wondered if he actually spent time with Thomas, or was he just shuffled to the side like my own brothers had been. Hell, I wondered if Sharon was even taking care of him or had she already handed him over to her own mom to raise as she had her other three kids. I mean seriously she couldn't very well be chasing dad with a new born strapped to her back.

Every single day I would spend time with Danny and J.J. Seems they really enjoyed all the hours they had to play with all the cousins.

And every night I cried myself to sleep.

One night while Matty was at Mary's, Lori with her dad, I was home alone. For some unknown reason I decided to turn on the stereo Matty had in the living room. I really don't know why I did it, I guess I was just bored. The second I turned it on I realized I should not have done it.

Now you must wonder did I never listen to a radio at all. Actually no I did not. Seems Matty just never turned it on when we were in the car and I just never turned it on in the house.

Memory wise, I had just made a very bad mistake. The second the stereo came on, it was playing my mom's favorite song...I hadn't heard it since before my mom died. Now hearing it, I was unable to move my hand to turn the volume down or turn it off all together.

Tears gushed from my eyes.

The horrific lump in my throat, now more like sand in my throat. Herb Alpert was singing, "This Guy's In Love With You" the very song that had my mom in tears every time she heard it. Now I was unable to turn it down.

Instantly every moment in my life I could possibly remember about my mom was in my brain, pounding my head. I was frantic, at that very second Matty walked in, took one glance at me, the look on my face, the fact I was now paralyzed unable to move, tears pouring down my face. Matty literally ran to the stereo and yanked the plug out of the wall.

I screamed for my mom. Matty had no idea what to do. She approached me and reached for me, but I ran to my room. Matty didn't follow me right away, rather left me to deal with my pain on my own. I cried and cried and cried. Seems hours passed, perhaps I was drained of all my tears, just so much pain.

Finally Matty came into my room and sat next to me. I couldn't even see her because my eyes were swollen shut.

"Wanna talk?" She asked.

"No." I answered her.

She touched my hand and said, "When ever you're ready." And with that she left me alone.

I did not leave my bed that night or half of the next day. The song played over and over in my mind.

My mothers beautiful face right in front of me the entire time. Her beautiful green eyes, her beautiful smile, it was all there. The words to Herb Alpert's song played in my mind a million time that night.

Words I always thought made no sense, made all the sense in the world to me now.

As I lay there I knew I could not avoid the radio for the rest of my life. It would be impossible, but I did know one thing. I would have that same reaction every time I heard it.

There are just some things you can never forget about a person. A song, a beautiful song, would break my heart every single time I heard it my entire life.

As painful as it was it was something I had to deal with alone. Matty and I never talked about what had happened, I mean what could she say. Nothing. To this day the first few seconds of the song has me almost hysterical. It is a memory, for me a beautiful memory of a woman I loved so much.

72

Though it seemed I took one step forward, two steps back in my life, it did continue. Donna and I hung out everyday, we talked on the phone every night. I finally understood the concept of talking on the phone, and why Sher and even Matty seemed to love doing it so much and so often.

Donna and I would laugh and talk shit about kids at school, and we would talk of our weekend plans. I told her of hearing my mom's song. She cried, because I couldn't stop crying as I told her.

She assured me I was very loved by my mom, and that my mom's song was a good thing, a good reminder, and though her opinions mattered it was still impossible for me to listen to my mom's song in it's entirety.

I decided to put all the "Jim is a Detective" bullshit behind me. I didn't care who he was or what he did for a living. He, Elizabeth, and Donna were just too nice to me for me to end my friendship with them.

One Friday night instead of going to the movies, Jim came home from work and told us, well I was spending the night, he was taking us "Somewhere."

He instructed us to get in the car with him he wanted to show us something.

We drove for about five minutes then he pulled into a big parking lot. The first thing I saw, what seemed like hundreds of people standing in a long line. I couldn't imagine what all these people, mostly kids, but some dad's, and a few mom's, would stand in line for.

We got out of the car and stood at the end of the line which seemed to me, to be a block long.

Eventually we inched closer to the front of the line, and I was completely surprised, almost shocked, when I looked up and saw what appeared to be a fifty foot tall slide. A fricken slide wide enough to accommodate about six people at a time.

When we got to the front of the line we had to climb a lot of stairs to get to the top. Once at the top we were handed a burlap bag, the same material I used for my jump rope routine when I was in the eighth grade. Given the burlap bag, we placed it at the top of the slide, sat down and, slid down the slide.

This slide had three humps on it, one at the top, one in the middle, and one towards the bottom, which gave me the sensation that took my breath away as I slid over each hump. Almost a sensation of flying, I could only describe the feeling each time we rode the slide that night.

Eleven times Jim paid for me, Donna, sometimes even he rode down with us. Being that the slide accommodated six people at once, Donna and I would slide down at the exact same time, almost racing to see who could get to the bottom first.

What an incredibly wonderful thing someone had invented, and right in the heart of North side.

If I wasn't at the Drive Inn movies with Donna and her family then we definitely were at the Big Slide.

Donna loved it, I loved it, her dad loved it and eventually with a lot of persuasion, we convinced Elizabeth to try it. Though scared at first, seems she couldn't get to the top of the stairs quick enough to slide back down.

Crowds would remain at the Big Slide till eleven at night.

I told Matty and Mary about the slide and once a week, uncle George, Matty, Mary and all the kids would go, let the kids slide a few times and sit back and watch all the slide goers enjoy their breath being taken away.

People from all parts of town would be there six nights a week just to enjoy this new ride. How simple... a slide.

Who would have thought so many would get such enjoyment from something so simple. It's a given it was different. Just about every person alive has ridden a slide at one point in their life. But a fifty foot one. It was rare to say the least.

It was quite an enjoyable past time. Too bad it didn't last.

I would love to see the neighborhood enjoy something so simple, so fun, so unique today...

73

Spring break had arrived.

On the first day of spring break Matty came home and started dinner. I was in the kitchen helping her.

"I have a friend that is a manager of a restaurant on the west side of town. I was telling her about you, and though you're young, she said if your interested she can give you a job there, some after school and weekends. It's not a lot of money, but if you're interested I can call her." Matty said.

A job, money of my own, I thought. How exciting. Then I thought of Sher's job and all the hell it caused.

I gave it a second's thought, and I really mean, just one second, and concluded, I'd rather have a job and money then not. So I agreed that Matty could tell her friend, yes I was interested.

Two days later Matty took me to my very first interview.

After talking to Iris, the manager of the restaurant, it was agreed I would work Wednesdays six till nine, the day I usually went to dinner with Donna and her parents, and Friday's and Saturday's six till ten.

Matty agreed she would take me and pick me up.

I called Sher to tell her of my good news, though she was so excited for me, she also reminded me what had happened to her. Difference was, I had already figured whatever I earned I would give Matty half because it was her gas she would be using to get me back and forth to work, and it was like double the gas for her going back and forth.

Matty said "no" she would not take one penny from me, so I told her in a round about way if she didn't take any money from me, then I didn't want the job, because it made no sense for me to make money yet it would cost her money to get me there and back home.

After some long discussions, she agreed.

"I'm not doing this because of what happened between you and Sher." I told her.

"I know that Malina." She said.

"Then do you agree?" I asked.

"Yes." She said.

Since we were on spring break Iris wanted me to start Friday, just to see if I would even like it.

Matty took me at five thirty on Friday afternoon.

A job, a friken job.

I was nervous because I had never worked before.

Iris was very nice to me, she showed me around the restaurant, took me into the kitchen, gave me an apron to put on and took me to the grandest sink I had ever seen in my life. Already dirty dishes stacked everywhere, one waitress and one waiter were attempting to wash the dishes and wait tables at the same time.

Iris instructed the waitress to assist me so Iris could go out and greet guests. Well I realized real quickly, there is no money in washing dishes for a waitress, so it was very clear to me this waitress, Janie, was not about to spend a lot of time teaching a young, dumb, green as they call it, kid, anything about the do's and don'ts of washing restaurant dishes.

Janie mumbled a few instructions my way then hauled ass back to the restaurant area, to go earn her money.

I sort of stood there a second or two not knowing exactly what to do, but common sense told me, glasses and cups first. Plates, silverware next, then pots and pans.

One of the cooks, Carolina, who didn't speak English very well, came to my rescue.

Seems you gotta put some type of chlorine in the water to sanitize it. Can't let all the customers get sick from dirty dishes. So, with apron on, gloves on my hands, my hair pulled back in a pony tail, I went to washing dishes. And I washed and dried and put away a lot of dishes that night. Seems I didn't stop for one second, it was non-stop work for almost five hours.

Working in the kitchen of a restaurant, a very busy restaurant, isn't just about washing a few dishes, Everything must remain clean and sanitized. Everything had to be scrubbed and put in it's proper place. Then there was the sweeping and moping, which wasn't actually my job, but I figured I would do everything I could so Iris would let me remain an employee.

It was hard work but I enjoyed it, and I sure as heck wasn't going to complain. At my young age, a job was a job, money was money. It probably was illegal for me to work at fourteen, but I didn't care, and I don't think Iris cared either, because she wanted me to work whenever I could.
Because of my age Iris said she was going to pay me cash, and she would pay me daily, which would be even better for me.
I suppose it was a bit illegal for me to be working, child labor laws and all, but I cared less.
Damn I was gonna be stinking rich, and I was gonna have money every single day. How perfect was this, when twenty four hours ago I had not one cent to my name.

Sixteen dollars.
I made sixteen dollars that first night and Iris paid me all in ones. In all honesty, I probably didn't deserve near that much money, because washing dishes, you don't get tips for that, and the hourly pay was just a few dollars, but I did keep up with the demand of the restaurant. And several times throughout the night Iris did come into the kitchen and check my work. Without an industrial dish washing machine, Iris had to depend on me to do my job and do it well. Which I did, hence the sixteen

dollars, and the fact only a fool would actually want that job. So I suppose to entice me Iris paid me well. I held sixteen dollars in my hand. For once in my life I accomplished something, and I was very proud of myself.

Matty and Lori were waiting at ten when I got off work. A smile on both their faces when they saw all my one dollar bills.

I handed Matty half of them and she put up a fight, which I knew she would, but a deal is a deal. Gas prices weren't what they are today, but it was still costing her something to get me back and forth, and it was after ten, which Lori should have already been in bed. Matty was sacrificing again for me, the least I could do was try and help her.

I did the math on the way home that night, if I made sixteen dollars three times a week, I'd have forty eight dollars by the end of the third night. Give Matty half, I'd still have twenty four dollars just for me. Shit dad didn't hardly give Sher that much to feed all six of us for two or three weeks.

It was a very good feeling for me to have a job and give back.

I told Matty about all the dishes and pots and pans I had to wash, she even joked how quickly I should be able to do dishes at home.

What I did at Matty's was nothing compared to the restaurant dishes.

Even though the work was a little hard it was still a job and I had money now.

It's a fact if my mom were alive there is no way I would be working at such a young age. I would not have wanted to anyway. I'm sure she would have washed and ironed ten times the clothes she did just so I would not have to.

Life was just so unfair.

74

We continued the tradition Sher had started of us going out to eat on Fridays, only difference, we did it on Sunday nights, because we didn't have time Friday or Saturday nights, and like Sher, now I was paying for the meals. I was glad to do it because Matty cooked all week and she deserved a break.

And as it turned out, working on Friday's and Saturday's meant I was working more hours, more hours meant more money.

On the Saturday's I would work, if Matty were going to go out with Alley, she would still pick me up after work, actually Alley would be with her most of the time.

"We ain't no early birds." Alley would laugh when her and Matty picked me up. "And we do have to make our grand entrance, now don't we Matty."

They would drop me at home, Lori would either be with her dad or at Mary's. If she were at Mary's I'd get her and take her home so she could sleep in Sher's bed.

One Saturday when Matty and Alley picked me up, they asked if I wanted to go out with them.

Me? I'm just a kid. Go where?

They had it all planned out, I'm supposing they just wanted to see me have some fun, and of course I'd be safe with them.

We went to the house so I could change clothes, and lying on my bed was a very very nice brown little mini dress and some brown high heeled shoes Matty had bought for me.

"Try them on," Matty and Alley both laughed.

I put the clothes and heels on which made me a lot taller, the dress fit perfect. It showed the little bit of a figure I had, just never let anyone see it.

Then those two crazy women put a lil bit more makeup on me than I was accustomed to wearing, then teased my hair a bit to make me appear taller, and by the time they were through with me I didn't look like a fourteen year old teen, I sort of looked grown up, but not like slutty grown up, I actually looked like a little lady.

Oh my dad would kill me if he saw me, I, at that moment realized what I'd look like when I actually turned twenty.

Both Matty and Alley smiled with delight.

Was Matty doing the right thing taking her young niece to a club with her? How the heck could she even get me in the front door?

Well for one thing you gotta know the right people when you go to a club. Of course my hand was marked to prevent me from drinking, but I wasn't there to drink....I was there ... what was I there for?

Alley got a table near the front of the dance floor, while Matty orders soda for me and soda for herself, and a drink for Alley.

Matty wasn't about to drink and drive with me in

the car, and my driving techniques were not quite up to par for me to safely drive us all home, should Matty and Alley both drink. Besides, I think that night was supposed to be for me, so I could see first hand what all the laughter was about when Matty and Alley would laugh their asses off while making fun of their nights out..

Though I assumed when Matty and Alley went clubbing they both drank, I'm also assuming one of them drank less than the other as to be able to drive home without getting pulled over. .

Now, as you know Alley is the dancing party animal of the duo, though Matty could hold her own. And many men requested both of them to accompany them on the dance floor, which they did.

I was no "dancer" per say but I could "Shake a Leg" so to speak.

As Matty and Alley were on the dance floor a man, not a teen, but a young man approached me and asked if I would like to dance. I said no, I mean really I didn't know him, I had never danced before, well not with a guy, I had only danced at home with my mom and brothers and sisters. Now this was a real club with live music and people everywhere dancing and having a good time, I was sort of frightened. Then Matty and Alley both came from the dance floor and told me "yes, yes go dance with him." A lil bit to much eagerness in their voices I would later recall.

I was embarrassed because, well come on now, I

really hadn't had many opportunities in my life to go dancing, so as you can imagine I was a bit frightened.

But I was not there to sit at a table all night, and if I looked stupid, I could care less, I knew none of these people, and I probably would never see any of them ever again, so what the hell did I care how stupid I might look to them. So with a lil "push" from Matty and Alley I went to the dance floor.

Once on the floor, the band was playing a song I was familiar with which had a beat perfect for dancing, or attempting to dance. I did not look at my dance partner for about five seconds, mostly because I was so embarrassed, but when I did I wanted to laugh in his face, instead I looked toward Matty and Alley and they were laughing so hard I thought Alley might piss her pants.

No, this dude was not John Travolta, he was…hell I don't know what he was, or what the hell he was doing, but it was fricken funnier than hell. Four longgggg minutes I had to dance with that idiot and by the time the song was over, I had pretty much figured that Matty and Alley had put him up to asking me to dance because he was the one Alley always imitated when she would show me and Matty his dance moves. Poor guy he was horrible, but I can tell you this much, every girl in that club wanted to dance with him, not because he was such a good dancer, but because he was so horrible, he made even the worst female dancer look fantastic.

It was 2 a.m. closing time. Alley was a bit drunk, Matty and I were not, obviously.

We dropped Alley at her house and when we got home Matty made us both a late night snack.

Matty asked me if I had a good time.

I told her I did, and she said anytime I wanted to go with her and Alley I was more than welcome.

I thought on that long and hard long after Matty went to bed that night. An open invitation to go out with the grown up ladies, just to have fun. The more I thought on it the more I realized it really wasn't a good idea after all. Though I understood very well, Matty really just wanted me to have a good time.

I never went back to that nice club with her and Alley again, even though the invitation always stood.

Not because I was too young, there were actually a lot of young girl's and guy's there that night, but somehow I thought if my dad finds out about this, he's gonna have a fricken fit. And the way he drug Sher out of Matty's, I was concerned he would do the same to me.

I did have fun with my aunt and Alley, they know how to have fun, that's for sure. But no fun in the world was worth my dad finding out and forcing me to live with him.

I'm sure Matty thought of it long before she bought me the outfit that night. But I think Matty's opinion was, I had been through a lot, she wanted me to have a little fun. Which I did.

As big as that club was I'm so surprised no one there knew my dear dad, but perhaps a lot of people did, they just didn't recognize me. Otherwise, I'm sure some fricken tattle tale snitch would have ratted me out to him.

But, he never mentioned it to me or Matty.

We were safe.

The Casino Ballroom, my first visit to a club. Quite an elegant place, right on the waters of Lake Worth. Not a place I was willing to take an ass whoopin for, should my dear dad find out about my historical night.

It was a nice place for it's time, and yes it was fun watching my aunt and Alley have fun, as women their age should have. And then of course getting to see and dance with the great "Jerry" that night.

As fun as it all was, it just would not have been worth the terror that could have reigned in my life if "Johnny G" got wind of it all.

Nope not worth it at all.

75

    Because of my new job I had to stop spending the night with Donna as often, I preferred the money more than I wanted a sleep over.
    But we still had fun when we did hang out.

    Sometimes on Saturdays, before I had to go to work, Donna and her parents would pick me up and take me to a movie at a local theatre. Or we would go window shopping at the local mall. Sometimes we would buy things, hey I was a rich kid now right?
    Then there would be times they would all pick me up and take me to eat.
    I believe her parents enjoyed me as much as I did them. Jim was always so nice, but not just to me, to everyone. I was never concerned my dad would see me with them and recognize Jim. I mean unless Jim was gonna take us to Sal E Bar, it was highly unlikely we would ever run into dad.

    I suppose Donna was missing our friendship, and actually I was missing being around all of them, so on some Friday nights at ten o'clock, they would pick me up from work, instead of Matty, so I could spend the night with Donna.

    Now, I know Donna never worked a day in her life, so she had no idea I'd be tired and couldn't stay up all night and talk. But I guess she just wanted a friend. I didn't stay every Friday night, perhaps just now and then, but our friendship continued.

Sometimes, early Saturday mornings, her dad would take us to eat breakfast so her mom could sleep in.

One morning me and Donna attempted to make breakfast for them and we screwed that up. We burned the eggs and the toast. Neither of us knew how much coffee to put in the coffee pot and when Jim took a drink, I thought he was gonna be sick. Me and Donna laughed at him because he couldn't get to the sink quick enough to spit it out, and he spit it all over his clean, white, starched shirt.

But in all they were a very nice family.

Jim, jokingly told Elizabeth to clean out one of the upstairs bedrooms, so I could have my own room when I was there. He said I was family and he wanted me to feel I could stay with them anytime I pleased.

I wondered where Donna's brother's and sister were, she never discussed them, but just as I never wanted to discuss my dad, I did not pry. It was as if their stuff was there but they never came around.

Oh well, it wasn't my business. I was glad they never pried in my life, I stayed out of theirs.

One Saturday morning Donna was showering and I was downstairs talking with Elizabeth. Jim had gone to buy a newspaper and fill his car with gas.

I think Elizabeth knew I really enjoyed being with them, because she was just so kind to me.

"How are you Malina?" She asked as I sat at the table while she washed the dishes.

"I'm fine." I said.

She had her back to me as she continued doing the dishes.

"No I mean, how are you since your mom passed."

She said it so kindly, but even hearing it from a woman I actually admired, brought tears to my eyes.

For a second I wondered why she was asking, because in all these months she never once asked me anything about my family. I wondered also, was it because Jim was a detective and dad was a hoodlum?

No way, there is no way this kind lady was gonna pull a Johnny G on me and try those trick questions dad always tried on me to get me to twist my answers.

She still had her back to me then I realized in all the months I had been invited to stay at their home, eat dinner with them, go places with them, this was the first time Elizabeth and I had ever talked alone without Donna or Jim being in the room.

She turned and faced me, tears in her eyes.

"I know the pain of losing someone you love very much, I too lost someone, and I must say if it weren't for Donna I would never have been able to survive."

She sat on the chair across from me.

I listened.

"My oldest daughter, her name was Connie, she was not quite eighteen when she died."

Elizabeth seemed to be looking at me, but not really looking at me, more like looking through me as she spoke.

"Yes Connie, my dear dear Connie, such a beautiful girl. You see today is the fifteenth anniversary of her death. Jim really didn't go buy a newspaper, he went to put flowers on her grave."

Tears in Elizabeth's eyes, she looked directly in my eyes, with such a painful look.

"See Malina I understand your pain, and how difficult it is to talk about it, because we never talk about it here. It is too painful. Just too painful."

I got one of those lumps in my throat that I always got whenever I tried not to cry, but knew I would.

"So if you ever want to talk about"... she hesitated... your mom, I promise I'll listen."

Now I was crying.

Elizabeth got up from her chair and came over and hugged me, and she too cried.

When she sat back down, she said something that I just wasn't expecting.

"Donna doesn't know, but Connie was her mother."

WHATTTTT??? I thought.

"Please don't tell her. You see, Jim and I are her grandparents. She has no idea, and, well it would be so difficult to explain, especially after all these years."

My head was spinning. What should I say "I'm sorry?" I had no experience helping someone else grieve. The horribly sad look on Elizabeth's face, I would have thought Connie had just passed away, yet it had been fifteen years.

The look on Elizabeth's face confirmed, you never get over a death, ever, and that I knew in my heart from the very day my mom died, I would never get over it, and to tell you the truth, I didn't want to.

I wanted to always feel what I felt for my mom. Yes it hurt so badly, but to hurt like I did confirmed I still had all that love in me, and I wanted that love for the rest of my life.

I wondered why Elizabeth was telling me all of this knowing Donna was just upstairs and could walk in the room at any given moment.

"Donna was not quite a year old when Connie died. Donna believes Connie was her older sister, it just always seemed easier for us to not tell Donna the truth."

Elizabeth's voice trembled as she talked, even her hands were shaking.

I then remembered the distant look on Donna's face the one time she spoke to me about her brothers and sister.

Elizabeth continued. "Connie had gone to a friends house, we thought just for a visit, turns out her friend had some boyfriend problems, and, well, Connie never made it home that night. Seems her friends husband or boyfriend, what ever he was, walked in, shot Connie's friend in the head, killed her instantly, then turned the gun on Connie."

I was crying now. I was in shock as to what Elizabeth was saying.

"Yes my Connie was at the wrong place, wrong time. He shot her three times. She didn't die instantly as her friend did, but she did die, and, my old heart has been broken for fifteen years. If it weren't for Donna, well Malina, Jim and I could not have survived. We love Donna so much, she is the spitting image of Connie and though Donna is so spoiled sometimes, she is all we have, I just don't know what we would do without her."

I got up and hugged Elizabeth, we both cried.
We cried a lot.
Now I understood why Elizabeth and Jim spoiled Donna, why they allowed Donna to walk all over them. They were terrified at the thought of ever losing her.

At that moment we both heard Donna running down the stairs yelling, "Where is everyone. Mom, dad, Malina." She was laughing and yelling all our names. Simultaneously Elizabeth and I wiped our tears away, just as Donna entered the kitchen.

"What happened, why are y'all crying?

"We're not crying baby, we were laughing so hard, and it looks like we're crying.." Elizabeth said so convincingly.

Donna just laughed and said, "Okay mommy, where's daddy, can we please go somewhere, I hate just sitting around this house." Donna said as she got a cookie from the cookie jar, and instantly her mom went to the refrigerator, got the milk and poured some for Donna.

"Here Malina, drink some milk" Elizabeth said.
"No thank you." I said. I didn't like milk unless it was chocolate milk.

Almost as if Elizabeth read my mind, she reached in the cabinet and handed me the chocolate syrup as Donna got me a glass and the milk. I made me some good old chocolate milk and ate half a dozen cookies, as Elizabeth continued cleaning the kitchen.

I watched Elizabeth as she finished up the kitchen, noticing her wiping her eyes a few times with her apron, Donna oblivious to it all. I walked over and picked up the broom and began sweeping the kitchen floor, Donna gobbling her milk and cookies. Elizabeth watched me for a second or two then walked over to me, took the broom from my hand, then winked at me while whispering "Thank you" then she finished sweeping the kitchen.

Elizabeth had given me a lot of information about their family, and I was very very sad by it. Things she didn't want Donna to know. Things she trusted me with.

I gave my word to Elizabeth that I would never tell Donna, but in the back of my mind I wondered why she told me all she had about Connie and the way she died.

She told it all to me, but not any real explanations of why she was telling me. It was a lot for me to absorb, but I knew the things she had said she wanted them to remain between me and her.

There is no way I would ever tell Donna, because I knew that would be some very painful news to hear. I had already been down that road with the kids at school talking shit about my dad, I knew the things Elizabeth had trusted me with, I could never mention to Donna and I wouldn't.
Tragic.

I realized all families go through some kind of tragedy, my family had been through a lot, and knowing how Connie died made me even more sad.
The rest of the day every time I saw Elizabeth, I just wanted to hug her. My mind was scrambled, I was hurting for Elizabeth, Jim too. Two of the nicest people in the world, were carrying such a heavy load.

When I was leaving Donna's house that day, Elizabeth hugged me a bit longer than she normally did. I had been on a "hug good-by" tradition with Elizabeth and Jim for awhile now. Seems they cared for me as I did for them.

When I got home that afternoon Matty could tell I

was upset, and knowing I could trust Matty, I told her of Connie.

Matty was only ten years old when Connie had been killed, and no, Matty did not remember hearing about her in the newspaper or on the evening news.

She agreed it was a terrible thing to happen to anyone's daughter, and asked me several times if I was ok.

My mom passed away in her sleep, such a tragedy I would never get over, then to learn how Connie had been straight up murdered, was just so hard for me to deal with.

My entire life I would remember the distant look in Elizabeth's eyes as she talked to me that day. I would always remember the pain I could see on her face. The same pain I knew I also had.

76

Me and Donna were standing at my locker when I noticed a group of girls walking real fast toward us. At first I thought these bitches were about to jump us, but they quickly walked right past us. And damn near chasing right behind them was old Screwy.

Actually, I hadn't seen much of him since my mom's funeral, he of course was no longer our paper boy.

He stopped the minute he saw me and Donna, and with a big, quite cute smile he said.

"Hey girls."

"Hi Louis." I said.

"Where you ladies headed?" He asked. His friend Tony stood beside us, but said nothing.

"Class." I said.

"Mind if we walk you?" He asked.

Donna and I did not say yes, we did not say no, we just laughed. I shut my locker door and we turned to walk toward our class. Louis got right between me and Donna and put his arms around both our waist, at the same time.

I suppose he wanted the more popular kids to think he had two girlfriends.

As you know, school hallways are not that wide and they sure were not wide enough for us to walk all three of us side by side without knocking someone down. But Louis held on tight, not letting either of us go.

It was uncomfortable for me, I removed his hand. He smiled and continued holding Donna's waist still smiling his cute little smile. She saw that I got away from him, she did the same.

Just at that very second, two other girls were walking past us from the opposite direction, he looked at us, smiled, and grabbed those other two girls by the waist and proceeded to walk them down the hallway to their class.

The girls could be heard saying "Leave me alone." "Get away from us." Perhaps annoyed by his behavior.

Didn't stop ol' Screwy, he continued the same process girl after girl after girl.

It was annoying but quite funny. I suppose he had himself a little reputation going on. Not so much a ladies man, but more a pest. Some girls didn't mind it, some hated it, others actually let him walk them all the way to class.

His friend Tony tried doing exactly as Screwy did, but Tony just didn't have the same smile as Screwy, so he was refused by more girls than not.

At lunch one day we saw Screwy in the cafeteria talking with a few girls and Donna asked me "what's his deal?"

"Before my mom died he was our paper boy."

She laughed out loud, drawing attention to herself. It was actually rather funny to see this young guy trying so hard to be a ladies man, but with the label of paperboy, well I believed that he thought him self to be that of a play boy, some what similar to Mr. Hugh Hefner.

"Pleazzzzzzzz fool!" I would think to myself.

I told her of the time he threw a rock and busted my lip, and he was so afraid my dad would find out, but that my mom had a long talk with him about his carelessness, and all was forgiven, that, and my dad never did find out..

"Oh my goodness, I bet he was scared, that's what the little fucker gets for throwing a rock at you."

So without really thinking about what I was saying, my dumb ass tells her, before I knew what it actually meant, I told her how all the neighborhood girls used to yell at him and say, "Screwy Louie, Screw Louie, watch out he might try to screw me."

Emphasis on "Screw Me" I said to Donna.

Which, I will stress once again, perhaps I was a dumb ass, perhaps I was just an innocent stupid little girl, but at that time I did not know the street translation of the word "Screw."

I thought Donna was going to die laughing.

Well Donna was my dear friend and I trusted her completely, but this comment was something she would blab all over the entire school.

Within one hour every girl that saw Screwy walking through the halls, chanted. "Screwy Louie

Screwy Louie watch out he might try and screw me."

I created a fuckin monster.
A fuckin monster that loved the nick name, without a doubt.
He came up to me during our last passing period.
"So you told her our secret."
"What secret?" What the hell was he insinuating.

Now, for all intentional purposes I really thought he was upset about the screwy part, being that my translation of screwy was, well a crazy person, not that of someone that had sex, and he was standing there before me trying to insinuate that he screwed me, maybe?

Buddy, I'm a fricken virgin and I'm gonna remain that for a very long time. My blood was boiling at the thought of him spreading rumors he had screwed me, thinking of Sher hearing such gossip and beating the shit out of him, or worse my dad finding out, hunting his ass down and chopping off his... well you know what would have been chopped off.
Of course I did not say any of this out loud. I waited for his reaction.
"That I'm Screwy." He smiled, that very cute smile, while pointing his finger at the temple of his head, then hauled ass to class. "Thanks girl." He yelled, when he got to the end of the hall.

He had a reputation now, the word "Screw" spiked

some interest in him from some very unlikely females.

No longer the pest that bugged girls from one passing period to the next.

He was now known as "Screwy Louie." by every one, whether they knew him or not. Mostly by all the girls. I wondered did he get lucky from a lot of those girls that thought the nickname was so cute and funny.

He's a fucking guy, of course he did.

Now, not really sure if any of this is true, this is just what surfaced after a few days of everyone knowing his new nick name. Rumor has it that he was trying his "screwy skills" and I'm not referring to crazy, on a chick right behind the back stop of the high school baseball field.

Possibly a rumor, I cared not. He wasn't my boyfriend, and I wasn't about to loose my virginity over a stupid fucking nickname.

77

It was now that time of year, the school Prom. I wasn't concerned, I knew no one was gonna invite me, so there was nothing for me to worry about.

I saw Sher and Ray in the hallway, as I dodged Screwy, they appeared to be having an argument.
"What's wrong?" I asked her when I caught up with her.
"He's acting stupid." Sher said.
"About what?" I was being nosey.
"His senior prom." She said.
"What about it?" I asked
"He wants me to go and I don't want to." Sher said.
"Why don't you want to go? " I stupidly asked.
Sher was a sophomore Ray was a senior. I knew there was no way she felt out of place around a bunch of seniors, goodness everyone loved her.
"Sher it's his senior prom, he wants you there with him." I seemed to know what I was talking about.
"Are you crazy?" I asked.
"No I'm broke." She blurted it out without noticing if any one was standing near enough to us that they may over hear our conversation.
She didn't have to tell me. For months now she had been buying things, for herself, for Danny and J.J. even Becky and Carrie. Seems if they needed clothes or shoes, Sher was still the provider. And

more than likely she was being Sher and helping dad out, I couldn't fathom why though, he never did anything for us. But then that was Sher and her big heart.

"Do you need money?" I asked.

She actually looked directly at me and laughed right in my face.

"From who?" She snapped.

I thought she felt I was making fun of her for not having any money, and I thought she wanted to knock me out for asking stupid questions.

Goodness I think too much.

"Excuse me bossy, I'm rich." I said matter of factly.

"Please twerp, you don't have enough money for me to buy a dress." She said.

"No, I'm sure I don't, but I'll bet I have enough for you to buy some material to make you a dress."

Now this was a very proud moment for me, I soaked every second of it in.

Her eyes lit up!

I opened my purse and showed her the money I had been saving.

At that very second, I could just as well had a million dollars in my purse, which I was very confident I did not have, didn't matter, the sparkle in her eyes told the story.

"Oh Malina, are you sure?" She smiled.

"What about Matty, maybe she'll get mad if you

give me money, and not her."

"But I do give her money, every week." I said.

"Damn little sista, you are rich!" She laughed, then she kinda chuckled.

"How much you need?" I asked

"Heck I don't know." Sher said. "Enough for material and shoes and a little purse."

My purse was still open.

"Here take what ever you need." I said, as I handed her my purse.

"I'll pay you back in a few weeks little sista." Sher said, as she reached in my purse, counted out, I don't know seventy, maybe one hundred dollars.

"Thanks changa."

"Are you kidding me Sher, I'm the one that owes you." I said.

"You owe me what?" Sher asked.

"For saving our lives." I said.

Sher got a little teary eyed, as she took the money. I was very proud to give it to her, it was the least I could do.

Sher had been through so much and now, just because she had no money was no reason for her not to go to her boyfriend's prom, her very first prom.

Sher called me the moment she bought the material for her prom dress. She was as excited as a little kid. I felt good finally doing something for her, instead of her always being the one doing for every one else.

Dad was at Mary's when I got home from working at the restaurant on Saturday night.

"What now?" I wondered.

"He wasn't at Mary's when I left to get you." Matty said.

I was not gonna rush over to Mary's just to see what he was up to, yet in less than five minutes he showed up at our door step.

I was in my room, preparing to take a shower and go to bed. I could hear him talking to Matty, his voice, as it had all my life, sent horror chills through my body.

I went to the living room before he could search me out in my room.

"Hi baby." He smiled.

Malina, dad! My name is Malina.

I was always on my toes, always the wise cracks where he was concerned. Yet no one ever knew I had so much shit to talk, because I never had the guts to voice any of it.

"What's this I hear you're working?" He asked.

I froze, temporarily unable to speak, unable to move, yet my smart ass brain was in high gear.

Who went and ran their fricken big mouth? I wondered.

"Three nights a week." Matty jumped on in there to save me.

"Do you like your job?" He asked.

"Yes." I said.

"Are you keeping your grades up?" He asked.
"Yes." I answered.
He knew damn good and well I hated school, and I suppose as long as I wasn't making straight "F's" he should be pleased, shouldn't he?
Damn I wasn't his princess, I didn't make straight A's.
"Ok, as long as the grades are good." He said.
"I know." I said.
"And help your aunt out here." He demanded.

Wait a fricken minute here sucker, this coming from the hoodlum that rarely saw his kids, and furthermore never paid his hard working brother-in-laws to raise his kids, he dared tell me to help out. Looky here fucker, I have morals, I know how to do the right thing.
"We have it all worked out," Matty jumped in the conversation to save the day... Again

Perhaps she resented him just coming in and throwing his weight around, considering she was the one raising me with no help from him. It was certain she wasn't gonna say anything to piss him off, she learned her lesson with Sher.

"That was a real nice thing you did for your sister." He smiled. His very handsome good looks, his beautiful smile, his tendency for a split second, to be a loving father.
He looked directly at me.

Usually I never allowed my eyes to meet his, it was that fear control he had over me my entire life.
Yet, this time I did not look away.
I almost cried. There was that lump in my throat again. I hated him for all the bad he did to us, but for some reason, I loved him.
I literally wanted to cry, because for a rare second he seemed to be the father I had always wanted.
And just like that, he said "Ok, I gotta go."
Perhaps before he too might just get emotional.
Ya think?

He walked over to me and hugged me goodbye.
One of those hugs that is given to a child that is loved, one that is given in return to a father you actually love.
"Don't be a stranger Malina, you can come to the house any time, you want." He said.
"I know." I said.

As soon as he stepped out the door, my thoughts were, if he had only been any other type of father I would go home. Yes, I would always miss my mom, but if he had only done right by all of us, I would be home, not with Matty.
But he wasn't any other type of man, he was who he was. And as long as I was able, I would stay with Matty.

He was gone, yet his cologne lingered in our living room, his smile and kindness toward me lingered also, thinking why can't he just be like that twenty-four hours a day. Not a few seconds throughout a life time.

So it seems, dad was making his rounds that night, to visit all his kids that didn't live with him.
No financial support was offered, but then no one ever thought he would. Now that I had a little part time job, I'm sure he never would offer.
Possibly Matty felt as I did, we didn't need his money.

I was teary eyed when Sher called.
"Has he been there yet?" Sher asked.
"Yep he just left, why?" I asked.
"What did he say, was he bitching?" Sher asked.
"No, actually he was here to check on my grades and give his fatherly approval of my job, and to, get this, thank me for helping you." I said.
"Damn Malina, I didn't mean to tell him, but when he saw the material he asked where I got it, I had to tell him." Sher said.
"Yeah I know, can't lie to the liar, now can we?" I asked, she laughed
And, I thought, I sure hope he doesn't think with my measly pay I'm gonna bank roll the mafia for him. Even I giggled at that one. Gosh Malina you're so mean, again a thought, again a giggle.

"I should be finished with my dress by tomorrow."
"Do you want to come over and see it?" Sher

asked with such excitement in her voice.
"No!" I was direct.
"Okay, I'll bring it to you."
"Ok."
"Talk to you tomorrow little sista." She said.
" Bye." I said.

When I finally went to bed that night I cried more than usual. Seems more than saying any kind of prayers for anyone, I did my sermon of tears, crying for my brothers and sister, crying for Sher, mostly always crying for my mom, but this particular night I actually cried for my dad. Not so much cause I hated him, but because for a rare moment in my life I felt what it was like to actually love my dad, to feel he loved me, and I cried because I knew I should have experienced that my entire life, not just a sporadic moment of love.
Bittersweet, again my life was just so bittersweet.

78

Sher came the next day, with her dress and her shoes, she even tried it all on so I could see how beautiful it all was.

She chose a gorgeous shade of pink, satiny or silky material, not sure which. It was a long formal dress, gathered under her boobs and sort of flared out. Sher had high heel shoes a shade of pink also, slightly darker than her dress, she even showed me how she was going to fix her hair.

Sher sure picked up the knack of sewing from mom.

Her dress, in my eyes, was one hundred times better than any store bought dress.

She looked beautiful, and she hadn't even fixed her hair or put on her make-up.

The prom would be the next weekend.

"Y'all gonna sleep in a motel." I asked knowing that was about the dumbest thing I could have possibly asked.

Granted, I was a dumb ass, granted I had never been on a date, granted I knew nothing about boys, and proms and, well like I said, dumb ass.

But I did have ears, and I did listen to the senior girls talk shit at lunch and in the hallways, and from what I gathered, most ended up at Hotels, Motels, or the back seats of cars, which, by the way some of these bitches carried on, would not have been their first time.

"Who?" Sher asked with the most puzzled look on her face.

"You and Ray." Who the hell else were we talking about?

"Why would you ask that, I'm appalled that you would even suggest it." Sher smiled.

"Isn't that what you're supposed to do after the prom?" I asked.

"Yeah I guess." Sher said. "But not me and Ray."

I didn't say anything as Sher gathered her things and headed toward the front door..

I felt so guilty assuming my sister would do as all the other girls would do just because it's what most girls did. I followed her to Ray's car, which she had borrowed from him so she could bring her dress for me to admire.

She got in her car, started the ignition looked at me, smiled.

"We're not staying at a motel dummy, we're staying at his parents house. They're gonna be out of town."

And with that, she stuck her tongue at me, and drove off smiling.

I attempted to yell "Sherrrrrr." But she was long gone.

The buzz at school all week was the prom, of course it would be.

Sher more excited than most of the other students,

she definitely had the right to be. She had been through a lot to get to this point in her life, even as much as making her own prom dress, which I just couldn't fathom any other sophomore girl doing, yet this was Sher.

I worked an extra week day at the restaurant that particular week because they were short handed and needed the help. Matty always said she didn't mind taking or picking me up from work but on this particular day she looked really tired.

When we got home she went directly to her room, Lori went to sleep on Sher's old bed. She slept a lot in the room with me now, I guess she enjoyed sleeping alone.

Matty was talking to someone, yet I knew she didn't have a phone in her room.
Actually just before I heard voices, someone knocked on her door. Since her room was at the back of the house she had a private door that led to the driveway side of the duplex. Though she never used it, she kept it double locked so Lori couldn't get to it and try to open it.

I was getting ready to take my bath, and preparing my clothes for school when Matty came in my room with a man.
"Malina, this is Adam, Adam this is my niece Malina."

I said "Hi."

He walked over and shook my hand, as he smiled I noticed he had one very crooked tooth, which looked very funny. I'm sure he was uncomfortable with his appearance, because he tried not to smile to big, so I couldn't see it. But I already had.

"Hi Malina." Both Matty and Adam looked embarrassed, like they had done something wrong.

It wasn't my business, it was her house, she could have anyone over she wanted.

Adam wasn't Lori's dad. Lori's dad was tall and thin, Adam was short.

They went to the kitchen and got something to drink, then went back to Matty's room. They left the door to her room open, I suppose so I could see there was no hanky panky going on, again none of my business.

Matty was young, she could do what ever she pleased, but I personally didn't think she would have a man spend the night, just because of Lori.

Lori was just too young to understand, I thought.

Matty did go out with her friends and I'm sure they met guys, but I had never heard her talk about any guys in particular, except the ones her and Alley would make fun of that didn't dance to well. I wasn't sure if he was one of those or someone else.

I went in and showered and when I came out Matty went to my room.

"Well" She said.
I looked at her like, well what?
"He's my boyfriend." She sounded like a teenage girl and this was her very first boyfriend, ever.
"He's gonna come over now and then." She said.
Again it was her house, I couldn't tell her who she could and could not have over.
"Will you be ok with that?" She asked.
Every thing negative I could think to say went through my mind.
"Does he drink, does he work, is he going to hit you?" Were just a few of my thoughts, but I didn't dare ask.
"Don't worry Malina, he's not moving in." She laughed.
Oh that was a relief!
I smiled at her and said "ok."
"We'll talk about it tomorrow." She said and went to her room.

Adam was gone by the time I got out of the shower. I was glad.
I went to sleep thinking of all my family again mostly mom. Wishing I could talk to her, see her smile, hug her just one more time.

79

The more I thought of Sher's plans with Ray after the prom, the more worried I became. Sher staying all night at Ray's parents house meant two things. She was about to, or had already had sex with Ray, and sure was risking getting pregnant, and all hell breaking loose with dad, and she was about to completely lie to dad on her whereabouts on prom night.

I seriously doubt the teachers pet Sher, was actually going to ask permission from dad to spend the night at her boyfriend's house.
In my opinion, Sher was walking a very thin line of deceit.
You could not just go to a man like dad and say,
"Hey old man, this is how it's gonna be," and then just go spend the night with a guy. Just wasn't done.

It was the Friday night before the prom. I worked till ten and Matty, Lori and Adam came to pick me up when I got off work.
Lori was very excited about their plans to take her to the zoo the next day. I was invited to go with them, but reminded Matty I worked on Saturdays.
Lori kept saying "Come on Malina, go with us, please."
I would have gone but did not wish for them to cut their plans short just to get me to work on time. I

assured Lori I would go with them some other time.

I called Sher before I left for work on Saturday just to wish her a good time, because I knew I would be busy working by the time her and Ray set out for the prom.

Well, well sure enough Sher was lying through her fricken teeth to dad about where she would be after the prom and she was using me to tell those lies.

Was she stupid or what? Whatever lie she was going to tell, she had to know her nosey ass father would check up on her. Even princess Sher was not above following dad's rules. What the hell was wrong with her? He had already whooped her ass over bullshit shoes and a fricken piece of paper, now she wanted to test his "I Spy" skills.

Her devious plan was to go to the prom just as she had already planned, do what ever it is groups of kids do after the prom, then mosey on over to Ray's house, get laid, then come to Matty's early in the morning and pretend she had been there all night.

First off, I knew that shit wouldn't work, Matty, for one would not lie for her. Sher thought Matty owed her for her ass whooping over the boot situation, and that she would lie.

"Sher, Matty might lie if you got caught skipping school or something simple like that, but to straight up lie about staying with Ray, there is no way Matty will lie and then say "Oh yes, go ahead, go get fucked and while you're at it, get pregnant.

Really Sher?

Sher ignored every single word I said.

"All you gotta do is answer the phone when I call, wait five minutes, then let me in, I'll take care of the rest." She demanded.

"It will never work." I said.

"Yes it will." Sher sounded annoyed that I didn't trust her plan.

"But Sher, dad beat the shit out of you over some damn boots, don't you remember, and you think he won't beat you and Ray and me and Matty if he catches you." I was almost in tears just at the thought of it all.

"The only way he'll catch me is if he shows up at Matty's in the middle of the night, in that case, you just tell him I came and left or I haven't come in yet."

"Sher, really you want me to get beat too?"

"Just do what I tell you, I'll give you Ray's home number, if dad shows up, you call, and I'll be there within five minutes. I'll simply tell him we went to get a burger or something."

Sher just seemed so convinced it would work.

"You're taking such a big chance Sher." I said.

"Well, as you said, I got beat for nothing, now he has a reason to beat my ass, if I get caught." Sher insisted. So damn much emphasis on the damn word "If."

Did she really think ol Sherlock Holmes Guetarro would not be lurking at every corner. He thrived on catching his kids in lies. He thrived on proving he was right and everyone else was wrong.

Sher wasn't thinking. She wasn't thinking at all. Goodness sakes it wasn't just Sher that would get beat, it was all of us.

"I sure as hell don't like this at all." I complained.

"Don't worry, damn I'm not gonna get caught." Sher said.

"I sure hope not." I had that knot in my stomach at the thought of Sher getting beat again.

"Bye twerp." She hung up.

This stupid ass teachers pet sister of mine had never had a deceitful bone in her body. She was dad's favorite and everyone loved her, now she wanted to lie to dad, get me to lie to dad, lie to Matty, get me to lie to Matty for her, and on top of everything else, she wanted to sleep with Ray.

I was literally sick to my stomach thinking of all the people dad would hit, no, beat the shit out of over a bunch of lies.

Should I go to Matty and save my own ass with her, I mean she was my ride to and from work. She was the one supporting me after all. I was risking her finding out that I was part of Sher's deceitful scheme, and pissing her off myself.

Or do I keep my big mouth shut, pretend I know nothing, and hope for the best.

Completely against my better judgment, I chose to keep my big mouth shut.

Whatever was going to happen would happen without me putting my two cents in. If Matty found out, and got mad at me for not telling the truth, then so be it. I was going to take that chance. But, if dad found out I was part of all Sher's bullshit, then I was in a lot of fricken trouble. Trouble I wanted nothing to do with.

But to rat out my own sister to save my hide, to our low life gangster father, was as low, no lower than telling all the lies. If he found out about all Sher's plans, he would in fact, be proud that I had not ratted out my very own sister, for that I would not get beat. But I guarantee I would get hit for every single lie I would be involved in, and that, well let's say, all those lies, I think my dad would have actually been exhausted by the time he landed the final blow upside my fricken head.

I knew out of hatefulness, after he beat me, he would make me pack all my shit and move back with him, and there is no way Matty would have been able to help me.
Dad would've been unstoppable. What the fuck am I thinking, he already was unstoppable, it wasn't gonna take a bunch of lies to figure that one out.
My head was pounding from it all. I didn't want to know anything.
I just wanted to go to work, earn my pay, go home to Matty's and go to sleep. Was that too much to ask?
It was going to be a long fricken day and an even

longer fricken night.

I got ready for work Saturday, even convinced Matty I had to be there a little bit early just so I didn't sit around the house and think of the miserable situation that would be unfolding later that night.

When I got to work, I went directly to work, even offered to stay later if they needed me.
Unfortunately they did not.
Again Matty, Lori and Adam picked me up.
He was starting to hang around a lot, I guess Matty was really liking him.
To my knowledge he wasn't spending the night, unless Matty was sneaking him in and out, being sneaky like Sher.
It crossed my mind, this is one night I wish Adam would spend the night, just so Matty would stay in her room.
Oh I was so confused.

When I got in the car Lori was so excited telling me all about the zoo and the animals she had seen.
I tried to listen, I tried to pay attention to everything she said, but I just couldn't. My mind was on Sher, I wanted to cry, because I was so terrified she would get caught and if that happened, I knew all of us would have to pay the price for Sher.

80

I was already worried sick about Sher. It was close to eleven p.m. when we got home and I realized the prom wouldn't even be over for at least two more hours then there would be the "lets go eat" afterwards bullshit.

Then I'm sure, as the gossip at school goes, everyone would go to Inspiration Point. All the guys and girls would go to hang out till a cop showed up and ran them all off.

Even if Sher were to go directly home to dad's after the prom, the actual end of the prom from all the running around really wouldn't be till around three a.m. anyway.

Then I wondered if dad had put a curfew on Sher. I mean really, Sher goes from being forced to the title of mommy and daddy for months, to popular high school sophomore with a fricken curfew. I seriously doubt it.

There were two, three, maybe four hours to see what was gonna happen.

The smarter part of me said fuck it, go to bed you can't do anything about it anyway.

The stupider side of me said, oh yes you can, stay by the phone and pray Sher answers, or at least dad doesn't come around at all.

Why me?....

I went to shower, and when I came out Matty's

door was shut. I believe that meant one thing, Adam was still there.

There's a first time for everything, and because it was approaching midnight, I think he was staying over.

It seemed strange for Matty to have a boy friend, I barely remember when she was with Lori's dad. Seems for as long as I could remember, she had been single.

Lori was asleep already, so I went to the living room to watch TV.

The sofa was near the window, the same window I would stare out of when uncle George wouldn't come directly home. The same window I would sit by and watch all the passing cars, the same window I would sit at, look out at the stars toward the heavens and think of my mom.

I sat looking out the window, only half watching the movie that was on.

Obviously the reflection of the TV, would let anyone passing by know someone was still up, and if that someone was dad, he'd stop sure as hell to see who was up and why, though it was none of his fricken business, he would make it his business..

Actually it was still early, even if he did show up, it was barely twelve, the prom technically wasn't over for another hour, unless of course he gave her that damn curfew.

Dammit, I hated all this, why can't everyone just leave me alone? I already knew how much I hated seeing anyone getting hit by dad. The sick knot in my stomach, the fear of him making me want to piss myself again, made me sick.

To get my mind off everything, hell there was nothing gonna get my mind off any of this lying bullshit, I went to the kitchen and made me a bowl of ice cream.

I heard Matty go in the restroom, wondering to myself, Ok do I tell Matty the truth just in case we need her, or not?

Remember Malina she ran and told dad about those boots, not meaning to get any one in trouble, but still someone did.

Now if I told, would she feel obligated to call dad just in case something happened to Sher and she knew and didn't tell him.

Hell, it was the same shit for me, if something happened to Sher, and I knew what she was up to, and I didn't tell anyone, wasn't I now the one in trouble?

Fuck you Sher Guetarro, why you gotta put me through all this?

Why? Why? Malina you stupid ass little girl. Because Sher became a grown ass woman a year ago when she had to take the role of being a mother to all of us.

Quit being so selfish you fucking whiny ass kid.

Maybe cussing myself would make me hate myself more than I hated Sher at this moment.

And what about Ray, was that idiot not concerned for his own fucking life. Was he such a horney ass bastard that he couldn't think straight, thinking only of getting into Sher's panties, if he hadn't already, than his own life.
Fuck you too Ray, fuck both you mother fuckers named Ray.
I had to vent. I was hating all men that night.

Tick Tock, I swear the damn clock stopped, like time stood still.

I was sitting on the sofa eating my bowl of ice cream, watching, no not watching TV, but looking at the screen of the TV, when Matty came in the living room.
"What you watching?" She asked.
Damn I had no idea, I didn't even know what to say.
"Nothing really just thumbing through the channels." I lied right to her face.
"Ok, well just in case you didn't know, Adam is spending the night, I just wanted you to know in case you see him in the morning."

Really? Matty was worried I would see her stupid boyfriend early in the morning, if I even lived till the morning, with all the bullshit Sher was doing, and I was a part of.

"Ok, will it be ok if I sleep on the sofa, I want to watch TV kinda late." I lied.

Actually, I really want to spy out the window like I have had to with you and Mary, I wanted to blurt out, but again didn't dare.

"Sure." She said.

"I'll get my covers." I said.

I went to my room to get my covers and pillows, thinking, ok now I have a reason to be in the living room looking out the window till dawn. Anyway, if her and Adam were doing whatever, I sure as hell didn't want to know.

Maybe she was glad I offered to stay in the living room, far away from her room. Maybe not.

Tonight I cared less about whatever she was doing. My concern was my sneaky sister.

I made the sofa as comfy as I possibly could, and lay down for a few moments knowing my real stress wouldn't begin till about two a.m.

I watched TV for awhile, trying to find something that would capture my attention for a few hours. Then I sat up a minute to look out the window, and there, bigger than shit was a car parked right out in front of the house, I damn near had a fricken heart attack thinking, look at my dad, he's already sitting out there spying on Sher.

Then realized that was Adam's car.

I started to lay back down, then I sat back up, Oh my God, dad is going to pass by, see Adam's car parked right in front of the house, think it's Ray's, stop, beat the door down, then beat the shit out of all of us thinking Matty is letting Sher's boyfriend spend the night.
Where the hell did I come up with this shit?
This shit only happens in the movies.

I'm a fricken worry wart. I worry to much. I think all the negative things instead of thinking positive. Get real Malina, there is nothing positive gonna come out of this, only negative.
And the worse thing that would happen is if Sher got caught and everyone got beat to hell and back, as dad and all the gangsters had beat the shit out of those guys in the bar, the next worst negative thing is, if Sher got pregnant at sixteen.
I was driving myself crazy with fear.

I would watch TV, I would sit up and stare out of the window. I would lay back down, get back up and stare again.
Come on Sher, get your ass over here so I can quit worrying.

I wondered if Sher would do the same for me? I mean, just let me take off with a guy and have sex and worry her to death.
No dumb ass, she would beat the shit out of you for even trying, long before dad could.

One fifteen now. So technically the prom was over, and who knows how long it takes for a bunch of rowdy teens to go eat, race their cars to Inspiration Point, make out for awhile, then race their cars home.

I don't even think my concern was where and what Sher was doing, she had bluntly told me of her plans, my concern was where the hell was dad.

81

Saturday night, dad wouldn't even be leaving the bar till after two himself. I mean just because he had a new kid, and a woman in his life, I seriously doubt dad gave up womanizing. He sure didn't give it up for my mom, didn't make sense to give it up now.

I turned the TV. off, it was now pitch dark in the house so I opened the curtain all the way so I could see out the window without having to sit up every ten seconds.
I lay on the sofa, looking up at the ceiling, now able to see the reflection of any car lights that came past our house. At least now I could see out, no one could see in.
Surprisingly at almost two a.m. hardly any cars passed at all. One car here and there, but not busy like it had been earlier.

Somehow, I guess from pure stress, I fell asleep.
How the hell was it possible for me to fall asleep at all?
When I woke it was three fifteen. I got up and went to the restroom, when I came out I thought to my weary self, no Sher, no dad, I felt a little better.
I lay back down, looked out the window, thinking it will be daylight in a few hours, then out of nowhere I saw him. Those damn Cadillac headlights, I recognized them any where.

Before he got in front of the house, he turned off his head lights, and passed by real real slow, as if he were eyeballing everything. The house, the car, the trees, looking, just looking for something.

Yes, I could see him, sneaky bastard.

It was possible for me to see him, but he could not see me, unless the fucker had night vision eyeballs, and don't you know it would be just like him too.

Suddenly he stopped his car, reversed about twenty feet, then continued to drive slowly past the house.

He drove away, but I know my dad, that was just the first drive by, I knew for a fact I hadn't seen the last of him. Then again, there he was, coming from the opposite direction this time, then he pulled up right next to Adam's car and stopped.

I wished at that moment a cop would have driven up and caught him with his arsenal of guns that I knew he always carried just in case, and hauled his ass off to jail.

I'm sorry, but I'd rather him be in jail, which by all rights he should have been any way, then Sher get caught, lying, sleeping around and any of the thirty or forty things dad would've beat her for.

I started to call Ray's house, but even if I did, if Sher and Ray drove up now, dad would have caught her.

Then the sneaky bastard drove off again, slowly.

I waited, thinking, I know he's gonna circle around

like a vulture flying over head for it's meal.

Sher, Sher, Sher, you have no idea what is gonna happen if he comes back and you're not here.

Three seconds after dad's car turned the corner, Ray's car drove up in front of the house, Sher jumped, I mean she literally jumped out, or Ray pushed her out of the car and she ran to the porch. Before she could get to the top step I had the door open.

We both looked toward the street and Ray was already turning the corner.

Yep, Ray was no fool, he disappeared into the night.

Fuck her and leave her, isn't that the way the saying goes... How pathetic.

Sher was laughing. She was fuckin laughing.

You bitch, I thought. You sorry ass bitch, you're happy and I'm dieing here.

"How did you know I was here?" Sher asked.

I pointed at my pillows.

"Were you still awake?" Sher asked.

"What do you mean was I still awake? Who could sleep with your vulture dad circling around lookin for you? Who gives a shit Sher, dad just left."

I tried to whisper because I sure didn't want Matty to wake and catch me and Sher just standing in the middle of the living room floor, guilty as sin.

"I know, but did he get off and come inside?"

"No, don't you think you'd be dead if he had." I was scolding her.

"Well, something told me to get over here, we were at Ray's since midnight, we left the prom early."

"I just had a feeling ol spy dad would be out here, so when we were coming this way, we saw him. I told Ray to haul ass, even if he catches Ray leaving here, so what, he has to catch me doing something wrong first." She said it oh so calmly like a very well rehearsed speech.

How fricken sneaky she was!

"We got company tonight." I told her.

"Who?" Sher asked as she peeked out the window.

"Adam, Matty's boyfriend." I said.

"Whatttt?"

"Yep, he's spending the night."

"Hahahahahahah." Sher said. "Guess everyone got some tonight." Sher laughed, then she lifted the covers I had been laying on.

"You got you a boyfriend under there Malina?" she teased.

"Are you crazy?" I laughed.

We laughed a few moments. She had an overnight bag with her, and had already changed into her shorts. She tip-toed to get covers from the closet and took one of my pillows, then laid on the other sofa.

Then she asked, "Were you worried baby sista?"

"You have no idea." Then to my self I said you have no idea how worried I was you bitch, jokingly of course, I would never cuss my dear Sher.

"Don't worry Malina, when Matty wakes I'll tell her Ray and I had a fight and he dropped me off here." "I got this covered so you don't have to lie to Matty."

Finally my stress was over.

Just as we were about to fall asleep, we saw car lights heading our way, and sure enough, there was dad again.

Me and Sher giggled, watching him drive by so slowly. Once then twice, and finally he drove in the direction of home.

I lay back down on the sofa, so did Sher.

"Poor dad." She said.

82

When we woke the next day Matty was already up, and looked completely shocked to see Sher there.

Sher and Matty had talked a bit at the court house and on the occasions I would ask Matty to call the house and ask for Sher because I didn't want to talk to dad or Sharon.

"Oh me and Ray had a little disagreement and I had him drop me here last night, luckily Malina was in the living room watching TV and heard me knocking." Sher explained to Matty.

Matty didn't ask any questions about any of it. Obviously Sher was lying and rather than Sher get another ass whoopin, Matty just stayed out of it.

Perhaps Matty knew damn good and well Sher was lying, she was a young woman, she graduated from high school, she knew pretty much what happened to Sher only a few hours ago, but wasn't about to call her out on it. I think Matty was still very shaken over her brothers behavior.

Matty made breakfast and offered Sher some, it was old times, eating breakfast again, Sher and Matty acted like there had never been a problem.

It was Sunday, Sher called and told Sharon she was still with me. Matty, Adam and Lori went to the movies.

Sher and I lounged around then she went to spend

time with J.J. and Danny.

I literally laid around the house all day, considering my sleep had been limited the night before. Eventually Ray, Sher's Ray, came and picked her up. I was again home alone, watching TV

Matty took me with her and Adam and Lori to eat. We then went to the big slide so Lori could ride it a few times, I didn't ride because I had just eaten and feared, well you know.

We stopped at the grocery store so Matty could get a few things, I stayed in the car.
They didn't see me but I sure saw them, dad, Sharon and Thomas going into the grocery store, looking like the perfect family.

I had never known my dad to even enter a grocery store, unless of course he was gonna rob it, let alone buy groceries.
Sharon smiled at dad as they entered the store, dad carrying Thomas in his little car thingy.
A disgusted feeling in my gut, turning into hate as I assumed he was paying for groceries for them, wondering if she helped her mom out with her own kids, knowing my dad did not help anyone with his.
Who gives a damn I thought.

Just then Matty, Adam, and Lori came out of the store with a buggy full of bagged groceries.

By their conversation they had run into dad and Sharon as they were leaving the store.

"Did you see your dad Malina?" Matty asked me.

"Yes." I answered.

"Adam and your dad met." She said.

One more person for my dad to dislike, I thought to myself.

I didn't particularly care to discuss my dad and Adam, and well I just didn't feel like talking, and as wise as Matty was, she figured it out and discontinued the conversation.

We were back at Matty's. She prepared a small snack for the four of us, then her and Adam went to her room. I remained in the living room, watching TV, Lori already asleep.

The phone rang.

"Hello." I said.

"Hey Malina." It was Donna.

"What you doin?" She asked.

"Watching TV."

"Just wanted to tell you were having a big party here tomorrow during school."

Surely she was kidding. I thought.

"Me and Greg are having a few kids over and we wanted to see if you wanted to join us."

"Naw thanks." I said. There was no need for her to ask me twice, I already knew I wasn't going to join in on any skipping parties.

First off, I didn't do shit like that and also I had ol

bossy on my ass, even though she didn't live at my address, she still ruled my life with just one evil glance. Besides, I knew I couldn't kick Sher's ass and I wasn't about to try. Especially over a bunch of bull shit skipping.

"Come on Malina, please."

"I just can't Donna, you don't understand. It's not just Sher, it's my dad, if he ever found out."

"He won't Malina, come on. We'll just hang out at my house, just a few friends. I promise."

"If I don't go to school, Sher will know I'm skipping."

"Then go to school, after an hour or so, get an early dismissal. Pretend your sick or something. We will have so much fun."

I thought for a second, but I knew I couldn't pull it off, even if I really wanted to.

"Sorry Donna, I just can't."

She paused, and sighed.

"Ok, I'll have fun for the both of us." She laughed.

"Why don't you forget about that ol skipping party and hang out with me in school?" I pleaded.

"I need a break from school, and with my parents going out of town, well, I don't have too many opportunities like this."

"Are they leaving you all alone?" I didn't understand.

"No silly, I'm gonna stay with Greg and his parents for the few days my parent's are gone." She explained.

"So how you pulling off a skipping party?"

"Oh Malina...Ok, when Greg's mom drops us off at school, we're gonna pretend to go into the school, when we know she has left the parking lot, then we're gonna walk back to my house. I doooo have a key you know."

It seemed to me Greg and Donna had it all planned out.

"Well Donna, I really can't, but I will call you when I get home."

"Are you sure? She asked.

"I'm sure." I said.

"Okie dokie, talk to you tomorrow afternoon." She giggled.

83

Should I, shouldn't I? Over and over in my mind I asked the question as I tossed and turned. I seriously though of it, but with Sher at the same school as me and not to mention dad, possibly even Ray passing through the school whenever they pleased, I just couldn't.

When I got to school the next day, Donna wasn't there. Either were about twenty of the kids I knew probably went to Donna's skipping party. Mostly the kids that were always walking away from the school, just as I'd be approaching the school. They were all known as, of course, "The Skippers."
I often wondered why they didn't just quit school and get a job or something. They would skip a day or two, get suspended or be thrown in study hall, then repeat their ritual of getting high at the next skipping party.
Perhaps getting some kind of money from the state for their actual enrollment, was all the school district cared about. Made no sense to me to keep them enrolled, I seriously doubt they were learning anything.

I purposely arrived at school a bit early to try and stop Donna from having her damn party, hoping I could convince her to stay at school with me.
As Donna had told me the night before, her

parents were going to be out of town on a business trip. I looked everywhere for her and Greg, but apparently they had already left the school, to host their skipping party.

All day I wondered about Donna, and couldn't wait to get home to call her.

Well, as very bad luck would have it, for Donna, there was a change of plans for Detective Jim, his trip had been cancelled and they went home early.

Their arrival was highly unexpected.

What Donna and Greg had planned as a small skipping party, turned into more of a mob gathering.

When Jim and Elizabeth got home, they caught a hell of a lot more than a few teenage kids at their house. Over seventy people were there, some of them weren't even high school students, they were guys in their early and mid twenties. Without a doubt the ones Jim would blame for the beer, the liquor, the marijuana, and yes, other drugs.

Jim did not hesitate for one second to call the cops.

Rumor says to keep any of the skippers from leaving the scene, and the fact he was a detective, and not knowing what the hell all those people were doing in his house, he held them at bay with his gun, except the ones that managed to run out the back door before Jim had a chance to enter the house.

Pure chaos.

Seven cops and two detective would take control of the scene, these were all mostly minors, it was in fact considered a crime scene.

It took several long, miserable, embarrassing hours for the P.D. to sort through, who was who, what they were doing, and what the hell to do, that one of their own had a house full of drunk minor kids and a house full of illegal drugs.
Some of the kids were sent back to school for the school to deal with, some were sent to juvenile hall, the probationers of course, and then some, well their parents were called. I'm sure those parents were very upset and very ashamed of their kids, but nowhere near as ashamed as Jim was.

Donna my dear friend Donna, what did you do?

Greg, well he dropped out of school the very next day. Never saw or heard from him again.

More rumors surfaced about Donna after that day. Seems she was in her room, knocked out cold, liquor, weed, beer, who knows what all they found in her room, not to mention she was found with all her clothes off, two boys in the room with her. Jim almost killed one of them.

Yes, quite a shameful exhibition for Detective Jim. Donna was removed from our school. She would be sent to a private school somewhere up north I heard. Donna and I were never allowed to say goodbye to one another.

All the gossip around school, though I never knew any of it before that day, seems Donna had been having problems with drinking and weed, even some occasional cocaine, so they say. It went back to her Junior High days..

Can you imagine?

Not wanting an ass whoopin from Sher would be my initial reason for not being at Donna's skipping party. That, and not to mention what my own dad would have done to me, to Donna, and her parents if I had been there.

Detective Jim moved his family as far away from North side Fort Worth, as he could possibly get.

Seems Jim couldn't very well be a highly respected Detective if his daughter was gonna be having, the equivalent to, an underage drug party.

Just wouldn't seem right, would it?

Jim had to do what he had to do, other wise he was no better than my own dad.

I knew I could count my lucky stars I did not give in to peer pressure that day. Who knows what would have happened? There would have been a lot of people getting hurt had my dad been one of the parents called to pick up his daughter that day.

I'm pretty sure the type of beating I would have endured, would have been severe. Not just because I skipped and was doing something I knew I should not have, but just the mere fact that a cop or detective would have had to contact my dad and pretty much gloat in his face. "Ha Ha Mr. Guetarro, your daughter is no better than you, the preverbal "Apple doesn't fall far from the tree."

An ass whoopin would have been inevitable for me, but not just me. There would have been Donna to worry about, and her parents.
Regardless of the fact I should not have been there to begin with, the fact that it even happened would have got the best of my dad. Male, macho, bullshit, gangster pride? Maybe so, or possibly just the fact for a second he had to be a parent and handle a situation as any parent might. NOPE....Not Johnny Guetarro.

Detective Jim, I'm sure my dad would have found blame in him, Elizabeth and everyone for that matter.
All those pointing of fingers from the P.D. and all the "shame shame, we can't catch you fucker, but we caught your daughter around some illegal drugs." Sure would have been a very hard pill for my dad to have to swallow.

Then there would be my dad's side or course, gangster or not, he did have some kind of rights, especially where his kids were concerned. I mean just because he didn't raise his kids, didn't mean he couldn't tell everyone else how to do it. And though ninety percent of his life involved some kind of illegal substance, didn't mean it would be okay for someone else to give his daughter drugs. Especially in the home of a detective.

And what about my dad's side of this situation? First off, all the name calling, and trust me, with his vocabulary, he would have mortified every police officer from this side of the Pecos.

Such words as "Fuck you mother fuckers, you sorry sons of bitches, and fuck your mothers too. Oh yes, he would have stooped that low to cuss their mothers, though he'd a killed a mother fucker for cussing his mother.

But then we do know the P.D. damn sure would have deserved everything they had coming. He would have even called it a cover up, no better yet, in his eyes I would have been set up, just for the P.D. to get to the powerful "Johnny G."

And we all know what ever dad would have done or said, he would have been completely justified. I mean come on, a bunch of kids, no supervision, beer, liquor and drugs, all inside a detectives home. Could have been an all out war between the local police department, and the Guetarro Crime Family.

That's a fact.

84

I was pretty much in disbelief as I listened to the school gossip about Donna. Though I was mortified when Donna had told me the entire school pretty much called my dad a murdering S.O.B. these would be the same gossiping fuckers that talked shit about Donna and her drug use, not to mention all the gossip about her party.

Of course there was never any drugs or weed, or beer when I would stay at Donna's house. I mean really her parents, or grandparents, were the ideal parents. But in spite of all the rumors and gossip, Donna was still my friend, where ever Jim had moved her to. Donna was my friend, my dear dear friend that listened to my problems, listened to me cry for my mom. Shared her own parents kindness with me, and always stayed positive about everything. Here one day, gone, the next. Almost every reminder we had ever been my friends now gone, not even a picture to remind me of our friendship.

Seems I was now friendless as far as having a friend to chum around with. I pretty much stayed to myself after that, I just didn't have it in me to try and find myself a new friend to hang around with. It was after all, drawing near the end of the school year, no need to get myself all worked up trying to get myself a new friend.

One day at lunch, as I was sitting alone, Screwy came and sat across from me.
"What's up Malina?" He asked.
"Not much." I said.
"What happened to your friend?" He asked which brought tears to my eyes.
"I don't know." I wanted to cry, but I knew screwy was a smart ass and if I cried he'd blab it all over school.
Fuck off is what I really wanted to say to him, but I didn't because we were in fact, in a crowded cafeteria, and if I talked shit to him, his macho ass would have to defend himself, and all I could do was cuss, which wouldn't actually ruin his reputation. But should he feel disrespected by my language, all he had to do is stand up and say "Fuck you slut." and though I wasn't a slut, just one cruel word from the ever so popular Screwy Louie, I'd have a reputation as a slut, just because a big mouth show off guy said so.
I kept my mouth shut.
He smiled his famous smile, then said, "Good thing you weren't at that party, huh?"
I said nothing.
" I mean, I can imagine how mad your dad would have been."
Finally I spoke. "Yes it would not have been a pretty sight."
"Well, then I guess I gotta walk you to class

everyday huh?" Screwy laughed.

"That's ok." I said.

"Naw, I don't mind." Sounding like he was gonna do it out of charity, conceited bastard.

I thought of Donna as he carried on a conversation I was not paying any attention to. Then the bell rang.

Shit, now I was stuck with this fucker.

He waited as I carried my tray to the counter, and proceeded to follow me, then like clock work he put his arm around my waist, then walked with me up the flight of stairs to my class.

Nothing was said as we walked, only "See ya later, girl," as he left me at my classroom door. I watched as he strolled down the hallway and picked his next victim.

I was once again, an unpopular nerd, now with absolutely no friends, except the occasional bull shit I had to endure from Screwy.

Life again just seemed so fuckin unfair.

85

Work, school, work, school I stayed as busy as I could. I was giving Matty money to help around the house, and I was saving what I could.

I thought of Donna everyday wondering why she hadn't at least called me. I missed spending time with her and her parents. I missed having lunch with her and Greg in the school cafeteria.

One horrible mistake made by an irrational spoiled immature girl, caused her dad to say "Enough is enough" and they all moved away.

Unfortunately, I would never see or hear from Donna ever again.

I realized how quickly life changes. Without any kind of warning what so ever my life had been completely turned around again. One unexpected night my mom died in her sleep. My life changed forever, not by choice. But Donna, her life, my life, completely changed by her. One choice, a choice to have a skipping party, left me without my dear friend, the friendship of Elizabeth and Jim, and no one to sit with hour after hour to talk to.

Life changes, it just seemed so damn unfair.

I was once again focused on my lonely life, my job, my brothers and sisters.

As Matty promised, she took me on my first

driving lesson. Only problem, her car was standard and I had no idea what I was doing.

She began with the normal instructions, check your mirrors, seat belt, adjust your seat, the list of things to do before I ever even put the key in the ignition, seemed endless.
Once Matty was satisfied I was in control of the car, she instructed me to start the ignition.
Nervous and scared, for the first time in my life I was behind the wheel of a car, and I was the driver.
I did ok on the straight road, but once I had to stop at a stop sign or a red light, I just couldn't get the hang of it.
Fearing I would strip the gears, Matty took over.

"Don't worry Malina, it's just your first lesson, this isn't the easiest car in the world to drive, don't worry."
"I'm just so nervous." I would say.
"We'll do this every weekend till you get the hang of it." She promised.

I was fortunate of Matty's age. She wasn't one of those sit around the house type of women. She liked doing things, going places. If I wasn't at work, or at school, if Matty wasn't tired from working, she always wanted to go some where.
Her ideas were unlimited. We would go to the mall, to the park, to the movies, bumper car rides, miniature golf, you name it she liked to do it. And

having some money of my own, if I saw something I liked, I'd buy it.

Hey, no one expected me to save my money for eternity.

I think as long as I was helping Matty out she was happy, and I never just spent my money on myself, I'd buy things for Matty, and Lori, usually a toy for Lori, and I'd buy for J.J. and Danny, toys of course and clothes.

One night late, Sher called me, she seemed very upset, but of course she wouldn't let me know just how upset she really was,

"I can not wait till I turn seventeen." She insisted.
"I thought you had to be eighteen to be considered an adult?" I asked.
"Well that's what every one wants you to believe, I checked it out, you must be seventeen to be considered an adult, legally."
Damn she did do her home work.
"I swear the day I turn seventeen I will be long gone." She sounded like she wanted to cry.
"What happened Sher."
Now keep in mind, Sher loved my dad, no doubt in my mind. In spite of all the ass whooping, and slaps, and bull shit he put all of us through, simply put, she loved him.
I knew it was not easy for her to talk shit about him. Oh I'm not talking about how her and I would

talk shit about him behind his back, that was all talk.

I'm talking about discussing his criminal ways, his evil doings, things I'm sure he wanted no one to know about, much less Sher to blab them to any one.

I furthermore knew, Sher had to understand the impact of telling me, of all people, any thing negative about dad. He was already my least favorite person in the world, but to hear things that had Sher on the verge of tears, let's just say, put another of many "I hate you dad" notches in my belt.

So she went on tell me how dad would make her and Sharon go to a bar with him and sit. Literally just sit there.

It was not "Sal E's Bar," which we were already familiar with, but another bar, and he would make them sit there while dad did…. whatever..

Sher said they would leave the baby with Sharon's mom, who would think they were going to a movie or some family thing. Dad would drive to an entirely different side of town, one Sher said she had no idea where they were or what part of town it would be.

Once there, he would order soda's for Sher and Sharon and then he would disappear to one of the rooms at the back of the bar for thirty minutes at a time. Sometimes he would only be gone for five minutes in the back room and then they would leave.

.

Sher said she didn't understand why he even made her and Sharon go, and why he didn't just leave them at home while he did his illegal shit.

Sher would say "I hate it there: a bunch of drunk ass people talking loud and acting stupid." I knew she was scared.

"Sometimes I wanna just run out of there and leave dad and Sharon there." She went on to say.

"What is he doing there?" I would stupidly ask.

"I'm sure it's something illegal." Sher said.

As she's talking I'm wondering, why not have Ray or one of the other guys do all his illegal shit? Why would he be so stupid, and why take your woman and your daughter with you? We couldn't figure it out.

"Show off." Sher said.

"What?" I asked.

"I think he's showing off, and he wants to be, "The man." Sher laughed.

"But why take y'all, and why risk getting caught with y'all?" I would ask.

"Show off I tell you." Sher said.

Did any of this makes sense?

As much as I didn't want to say, "Yes" it fricken did, in a sick twisted, fucked up life, sort of way it made all the sense in the world to me.

Here's my theory.

Big time gangster, would take his woman and daughter, as his alibis, not conspirators, just innocent alibis.

But why him, why do it himself? I would wonder. Obviously to build himself a name, that's all it could be. To expand his illegal horizons.

Couldn't very well be "the man" if no one knew who the hell he was.

By all appearances, he was still living like trash even with his new kid and woman, so what ever he was doing it sure wasn't for the money. So the only explanation for any of this was, he was doing it for the "Power" which really seemed even stupider to me, but it's all it could be.

Then Sher told me, "What do you think he's going to court for...again?

My stupid ass really had no idea.

"He got caught selling dope, not marijuana, dope." Sher said.

I'm sure Sher had no idea what kind off dope, she was just using the word dope, because she must've heard dad say it.

For as long as I can remember dad had smoked weed, and even bragged that it should be legalized because it was not a harmful drug, it was no different than taking aspirin for pain, in his eyes. Aspirin, he would say, legally reduces pain, same as marijuana.

As fucking twisted as it sounds he made a lot of sense. And to be witness to my dad's behavior with and without the use of Mary Jane, I could attest, marijuana should be legalized. He was a much better person because of it.

I gathered this much from my conversation with Sher. This, oh so fuckin intelligent father of ours had gotten away with an attempted murder charge, who ever, what ever the reason, he supposedly attempted to kill some one, instead of using one of his men to do it, he did it himself, and had apparently gotten caught. Then, just like that, charges dropped. Who knows how or why he got away with that.

Now, by what Sher was trying to tell me, he fucked up again. Instead of using Ray or one of his men, he had to be a show off and do his illegal shit himself.
 I wondered if it were really showing off or is this what a team leader has to do. Dad was in fact, a team leader wasn't he? He led his pack of rats around doing all his bull shit.
 So, technically for anyone to actually know who the great "Johnny G" was, he had to be out there right up front, at least for awhile. And like the low down dirty rat he was, he used his daughter and woman as cover.
 Stupid or smart move?
 Let's see, a car load of gangsters rolling around smoking weed, with a trunk full of weapons, is much more conspicuous than a man, his daughter, and his girlfriend. You figure it.
 But do gangsters really use their women and kids in such a fashion to further their illegal careers? I guess it all depends on who you ask. If my perception of a low life gangster is correct, you damn straight they do. I don't believe families of such are immune to this type of behavior.

Another criminal charge was now imposed on my father, well he imposed it upon himself, yet he made the choice to be a gangster. Though I could never call my dad a punk or a thug, and I would not. I never approved of his life style, but he had every right in the world to be who he wanted, what he wanted. It's just a fuckin shame all the talent he did possess, he never used it.

Again he was putting his future on the line by involving himself in activities he could have ordered any number of men to take care of, but made the conscience decision to do it himself. This was one decision that could very well land his ass in prison, yet he took that chance.

Sher was upset and she was venting, but I knew damn good and well she intended our conversation to remain just that, our conversation. Sher had nothing to worry about where I was concerned.

Anything my dad did, or anything I knew about him, would go with me to my grave…well…there are two sides to every story, and I do have the right to tell mine…Right???

86

Conversating with Sher and realizing the one year anniversary of my moms death was near had me very depressed. I relived that day in my mind. It was one year ago. It seemed like only yesterday, it seemed a million years ago. So many thoughts crossing my mind. I literally cried every night before I went to sleep. I would whisper to my self over and over "Please come back mommy, please come back." Always with the same result, my mommy would not come back.

Two people I loved had died in my young life, my mom's the most devastating, my grandpa's the second.
A vision of my mom and grandpa having their father daughter conversations on our semi weekly visits to grandpa and grandma's apartment. My mom with that beautiful sparkle in her eyes as she talked with him, actually the same sparkle would be in her eyes no matter who she talked with.

Grandpa loved when we visited. Grandma B would be on one of her twelve hour shifts at the nursing home, grandpa would be all alone, well him and his pack of beer. If we were fortunate dad would drop us off, if he needed the car, or on occasion we would take the car.

I know for a fact grandpa loved mom so much. His eyes would light up when he would see us enter his apartment.

Since grandma B worked so many hours, she never had time to clean their apartment, so mom, every two weeks, would take the task of cleaning it for her. Not that she minded doing it, and not that grandma ever asked her to, I guess it's just what you do to help out the people you love, you know, show your love and support for them.

Now, grandpa was definitely the family cook, he always had been, and when he cooked he made sure the kitchen was left spotlessly clean. But, as far as sweeping, moping, vacuuming, dusting, he never did it, and grandma never had the time.

Mom would start cleaning at one end of the apartment and hum her way to the other end. Oh how mom loved to hum her favorite songs.

Danny and J.J. would remain on the living room floor playing with their cars and trucks, Becky and Carrie their endless hours of jacks. Me and Sher, we would be mom's little helpers.

The part of being there I loved the most, well actually there were two things I loved about helping clean the apartment.

In grandma's living room she had about eight shelves for books, four on either side of her fireplace, which she never allowed grandpa to use, for fear he would get drunk, and forget about the fire, either burning the place down, or killing himself on the smoke should a log roll out.

These book shelves were not filled with books, they were filled with figurines, ornaments.. Hundreds of them, almost every spot of the shelves had some type of beautiful figurine. It would be my job to carefully take each figurine, and clean it with a damp cloth, dry it with a dry cloth and put it right back in it's place, without breaking any of them.

I loved doing that so much. I would get lost in my thoughts while I handled such delicate fine possessions of grandma's. And every time grandma would come home, if we were still there when she returned, she would just hug and hug me and thank me for cleaning every single one of her ornaments.

The second thing I loved about cleaning day, or any time we went to grandma B's apartment for that matter, grandpa's undeniably the best biscuits in town.

I have no idea what he did to those biscuits, but I guarantee, if you ate one, there is no way you would not go back for second's third's and fourth's. They were just that damn good.

Recalling for a second, how sad my mom was after my grandpa died, how much she cried. I remembered seeing her upset, I remember her tears, then she would start crying, any given moment throughout the day, no matter what she was doing.

I remembered her pain so well, a pain I felt, because it made me so sad to see her so sad. Grandpa's death was the first death I had to suffer through.

So many emotions, so much pain.

Part of me wondered why he drank so much. Didn't he know the effect drinking, and destroying his liver would have on his family? Did he not know it would destroy my mom to watch him die, to bury him?

Was drinking more important to him then spending more time on this planet with his family?

I just did not understand.

Then I thought of my mom's funeral, though I remember every second of that day, all the pain, mostly how much I missed her, how badly I wanted her to come home.

Oh my, this is how my mom felt for her own dad, how much she went through over the death of her own father.

Over and over I thought of her pain, over and over I thought of my own pain.

No, it's impossible. She could not have hurt as badly then as I did now. .She could not possibly have hurt the way I was hurting.

Yes, I know she loved her dad, yes she missed him, but there was no way her pain compared to mine.

Or did it?

I did not understand?

I know death hurts, and though my mom was in pain for losing her dad, she did in fact spend weeks by his bed side, preparing for his death. She was allowed to say good bye. She was allowed to tell him how much she loved him. She held his hand as he took his last breath. And she had her mom by her side.

    I didn't think anyone's pain compared to mine. Though my mom lost her dad, she still had her kids, her mom, her brother and sisters and as selfish as it sounds, she still had me.

She had me. Didn't she love me more?

I loved her more.

I again could not control my tears, my pain.

I just want to see her, to hug her one last time.

Dear god I don't want to hurt anymore. Please take this pain out of me.

Pleeeeeease!

It seemed no matter what I did, where I was , my mind, my heart always led me back to my mom, how much losing her hurt, how badly I wanted to see her.

I knew early on I would never ever get over my mother's death.

At that moment, at that very moment in my life, I felt like I was wandering in a sand storm, wandering unable to see where I was going.

I was just that lost.

87

It was the last day of school. Sher actually looked horrified at the thought of it. But I knew she already had many projects in the making to cover her time over the summer. Not to mention her job and the time she needed to spend with Ray.

Though hundreds of kids loitered in the school parking lot and convenience store parking lot, saying all their good-byes, I chose to avoid all of them.

I was walking home when Screwy approached me.
"Can I walk you home?" He asked.
I wanted to say 'Leave me alone." But not because I wanted to be a bitch to him, I just cringed at the thought of my dad and Ray passing by as we were walking and chunking Screwy in their car and taking him on one of those gangster "Rides," you know the ride of no return.

But we were literally one block away from Matty's, so I said yes.

As we walked he asked if I were okay.

Okay about what? I thought, but didn't answer him.

He asked another question.
"Have any plans for the summer?" He asked.
"Yes, I'm working.
He smiled. "Oh cool, a rich girl huh?" We both laughed.
"Naw nothing like that. I just have a part time

job."

I was glad he didn't ask me what kind of job. I mean I was the one that blabbed my mouth he was a paper boy, now if he knew I was a dishwasher, well he could really fuck my shit up. Not that I was popular or anything like that, but still, these fucking kids at school could be very cruel if they had shit on you to gossip about.

We got to the corner of my street and instead of him continuing walking straight towards his house, he turned with me.

For a second I sniffed the air to see if I could smell dad's cologne anywhere on our block.

Nope no cologne.

I eyeballed our block to see if dad's car was parked anywhere.

Nope no car.

Just then a car pulled up, I froze fearing a bunch of machine guns would be pointing toward us through the open windows.

Screwy smiled at me, "Gotta go girl." And with that he opened the passenger door and got in.

"Bye." I said.

The driver, I assume was Screwy's brother because they looked just alike, screeched his tires as he put the car in gear and hauled ass.

I walked the rest of the way to Matty's remembering I would be working as much as Iris could possibly allow me without getting herself in any kind of trouble with the child labor board.

Actually, I think washing dishes was a job without an age limit, or so I thought, because in all fairness, who wanted to do it, besides me.

My summer goal was to work as much as possible, save money, and help out with school clothes for my brothers and sisters, and myself.

A week into the summer vacation, someone had the brain storm idea for Carrie, Becky, J.J. and Danny to spend one month of the summer with one of my mom's sisters. Wasn't really clear who initiated it, mom's side of the family or dad's. Did it really matter?

Though it appeared all mom's relatives fell off the face of the earth the day mom was buried, and as far as I was concerned I didn't know any of them anymore. I suppose their guilt of being away for a year had them curious where we all were.

As far as my dad's sister's and their families, well it just seemed everyone needed a break.

Dad pitched his normal fit saying "Fuck those mother fuckers, hell no my kid's aren't going to spend time with them. Why? So they can treat them like shit like they did when Shirley died."

Agreeing with my dad, was at the very bottom of the totem pole as far as I was concerned, but he had a point, a legitimate valid point.. He hadn't spoken to any of them since mom died, and I also had not seen or talked to any of them either.

Every relative of mom's had just quit coming around. No visits, no calls, not even Christmas or birthday cards.

What kind of people do that? Especially a grandma. I suppose the fear of my father kept even my grandma away. I would never in my life understand that, seems a grandma would do just about anything to protect her children, her grandchildren. Even murder a mother fucker. Seems....

When confronted about sending the kids away for a month dad's response would be "Hell no." He would say to Gloria and Mary, whom by the way, really wanted the kids to go.

Maybe my aunt's thought it would be good for my brother's and sister's to get away for awhile, maybe they just need some time with their own families.

Raising some one else's kids isn't easy for anyone. I feel if you do it completely out of love, then it's something you do from your heart. I'm not insinuating my aunt's and uncles did not love us. I know they did. But to deal with dad, and to be responsible for his kids had to take it's toll on everyone.

Just before we got out of school for the summer Becky had been suspended from school for fighting.

She always had a smart ass mouth on her, but now she was acting out.

Being raised by Aunt Gloria in a good Catholic home wouldn't be enough to control Becky's outbursts, and she was beginning to put a strain on Gloria.

Gloria had to make such decisions as, does she tell dad Becky had been suspended, knowing Becky would get another violent ass whoopin, or does she not tell him, knowing if he found out, then she would have to deal with dad's bullshit.

It was stressful for everyone.

But Gloria was no quitter. She worked even harder with Becky, but Becky was so damaged over our child hood, it just seemed maybe she needed a change of scenery to get her away from all the bad memories.

Carrie, well she was always Becky's follower. She didn't act out like Becky, but she was right by her side regardless.

Yes, I believe my aunts needed a break, yet I wondered "who gets a break from such arrangements".

I assumed you're just supposed to work through the difficult times, you don't send kids away when times get tough, because sure enough those problems will be there when they get back.

Whatever the reasoning, dad wasn't financially supporting anyone and his sisters were direct.

And I know if I were my aunt's and I wanted to send his kid's away for the summer and he said no, then I guarantee I would say, "Then come get your own kids for the summer." And as we all know he sure wasn't about to do that, now was he?

Eventually, with a lot of bitching and cussing, he gave in, which gave them all some breathing room.

My aunt and uncle drove down to Fort Worth to pick up all four of the kids. They came in a motor home from somewhere near Las Vegas. They really had no choice but to come for them, dad would not allow them to be put on a bus.

I went to see them all the night before they left, crying because they were gonna be gone a month, and this would be the first time separated from them all for such a lengthy amount of time.

I wasn't there when they actually left. I was at work, besides I had no desire to see my aunt and uncle.

It had been over a year since my mom died and we had received not one visit not, one phone call from anyone, now out of the clear blue sky they want to jump up and play the part of long lost relatives.

Made no sense to me, but hey I wasn't goin no where. I had been invited, so Sher said, but I, as Sher couldn't go. We both had jobs, and I for one wasn't gonna quit my job just to make my mom's side of the family's conscience eased, after a year, by hopping on

the so called bus and hitching a ride to Pity Ville.
Hey that was my interpretation.

A year of guilt finally caught up with them, and they needed to ease that guilt by obligating one month to Shirley's kids.

Nope this was one ride I didn't want to get on.

88

Matty and Adam were seeing each other a lot. He was at Matty's more than not. Though technically he hadn't moved in, I knew it would be just a matter of time before he did.

One afternoon Matty and Lori were going to go to the park after they dropped me at work. Matty asked if she could borrow my camera, the one she had given me at Christmas.

"Sure Matty, it's in my closet."

She went to get it but it wasn't there.

"Are you sure it was in the closet?" She asked.

Though she asked, she knew that was where I had kept it since she gave it to me, always telling her she could borrow it anytime she wanted.

We took everything out of the closet and searched every inch of the apartment, no camera.

Matty even called Mary to see if we had left it at her house and just forgot.

Mary assured her it was not there.

"Has anyone been here?" Matty asked.

"Only Sher, a couple of months back," but Matty had used it since then.

"What the hell!" Matty said.

We both kinda scratched our heads wondering what the hell happened to it. I knew I had not lent it to anyone, Matty also knew she had not lent it. We had no idea what happened to it.

We put the closet back in order, it was time to take me to work.

On our drive to the restaurant Matty said "I'm gonna give you another driving lesson tomorrow."

I was excited, I was scared, but the thought of getting to learn to actually drive had me very happy.

I worked until eleven, Matty was as she always was, on time. The drive home was quiet, she seemed disturbed.

When we got home, Adam was sitting on the porch waiting for us. Matty unlocked the door, and they went directly to her room.

I showered and put on my Pj's and went to watch TV.

Within fifteen minutes I heard yelling from Matty's room, well not really yelling, Matty never yelled or cussed, it was rare for her to say damn or hell. I suppose all the cussing genes went to my dad, not my aunt's.

I couldn't make out what was being said and as long as I didn't hear hitting or such bad things I stayed out of it.

Disagreements between adults was none of my business, though I had my share of violence in my life, somehow I didn't think this was one time I should be concerned.

The loud conversation continued for about fifteen or twenty minutes, then, through the open front door, I saw Adam walking down the drive way to his car.

He had left the house through Matty's side door. I assumed he was leaving pissed, cause he was walking kinda fast.

I heard him start his car, and then he drove off.

A few minutes later Matty came in the living room, and said. "I found your camera."

"Really?"

I didn't ask where it was or where she found it.

"Adam has it." She said, sounding ashamed.

"Oh." All I could think to say.

"I don't know when or why, but he "borrowed" it, but he is gonna return it tomorrow.

"Ok." I said.

She looked very disturbed, almost like she wanted to cry. I didn't say anything, I didn't wish to make her cry with a bunch of questions.

"I'm sorry that he took it, but believe me, he will bring it back, I promise."

"That's fine." I assured her.

I was not concerned about the camera at all, but Matty was. Turns out, one day, Matty wasn't sure when, but Adam just up and took the camera. I believe he said he pawned it for gas money, which pissed Matty off even more. It didn't make a lot of sense, but none the less he took it and Matty pretty much said get it back here in twenty four hours or don't come back.

He left, kinda like with his tail between his legs. "Borrowing" the camera without permission, is the same as stealing in Matty's eyes.. But he did in fact take it, and I think what bothered Matty the most is when did he take it. Where were we when he just up and borrowed something that wasn't his and he had no right to take?

Adam showed up the next day camera in hand, he even bought some film for it.
A picture of him and Matty, him with his crooked tooth, a bit of guilt on his face as the film developed. He had a warm sincere apology and said it was wrong of him, and promised never to do anything like that again.

I found a safe place for my purse with all my savings....
Under my friken bed.
It's a fact, I had a little bit of money saved, this time it was a camera.
I ain't saying all men are fucked up.
Stealing, or should I say borrowing a camera sure ain't as bad as whoopin a child's ass, or tormenting your family, but it proves one thing, at least to me.
Had me asking?
Was there any man in the world that wasn't fucked up? Point proven again…
Unfortunately it seems, not in my world, none at all.

89

It was lonely for me not having J.J. and Danny to see when I would go to Mary's. Though I wasn't seeing Becky and Carrie as much, I could at least talk to them on the phone.

An entire month without them, would seem like an eternity.

All was forgiven about the camera and Matty and Adam seemed to be getting along pretty good, though Matty always took jabs toward Adam about taking the camera without permission. I guess it could be expected, that or break up with him. He would laugh right along with us knowing he damn well had it coming.

Aunt Mary and Uncle George were going to take their family to the coast for a week, but not before Matty and Adam gathered us all together at Mary's and announced they were expecting a baby.

A baby, Matty was glowing with excitement. Adam and his one big tooth, smiled as big a smile he possibly could, not even bothering to try and cover his tooth up.

We all clapped and laughed and congratulated them, even Lori kept saying. "I'm gonna have a baby brother."

There was a lot of excitement, seems aunt Mary was the most excited for her little sister.

I was no fool, I knew with this new announcement

would come another announcement. That Adam would be moving in, and I sure hit the nail on the head with that thought. Sure enough that night Matty and Adam announced he would in fact be moving in.

Though I had no say in the matter, I really had no objections at all.

I didn't have a problem with him. He was good to Matty, he worked everyday, and by what I saw, wasn't a drinker or a smoker.

Yes, it was gonna be okay. Adam in fact did have the right to live with his girlfriend and his baby.

Two and a half weeks after the kids left to stay with mom's sister, on a beautiful Saturday morning Matty told me when I got up and dressed to go to Mary's, she wanted to show me something.

So, I got up, fixed me some cereal and got dressed. Within thirty minutes I was at Mary's.

When I walked into Mary's, at first I did not recognize who was sitting a the table. I had to look twice. She smiled at me, the instant she did, I recognized her. It was my Grandma J. Dad's mom.

I hadn't seen her in over a year. The last time I saw her, was at my mom's funeral. But then grandma J. was one to travel a lot.

Grandma J was a beautiful woman. I remembered of all things, the way she dressed. Seems she always wore what appeared to be a silky shiny dress. Kinda looked like a China doll dress, beautiful, silky form fitting.

She always had shoes to match, even her nail polish would perfectly match her clothing.

I remembered her never wearing slacks, always a gorgeous dress. And grandma had the most beautiful hair. A full head of thick hair, actually all my aunts had the same hair as grandma. I would compare their hair to Farrah Fawcett, only all of theirs was pitch black, but it was always full and bouncy, quite noticeable everywhere she went.

She always had on make-up. Never did I see her, that her face was not perfectly fixed.

She did not fit the preverbal grandma look, like grandma B, Grandma J looked as if she could have been a movie star.

It was apparent my dad got his very handsome looks from her. The resemblance was unbelievable.

When grandma would come to visit, she would talk to us for hours. It would not be a visit as some relatives stay for an hour, hug you, and they're gone, I suppose since her visits were so far apart, she wanted to make the most of them.

Grandma J loved my mom, that's a fact. I'm not sure just how much she knew of her son's horrible ways where my mom was concerned, but it always seemed the only person in the world my dad ever listened to was Grandma J. He was after all, her only son.

Dad never disrespected his mother, ever.

He may have done everything wrong under the sun he could possibly have done to every one else, but two things he never did. He never cussed toward his mother and he never talked back to her.

He was a ruthless low down dirty husband and father, but to her, he was the perfect son.

Denial, all I could say. She was in denial. That and all the bad things he ever did, no one ever told grandma of such, or so it seemed.

When there would be newspaper articles about him being arrested for any of a dozen reasons she would always say "Not my Johnny."

Grandma had been married once to a man, I don't recall him very well but I do remember staying with them, me and Sher, and the fact they had a big boat in their back yard.

Her husband, not our grandpa, loved to travel, most of it by boat and he was an avid fisherman. This wasn't a little boat either. This was one that had a cabin and all. He didn't dock it at the lake, rather kept it in their back yard. Don't get me wrong, it wasn't a yacht, but it was bigger than a row boat.

Sher and I would spend hours in that boat pretending we were Ginger and Mary Ann from Gilligan's Island, me I would pretend so I could escape my childhood.

Grandma J would fix us a basket lunch and take it to us while we were in the boat.

Sometimes grandma would invite me and Sher to

go out with them when they would take the boat out to the lake. I had no desire to be on a lake and refused them every time.

Grandma J was a giver, she could not stop giving. I swear she had to have asked us a thousand times, over one weekend are we ok, do we need anything, is every thing ok, do you want to go anywhere? She was a very good grandma, we just didn't see her as often as we did Grandma B.

As Grandma J sat at the table, I went to her and hugged her, she cried, I cried. She was still wearing her beautiful silky dress, hair perfectly combed, her make-up perfect, and still the matching nail polish, only difference grandma did not have on heels, she was wearing flats.
   Mary, Matty and grandma all sat around drinking coffee, I sat with them listening to grandma talk.
   About an hour into the conversations grandma had to go to the restroom, but she had trouble standing up.
   Matty helped her, and I noticed she walked real slow. I thought she was just tired from her long trip, she had been living in Florida.
   When she came out of the restroom, again I noticed she walked very slowly and I wondered if she had just worn those pointed high heels so long, it ruined her feet.
   She was still cheerful and she cried off and on when she talked to me.

It was time for dinner and Matty helped Mary, I continued visiting with grandma. I told her about my job and how badly I hated school, and I told her of Donna.

She asked if I ever visited my dad.

This was not a subject I chose to discuss with her, but then, she was his mother.

Now, I was not about to rat dad out, not even to his own mother, and I knew there was really no way to get out of it.

"No." I said.

"Why don't you visit your father?" She asked, almost like she wanted to cry.

Now how do you possibly tell the mother of a monster, your son is a fricken monster?

You don't. So I avoided telling her the truth.

"I don't know." I answered.

"Where is Johnny by the way?" She asked Mary.

A complete glow came over her entire face just by saying his name.

"He'll be here soon." Mary said from the kitchen.

Oh lord, I was gonna have to sit and deal with my dad, right in front of his own mother.

"Have you seen your little brother?" Grandma asked.

Matty walked in the room at that second and saved me.

"Mom we can talk about that later."

Grandma looked at me very sadly, then she hugged me.

I missed my grandma. She was not at all like my dad, she was more like dad when he was high.
No, she was not high, she was just nice, and loving and caring, without the drug..

Dinner would be long over by the time dad showed up. He cried, grandma cried, every body cried. It was quite touching.
I couldn't help but notice grandma didn't get up from the table much, and when she did, seems someone had to help her get from one spot to the next.
I didn't ask, but it seemed something might be wrong with grandma.

Dad stayed an hour or so, non stop talking of course. His voice carrying over every one else's voice. Grandma cried when he left.
At first I hadn't noticed, but in the back room of aunt Mary's house was lot of boxes and suitcases, again I didn't ask, but it looked as if Grandma J had just moved in to Mary's.

Matty and I went home about an hour after dad left. As I was preparing for bed I asked Matty if something was wrong with grandma.
At first Matty didn't respond, but I guess she knew I was gonna find out eventually.
"Grandma has Parkinson's." She said.

I had no idea what it was, or what that meant.

Matty explained that it is a nerve disorder and that it effects the brain, the way one walks and talks and moves.

"Is there a cure?"

"Well, there is research, and grandma is gonna try some new medication real soon."

"Will she be ok?" I asked

"We sure hope so."

I cried that night. Grandma had always been good to me. I was sad that she was ill. After having such a free independent life it seemed heart breaking to have such a terrible thing happen to her.

And as I always did for over three hundred and ninety five nights, I cried myself to sleep.

The next day, though J.J and Danny weren't there, I went to Mary's to see grandma.

She was in the living room, sitting down watching TV. I sat with her awhile asking if there was anything I could do for her. Each time she smiled and said no.

Once she got up to go to the restroom, and Mary was not in the room, I helped her. It seemed she was so frail, actually dragging her feet as she walked.

I was scared. What if she fell while I was assisting her? What would I do?

Mary prepared grandma's lunch and a few times Mary had to help her eat because she had difficulty keeping the spoon steady. Mary didn't have to feed her, but grandma's hands would begin to shake a little and it seemed she couldn't control the shaking.

I knew better than to stare, though this disease had

me puzzled, I also knew grandma might be embarrassed or uncomfortable if we made a big deal out of it.

But to me, it was a big deal.

She was my grandma. I didn't want anything to be wrong with her, I wanted her to be like she always was, happy go lucky, some times very serious, but mostly she was always happy.

90

It was late Saturday night, Matty was out with Adam, I was home alone watching TV, grandma was already asleep at Mary's.
Sher called to see what I was doing.
"Why haven't you gone to see grandma?" I asked.
"I'll be there tomorrow." She said.

We talked about the kids, who would be returning soon, and then we got on the subject of dad and Sharon.
Sher said they had a big fight and Sharon took Thomas and some clothes to stay at her mom's.
I was shocked that she had the guts to leave dad.

We talked awhile then perhaps Sher felt she owed me something for protecting and covering for her on her prom, and regardless if she told me or not, one day I would find out any way.
She proceeded to tell me something I don't believe I was prepared to hear.
We got on the subject of Dad and his attempted murder case. There was just something about that case that had bugged the shit out of me since the day the charges were dropped.
Dad had all these hired hands, and Ray. What kind of stupid ass gangster goes and tries to kill a mother fucker and gets caught, risking going to jail for God knows how long, just to try and kill someone?

Who does that shit?

Goodness gracious, just pay, or order one of your punk ass employees to kill them, but what would have possessed my dad to try to kill someone, especially when it could be done correctly by a number of his hit men. What would possess him to be so damn stupid?

Sharon.....

It was because of Sharon, Sher said.

It was like pulling teeth with Sher, wasn't easy at all for me to get it out of her, but if anyone knew any thing about dad and his bullshit life, it had to be her or Matty, and I think after all the shit with Sher and the boots, Matty's lips were sealed.

This must have been one of those good days for Sher, she opened up to me. I believe she realized once she told me, she never should have said one word about it.

It was one of those "Can't take it back moments."

And so it goes, yes, Sharon the home wrecking, can't take care of her own kids, good for nothing bitch, was fucking around with my dad. And yes, my so innocent, never hurt anyone her entire shortened life, mom knew all about her scandalous ass. And yes, this is what my mom was threatening to leave my good for nothing, slithering ass snake, pitiful excuse of a father, over.

Seems our new step mama wanted my dad very badly, and so upon finding out she was expecting a

child, she went to my dad with her good news..
Well, regardless of Sharon's evil intentions, dad wasn't gonna just walk out on my mom, leave her to support six kids with no money, no education, nothing. Mom was trapped and dependent on him and he knew it, but the low life fucker he was, he still wasn't low enough to walk out on my mom.

I suppose Sharon thought her baby was dad's only illegitimate kid, damn even I heard rumors for years we had another brother and sister somewhere, a brother in between me and Becky and a sister between Carrie and J.J.
So no, dad probably, in all fairness, would not have walked out on my mom. Sharon finding out that he, though he was a fucking low life mother fucker, not even he could abandon my mom and six kids, for one woman one kid, decided to sort of threaten my dad by going to see one of them, quack doctors, you know get herself an illegal abortion.

Well, this is something Sharon should not have opened her big mouth about, and told to my dad.
Taking her word, and only her word that she had found herself a quack doctor, dad made Sharon take him to this so called doctor.
The doctor, or what the fuck ever he was, got beat, damn near to death, by my dad and only my dad.
Ok, so you have an illegal gangster and an illegal doctor performing an illegal act. You decide who is the more evil of the two evils.

Now, even though dad did not kill the doctor, he did hospitalize him for over two months, well that's about how long it took them to pry his mouth open from having his jaw bone altered to one side of his face. Dad's name was given and that is when dad was arrested and sent to jail.

Of course mom knew. Of course she wanted to leave. But we all knew she could never get away from dad. Ever.. It would take her death to get her free from him.

So now I have to wonder, did he kill my beautiful mom for Sharon?

Could my dad kill my mom for another woman?

Another baby?

Would I ever find out?

How could I find out?

And what about Sharon? She had used an awful tactic to get to my dad. Threaten to kill his unborn baby, just to be his "Woman."

Could she have killed her baby?

Would she have killed her baby?

Fuck no she would not have!

But, why was her ass not beat? Surely dad had some rage built up in him for her even threatening to kill his baby.

What? This bitch gets a free ride?

Surely not.

Well monster that he is, he had almost killed a man, because…Sharon said…

Would not look too cool on his resume to beat the

baby mama damn near to death also, now would it?

I mean if he had hit her wouldn't he just be risking killing his own kid?

So how in the hell did Sharon get away with all this shit?

How did she cause so much fucking trouble and not get any type of... should we say, action taken against her...

One woman caused so must disruption, so much chaos, so much harm to so many, and she now has the life she wanted.

How the hell did she do all this, and get away with it?

Whoever said she did get away with it?

And as Sher went on to tell me, I never once interrupted her. I was breathless, I was shocked, and to me now Sharon was my dad's equal.

I hated her as much as I did my dad.

"You ok twerp?" Sher asked.

"Hell no." I said.

"Well, I think you have the right to know. I'm sure it hurts to hear it all, and to be honest, I think he hit her tonight.

I wasn't shocked at that, and if everything Sher had just told me was true, then Sharon deserved a lot more than the beatings my mom got.

I was crying by the time I hung up with Sher,

She apologized a few times for telling me. Each time I assured her it was not her fault. She couldn't be blamed for our dad's actions. He chose to be a fucking monster.

91

I continued to work, I continued to save money.

Daily, I went to visit grandma at Mary's. Sometimes she would be very happy, her old self, then sometimes she would seem different, almost as if she were in pain but didn't want to say anything.

I wanted to have a really good sit down talk with my grandma, perhaps she would open up to me and tell me things she might know about, "How the hell did my dad get so fucked up where his priorities were concerned."

But every time I saw grandma she appeared sickly and I just didn't have the heart to ask a bunch of questions she may or may not know the answers to, or she may not even remember. I was just so confused about my grandma's health.

It was Friday evening, and when Matty picked me up from work, she informed me the kids were back, and though it was a bit late I could not wait to see them. I cried the instant I saw Danny and J.J..

They were tanned and sunburned and they looked so damn happy and cute. I could not stop hugging them and kissing them.

They showed me the toys and clothes my aunt had bought them, they showed me pictures of themselves that my aunt had taken of them. I missed them so damn much and I was so happy to see them.

Danny, now going on six, looked so grown up and cute, but I don't think he remembered or recognized

Grandma J. I told him she was our grandma as was grandma B, whom by this time he had completely forgotten her also.

I explained who they were, yet I don't think he understood. Hey he was still just a little kid.

We said goodnight and I told them I would see them the next morning.

Seems my dear aunt and uncle were in a great big old hurry to drop the kids off, they pretty much just dumped all four of them at Gloria's. I can only assume their hasty departure was because they had no desire to see my dear ol dad.

I lay in my room staring at the ceiling. Again I was alone. I thought of my brothers and sisters, and was so glad they were home. It was late I knew I couldn't call Gloria's to talk to them, so I decided to hold off on that thought till the next day.

Just as I dozed off I heard a very familiar sound. One that brought a lot of tears to my eyes.

From my bed I heard a fire truck passing Matty's, with it's loud engine and sirens blaring.

My mind went immediately right back to our old house, mom, me and the kids. What a wonderful thought, what a wonderful feeling.

The sounds I heard now from my bed at Matty's, were the same sounds I heard every night my entire life at home.

Several times throughout the night the fire trucks

could be heard. Alarms going off indicating that the fireman were needed somewhere in our neighborhood. Within moments of the alarm sounding, I could actually hear the firemen scurrying around, and within seconds the driver would sound the horn and start the sirens, as the truck would depart for it's destination.

The fire Station less than a block away, with the silence of the night, created an echoing effect, enabling me to hear even a Fireman's sneeze from our raggedy old house. It would literally sound as if they were standing right outside our bedroom window. It always seemed safe knowing they were near.

The return of the fire trucks was always as loud returning to the fire station as they were departing. With the exception of the sirens.

The loud motor of the fire trucks backing into the fire station, always a loud lengthy task.

The firemen's voices all could be heard as they would get out of the fire truck leaving just the driver to reverse the massive truck, their voices echoing, especially in the wee hours of the night.

It didn't matter if it were two in the afternoon or two in the morning. What ever stress call that needed the firemen's assistance, we were aware of it day or night, because we lived so close. It was impossible not to know when they were coming or going.

We had grown up seeing more of the firemen then we did our own father. Several times daily as they would pass our house, they would honk and wave, knowing just how much, especially Danny, loved for them to honk.

Sometimes Danny and J.J. would sit on the grass, outside the fire station and watch the fireman as they washed the gigantic truck, which usually took over an hour because it was so large, and the fact they kept it so clean.

Then I remembered, these were the same men, the day my mom died, that were first dispatched to our house to attempt to resuscitate her. Sher told me, they tried to pump life into her body for perhaps thirty minutes or so. After knowing my mom and seeing her daily, they would be the ones that would have the responsibility to try and bring her back to life. Something they could not do, something I'm sure most of them wished to God, they had been able to.

As I dozed off that night, I thought of my brothers and sisters, I was glad they were all home and safe. I couldn't wait to see Becky and Carrie.

92

I asked Matty if it would be okay for Carrie and Becky to spend the night with me. She said it would, so I called them and asked if they would like to come, they both said yes.

Matty talked to Gloria, she had no problem with it either.

When we went to get them, Carrie seemed so grown, her hair had been cut short, I guess my aunt thought she had the right to do that, though I knew dear old dad was gonna pitch a fit over that one.

But Becky, she was no longer my younger sister, she had completely changed. She actually looked older and more mature than Sher if I may. She had on a touch of makeup and lipstick which she later told me uncle David had taken away from her when he saw it. He said she could not wear makeup until she entered high school, because his daughters were not allowed to wear it until they entered ninth grade, which would be in just a few days actually.

She had a beautiful dark tan, and well she didn't look like little young Becky she just looked so grown. We all hugged and they brought their overnight things.

Once at Matty's, they relaxed and we talked and they told me of their trip with mom's sister. Carrie insisted she wanted to stay with mom's sister because she loved the city and that my aunt was real nice to her.

Of course they were nice, it was just for one month, try it for a year as Matty, Mary and Gloria had.

We ate snacks, and sat on the sofa talking.

Matty was at Mary's and she stayed kinda late to help Mary with grandma.

While Becky, Carrie and I were talking, Becky asked me a strange question.

"Malina, have you ever kissed a boy?"

What boy I thought? I didn't even know a boy other than Screwy, and according to all the school rumors his screwy nick name was pretty much making a male whore out of him.

"No. Why?" I asked.

"Well if you haven't kissed one then you probably haven't slept with one either."

Carrie giggled.

"What Becky, what are you asking?" I was almost in shock because she was taking this conversation to such an adult level.

"I just wondered." She laughed.

"Becky have you done something stupid." I asked.

"All depends on what you think stupid is." She laughed, then said "No Dummy. I was just curious."

"What in the world made you ask such a question?" I asked.

"I don't know, I guess I'm just curious." She sounded so innocent.

I looked at Carrie who was looking at Becky.

"Carrie, do you know what she's talking about?"

Carrie just shrugged her shoulders, I knew I

wouldn't get anything out of Carrie. Her fricken lips were sealed and she was just straight up too damn loyal to Becky.

"Don't worry Malina I didn't have sex or anything, but there are a lot of boys near aunt's house and, well I did kiss one."

I got tears in my eyes. She was my little sister, she wasn't supposed to be doing things like that.

She laughed. "Damn old maid, it was only a kiss."

I wanted to slap the shit out of her. Not only was she carrying on, she was acting out in front of Carrie.

"Look, don't go tattle tale on me or anything, but I snuck out of aunts house one night."

"Becky!!!!!!" I screamed.

"Don't worry I didn't do anything, I just sat in their back yard with one of the neighborhood boys, he kissed me and I let him, what's the big deal?"

I was shocked.

This couldn't be my young sister that had always been the big mouth talker, never the doer.

"Are you sure you didn't do anything wrong?" I asked.

"Believe me Malina, if there were any chance at all I could be pregnant, I would not have ever come back to Fort Worth."

Seems my plan for a little sleep over turned into a tell all, one I was not enjoying at all.

Goodness, now I gotta sleep in front of the door tonight, so this here little girl won't attempt sneaking out of here. My thoughts were racing.

I was in shock at what I was hearing.

I would be a sophomore when school started in a few days, Sher a junior and Becky would be a freshman.

Oh my what was I gonna do about Becky.

Becky assured me about a million times that night that she did nothing more than kiss a boy, of which was one thing more than I thought my little sister should be doing.

It would be a very very long night for me. My head was throbbing. I watched Becky as she prepared blankets on the floor for her and Carrie to sleep on. I lay on the sofa.

"You can sleep on my bed Carrie, if you want." I said.

"No thanks Malina, I'll sleep right here with Becky." Carrie said, then went to the restroom to put on her pj's. Becky lay down on the blankets, propped her pillow, and looked straight up at the ceiling. I watched her as she stared at the ceiling, remembering all the nights she did this very thing, lay down, look up at the ceiling, then begin a conversation with, angels she always said, though none of us ever saw them.

Carrie came in, took her place right next to Becky, then said "Goodnight." Becky and I saying "goodnight" at the same time.

Within a matter of moments Carrie was asleep. I watched as Becky continued staring at the ceiling.

I was worried about Becky's behavior but I did not

wish to ruin our sleep over with a bunch of questions. I was not the problem solver of the family. Sher was.

"Want some ice cream?" I asked Becky as she stopped staring at the ceiling and glanced at the TV.

"Sure." Becky said.

"Come on." As we both raced to the kitchen to fix ourselves a bowl each of ice cream and a handful of cookies each.

We stayed up an hour or so longer watching TV, then Becky said goodnight and she too fell asleep.

I lay on the sofa and watched my two little sisters sleep, remembering how difficult it was to sleep in our old bed at home. I watched as they slept, almost peacefully, and wondered what I should do about the news Becky had shared with me. I cried for my mom, knowing not only did I need her, my two little sisters needed her also.

The next day when aunt Gloria came to pick up Becky and Carrie, Becky said as she left.

"I know you're gonna tell Sher, it's ok. Just tell Sher she probably did worse than me on her prom." Becky smiled her famous smile, and went to Mary's to see grandma, Carrie following right behind her.

Becky pretty much left me there, speechless. I did not recognize my little sister at all.

While they were at Mary's, Marcie, my cousin, aunt Gloria's daughter, walked over to visit me.

She had come with Gloria to get the girls, so while

everyone was saying good bye to grandma, she decided to visit me.

She had never seen Matty's apartment and was quite impressed.

"Do you like it here with Matty?" Marcie asked.

"Yes."

"It's really nice here." She said.

I agreed.

"So what's up with your wild sister." She blurted out.

I looked at her, wondering did Becky confide in her also.

"What?" I wanted to sound shocked just to see what she knew.

"Yeah, the first night they were home, while we girls were all upstairs, out of nowhere Becky lifted up her shirt and said "See my boobies." And Marcie went on to say that Becky just lifted up her shirt and showed her knockers to all four of Gloria's daughters.

Marcie did not lift her own shirt while reenacting Becky's behavior, she did though, re-enact everything else.

It was funny to watch Marcie carry on, because Marcie was like Sher, she liked to get overly animated in her reenactments, and when she talked.

We laughed our asses off.

"Maybe Becky wanted to show off her tan." I said.

"Hell no, Marcie blurted out, that bitch was acting to slutty."

We laughed, but in the back of my mind I knew

Sher needed to have a long talk with Becky before she got too far out of control.

Then we got on the subject of mom, and Marcie told me how much she missed going to our old house, her mom visiting with my mom, and how all of us girls, their four our four would sit around and sing songs, and laugh, and always a performance from the Guetarro sister's she said.

"Seems every week you girl's would just create a new skit or song. Y'all always had something fun and exciting to perform for us."

"I sure do miss those days." She would say.

"So do I." I would inform her.

We cried, then we would laugh, then we would cry again. I did not tell Marcie of my conversations with Becky about Becky's behavior. I was afraid if I had, Marcie would be forced to tell Aunt Gloria, and with no other alternative, Gloria may have been tempted to send Becky to live with the nuns at the nearby convent, or forced to send her back to dad.

Oh what those poor nuns may have had to endure with Becky around.

My judgment got the best of me, knowing Sher was the only person I could go to with Becky's unruly behavior. Sher as always, would know exactly how to handle it.

93

It was now the Saturday before school would start. Matty and Gloria had errands to run, pay bills, and possibly have lunch at a restaurant.
They invited me to go with them, they said they also wanted to put flowers on mom's grave.
I hadn't been to the cemetery since mom died,
I hadn't been to the cemetery since the day they lowered my mom into the ground.

Just as they both said, they needed to pay bills. Matty paid the electric bill, Gloria paid her water and gas bills. We also went to the car lot where Matty had purchased her car and made her car payment.
After the bills were paid, we stopped at a small restaurant and had lunch.
Matty and Gloria, but especially Gloria, enjoyed going to different restaurant's to sample their cooking, then she liked to attempt that same meal from her own kitchen.
We finished with lunch and took the short drive to the cemetery.

Once at the cemetery, Matty knew exactly where to go. She had been there many times before she said, yet this was the first time I was asked to join them.
I noticed the narrow winding roads, almost like a maze, turning and winding, never ending it seemed.

Headstones everywhere, tall ones, short ones, something I hadn't noticed the one and only time I had been there, but then I cared less for what was at a cemetery I didn't want to be at anyway.

Flowers, beautiful colored flowers, in vases on hundred's of plots, as far as my eyes could see. Seemed like every headstone had a beautiful flower arrangement on or around it..

No, I hadn't been to see my mom, no one ever asked me if I wanted to go, no one ever invited me, no one ever said "Malina do you want to see your mom, do you want to take flowers, do you want to go talk to her,...... nothing,"

No one ever asked, I never asked to be taken.

Why?

Because I was afraid. Afraid to relive the worst day of my life, over and over again.

Matty talked to me at times about mom, but the longer I lived with Matty, the fewer conversations we had about mom.

I had never been to a cemetery to visit a grave, though there was a cemetery right across from the Fire Station.

I had never been in the graveyard.

I had only been to one funeral in my life, my moms, no one else's.

I had no idea what to expect.

I had no idea what you're supposed to do when you're actually there.

So when Gloria and Matty said they wanted to take flowers to mom I had absolutely no idea what to expect. I was frightened.

The day mom died I can't even remember what the cemetery looked like, except for standing at my moms coffin, I don't have any idea what was around me, or who for that matter.

I felt sick as Matty drove around the cemetery till she got to the spot mom was buried, then stopped the car.

Gloria grabbed the vase and the flowers, and got out of the car.

Matty turned off the car, took the keys out of the ignition, and got out of the car also.

They started walking toward, I assume, mom's grave.

I was still in the car, sitting there, not knowing what to do..

"Come on Malina," Gloria said, "Come see your mom."

Come see her????

Just for that brief millionth of a second I thought it possible. My messed up mind actually thought I might get to see mom...........impossible, I thought.

What a strange choice of words she had.

I went blank for a split second, she said "Come see my mom," But it can't be true, she wasn't really there was she?

I tossed those few words in my mind over and over, within a very few seconds..

No she wasn't there, Gloria merely wanted me to see my mom's final resting place.

I put my hand on the handle to open the car door. But my hand wouldn't move.

I was scared.

I tried again to open the door, I still couldn't.

Gloria came back to the car and opened my car door.

"I can't." I said

"Yes you can, you have to visit your mom." Gloria said.

She seemed insistent.

"Come on Malina." Matty said from the distance.

I reluctantly got out of the car, Gloria shut the door behind me.

I stood there wanting to run away.

"Come on honey." Gloria said, as she put her arm around my shoulder.

I slowly walked with her, my head down, looking toward the ground. I was horrified to look at any of the head stones, knowing at any second I was gonna see my mom's name engraved on a stone, with her birth date and the day she had died.

I stopped suddenly, "No I don't want to go any further."

"It's ok." Gloria said.

Matty also had stopped and was waiting for us.

I couldn't get my feet to move.

"It's right here." Matty said as she placed the vase of flowers on the ground and put them... put them on

what ......
There was no headstone. There was nothing at all....
I looked around. I looked in front of me, I looked to the both sides of me, I even looked at the headstones right behind me, looking for something with my mom's name on it, but there was nothing,
My heart almost beat out of my chest, then my heart felt like it was about to stop.

Had she really not died? Was this all the nightmare I always wanted to wake from.
No headstone anywhere, was this the proof she hadn't died. You can't be dead and have no headstone.
Again I turned and looked at the nearby headstones, studying the names on each of them.
My feet not moving, but my legs wanting to run to every headstone, kneel down to get a really close look at each to see which one had my mom's name on it.
Frantically searching with my eyes, I realized none were my moms.
Maybe my two aunts were just at the wrong graveside, maybe they were mistaken, maybe this was the wrong cemetery all together.

Then Matty and Gloria did something I could not understand. They knelt down on the ground, did the sign of the cross and closed their eyes to pray.
I could not move.

Gloria opened her eyes, looked right at me and said, "Kneel down Malina, pray for your mommy."

I was so confused, they had to be wrong. They had to be mistaken. But why would they kneel down at the wrong grave?

Kneel down to what?

There was nothing there.

What were they doing?

Why were they kneeling down to nothing?

What were they praying to?

I wanted to scream.

Why would these two women kneel down to a bare spot in the cemetery? I saw no headstone, I saw nothing in the area where they were kneeling.

I looked again at the ground. I looked at them, then I looked at the ground again.

Then a third time I looked, this time I looked very closely at the ground, and there was something.

There was a round thing about the size of a top from a jar, it was made, I guess out of metal?

I looked at it and it had numbers on it, a bunch of numbers with dashes like 123-456-789.

What was this thing? I wondered I wanted to know.

It was over a year since mom died, and this…this was supposed to be her headstone?

A flat metal thing with numbers.

My beautiful beautiful mother wasn't even labeled as a person with her name on it, she was labeled with a damn number, almost like a prisoner

My aunts were praying to a piece of metal, with numbers engraved in it.

No no no, this was not happening.

My eyes filled with tears, I yelled out her name, "Mommy, mommy," and within seconds I was on the ground screaming at the top of my lungs, "Mommy, Mommy, mommy."

I knew my aunts were horrified, they both tried to lift me from the ground, but I forced my body to stay on the ground.

"Mommy, mommy." I was screaming uncontrollably for my mom, and with my fingers I began to dig at the ground. I dug with every bit of energy I had in me, pulling at the grass, getting as much dirt in my hands as I possibly could, throwing the grass and dirt everywhere, almost like a wild woman.

Mommy, my mommy was under the ground, with nothing to identify that she was there at all but a bunch of fucking numbers on a piece of metal.

I was screaming and clawing the dirt and hollering from all the pain I had in me. I was pounding the dirt trying so desperately to beat the ground in an attempt to get my mother out of there.

One year mom had been gone and for one entire year no one, not dad, not my aunts and uncles, not even mom's sisters, brother or even grandma could put a headstone on her grave?

The hate in me for all these people, how dare all of them pass her off as no one.

How does anyone go through life day by day and not even attempt to put a marker, a marker of respect.

She had died alone, and now she's here all alone. And to make it worse you couldn't even find her if you tried.

I was screaming for my mommy.

I wanted her out of the ground so I pulled and pounded and scratched at the ground, my fingers bleeding from the force of my hand pounding the hard dirt.

"Mommy please come out of there, I don't want you here, I want to be with you, I don't want you to be here, I don't want to live anymore mommy." The cries of a child no one would ever understand the pain I felt. No one.

I was hysterical, my aunts screaming and crying.

They knew at that very moment they made a terrible mistake bringing me to this place, now they couldn't get me away if they tried.

They both tried desperately to get me away from the marker, the spot that claimed to be my moms resting place, they both tried as hard as they could to pull me away from the spot they were kneeling and praying to.

And with all my might, I swung at each of them as they desperately tried to take me from the ground where my mommy was.

I screamed, and cried and fought and banged and pounded as I was on the ground on my knees swinging my arms wildly trying desperately to dig through the ground to get my mom out of her coffin..

My aunts were hysterical begging me to stop.

"Stop Malina, please stop baby." They begged.

But now I couldn't stop.

I could not stop trying to get my mom out, to set her free. She was under the ground, and to me, she was suffocating, she wanted to get out and come with me, take me home, take everything I missed about her, and help me.

I wanted my mom out of that coffin.

I screamed and screamed her name. I could not control myself anymore. I didn't know what I was doing anymore.

Then suddenly it seems there were three then four then five people attempting to get me off the ground. People that were there paying respect to their own lost relatives, gathered to attempt to help my aunts take a terrified child out of the cemetery.

Someone yelled "She's in shock, take her, take her away from here."

"Nooooo I want my mom, leave me alone, I want my mom." I screamed.

"Mommmy, mommy, why did you leave me, I want you to come home."

"Please, mommy come home, I want you to come home, I want to be with you."

As I screamed and pounded on the ground, my mind could actually see my mom in her coffin again, as the funeral director opened her coffin and put her wedding ring on as dad asked him to. I felt I could almost touch her, I just wanted to hug her one last time.

The horrific pain in me, knowing that my mom was six feet below the ground I was trying to dig up with my bare fingers, was almost to much. She was right there six feet away and I could not dig the ground up to release her from this horrid place. The place no one would ever find her because there was no damn headstone, nothing to identify that the most wonderful woman in the world was just below me.

I hated every fucking person alive.

The five or six people that were there to help, total strangers, were forced to witness my pain, and it was something none of them were prepared for. Now they were all crying. Suffering their own losses is what had them at the cemetery on that particular day, and now they were having to deal with a terribly distraught, hysterical child.

I could hear them all talking, I was just in so much pain.

A stranger, perhaps one of my aunts tried again to pick me up, I fought them like a wild animal. All the hate and frustration that was built up inside me for over a year, now I was taking out on the strangers that were just trying to be kind and help a hysterical child.

"I want my mom," my voice echoed through the entire cemetery as it had the day mom was buried.

My fingers bleeding, dirt and grass all over me.

If I could just get her out, if I could just hug her one more time, one more hug, see her smile just one more time. That's all I wanted.

"Just one more time!" I yelled, "Just one more time." I screamed and screamed and screamed.

I just couldn't go on anymore.

I saw that pathetic excuse of a headstone, a damn piece of metal with numbers. This was supposed to be where anyone that loved my mom could come to talk to her, to pray, to remember her.

I hated every person in my life knowing my mom would never be there when I graduated, she wouldn't be there when I got married, she would not be there to love my own kids, she would not be there to help me through my life, I would never be able to go to her and ask her advice, I would never have a mothers love. Ever.

Now I could see the faces of the strangers at the cemetery, I could see my aunt's faces, I even felt the pain in my hands, from hitting the ground. I could see the blood on my fingers, I could see dirt and grass every where.

I could see people trying to talk to me, but I

couldn't hear anything anymore. I couldn't hear my aunts voices, I couldn't hear the strangers talking to me anymore, only everyone's lips moving.

   Then just as I did the night mom got beat, I passed out. This time it was just to much for me. Too much pain for a little girl to go on without the love of her mother.

94

My life ended again that day. For the second time in my life, a gigantic piece of my heart broke off. Seeing that pathetic marker, not a beautiful headstone with my mom's name on it, was just to much.

You may all hate me for this, and say to your self,
"But you claim to love your mom so much"
That is a true statement, and I have seen videos of people when they go visit their loved ones at cemeteries. They take flowers and balloons, and they sit at the grave sites and they talk to their loved ones and they cry and they mourn, yes that is what most people do.
Most, but not me.

So as my dear reader you may hate me, maybe you will understand, maybe you won't, but not once ever in my entire life have I been back to the cemetery to visit my mom.
"Disrespectful," some of you may say. That's your prerogative, but to me there is nothing there, just a marker.
Not a spot for people to actually visit her, talk to her, pray for her if you like, there is no shrine. Just a damn piece of metal.
No headstone. My mom has no headstone?
Though it is unlike me, but I must fast forward this story for a moment.

My beautiful mom would lay in that cemetery for twenty five years before anyone would put a headstone for her. Twenty five long years.

Nope, not my father, not my Grandma B, not uncle Bill, or Dolly or my other aunts... No one on my dad's side either. Well I guess it just wasn't their responsibility was it? They had, after all, raised his kids.

So for twenty five years no one cared, I guess whether she had one or not. You would think, even if everyone on the planet thought dad killed her, some one, anyone, would have spent the money to respect her memory. You would have thought, huh?

Two hundred fifty dollars is what was owed to the funeral home to lift the lien, yes there was a lien on her grave by the funeral home. The debt had to be paid before they would allow a headstone to be placed to honor her.

A fuckin lousy two hundred fifty dollars, over twenty five years, you figure out what it would have cost someone, anyone even if they paid a little every year..

I'm sure most of you are shocked, as I have been.

It would take a relative, yes my brother J.J. once all grown up, and with a family of his own, went to the same funeral home twenty five years later, had a long sit down with, yes the same funeral director, now owner of the funeral home, and told him our situation.

Strange, after twenty five years he still remembered mom's funeral. He told J.J it was the saddest funeral he had ever seen, nothing since then compared to that particular funeral mom being so beautiful and young, and of course the two autopsy's, and he said he remembered a little girl in particular..
"How is she by the way?" He would ask, referring to me.
My brother opened his wallet to pay the $250.00 debt, the funeral director said "Put your money away sir, consider the account closed."
It is sad and disgusting for me to write this, to let you all know just how unbelievable things were. Don't know if you wanna hate me or love me. I won't blame you if you hate me, I hate me.

I'll never ever get over losing my mom. I just don't know how.
Things like this sure don't make it any easier.

Yes, J.J finally, as a grown man, went to pay a long over due debt, that no one, not even I could bring myself to do.
It is inconceivable that all the people that claimed to love her, forgot about her the second she was in the ground.
Disrespectful, of course you may want to call me, I don't blame you at all. I hate myself so much for

this. I guess even though I've spent an entire life time missing my mom, and wanting her to come home, I'm just as rotten as everyone else, mostly my dad..

For me, my mom is not and never will be in that ground. If I were to ever go back to the cemetery, I do believe I would not survive. It's just a very bad place for me, filled with a lot of pain.

I was a tormented child then, today I'm a tormented woman.

The debt was cleared and it cost my brother $1200.00 to put a headstone on mom's grave. A stone I have never brought myself to go see.

I just cant.

I lost some of my heart at my mom's funeral.

Two days that have changed me forever. My mom's death and that day at the cemetery when my aunts thought they were doing a good thing.

I lost some of my life after that day. I can not remember anything.

I don't know what I did, I don't know if I were in a hospital, a crazy house, or was I medicated so I couldn't remember. I can honestly tell you I do not remember anything, and possibly, that is a very good thing. Perhaps if you were in my shoes you would not wish to remember either.

Yes, if you should ask me what I did for six or seven months of my life I could never tell you

because all these years later, I do not remember.
I try, but it's impossible.
I know I didn't die, I know life continued, but me Malina, there is no memory to look back on, there is nothing to recall.

Sometimes I wish I could never remember the years in my life before that day, then I would have no reason to hurt. But to not remember at all, would mean not remembering my mom, the love I had for her, the love she had for me.

No, I am grateful I can remember because I do remember my mom and then I think to myself, perhaps mom was dreaming of a good life, a happy future when she fell asleep that night. Perhaps she didn't wake because her dreams took her where she knew her life never would.

The peaceful look on her face as dad turned her over that morning, makes me believe that, otherwise to believe she was murdered for no reason, well let's just say I wish I could be that fortunate to fall asleep and leave this earth in a similar fashion.

I would spend my entire life missing my mom.
Yes, I would never get over my loss, I would never even try.
Me, Sher, Becky, Carrie, J.J. and Danny, well life was not always good to us, our lives, I can tell you, it didn't get too much better. Sometimes yes, sometimes

no.

So if you ever go to the cemetery where my mom is, if you want, you can say hello to her, you can tell her that I love her so much and I miss her.

You can tell her you know all about what a wonderful woman she was, that you met her in a story, and somehow I just bet you will envision her beautiful smile while you're talking to her and you too may shed a tear. And you can even tell her that you have grown to love her also, but then I'll just bet she already knows.

95

So on the Saturday before school was to start I was taken to the cemetery to visit my mom, I went there not really knowing what to expect, I left there with no memory at all.

No immediate memory, for six months to be exact. I do realize I did not die, and I really don't think my dad had me committed to a hospital. But as far as remembering leaving the cemetery that day, remembering my daily activities, my mind draws a blank.

I do realize my life continued. If you can call it a life. It was more like I just continued to exist.

I know I went to school, I know, or I think I continued living with Matty. I know I did the everyday routine things like eating and sleeping, but in all honesty, I can not remember where it all took place.

I can't pin point dates and times and events like Christmas that year or Halloween and Thanksgiving. I don't remember conversations with people, I don't remember places Matty or any family member may have taken me.

I can't remember anything concerning my brother's and sister's, if they remained living with my aunt's and uncles, were they happy?

I can't remember my dad, and you know there had to be a lot of bull shit where he was concerned, but whatever he did or didn't do those six months, I just can't remember. Possibly where he is concerned, not remembering his ass is a good thing.

Sadly, I can't remember Sher, where she lived or what she did. I don't recall seeing her if we were in fact still in the same school. I mean I believe I was, I simply can't remember any of it.

If I were in a crazy house, I do not remember that at all. I believe my life continued and I remained with Matty. I try so hard to remember, retrace my steps of those months, but it is just impossible.

Do you have any idea how terrible it is not to remember anything? Good or bad.

And so for six long months everything is completely blocked out of my mind, everything wiped out of my delicate memory.

Everything, it seems, but one particular night, one particular dream, I remember only because I lived through it.

To this day it is my escape, the escape for a twelve year old child that lost everything good in her life, that wanted all the hurt to go away.

I dreamt it, it was real and it is where I go every time my life gets to difficult for me.

I dreamt one night, a dream almost too real.

96

I dreamt my mom came to me, appeared at my bedside. I could actually see her, I could even smell her perfume. She was wearing the same beautiful green gown she had been buried in.

She woke me. "Malina, Malina baby wake up."

In my dream, at first, I could not open my eyes, but the sound of her voice drew me to her.

When I opened my eyes she was standing by my bedside. She was smiling that beautiful smile. I opened my eyes and the second I saw her, I began to cry.

"Don't cry baby, everything is ok." She wiped my tears away with her gentle touch.

"Mommy, Mommy." I cried.

"Shhhh." As she put her finger to her lips, "you'll wake Matty and Lori."

I instantly stopped crying.

She pulled the covers from me and said,

"Come with me Malina."

I sat up and put my legs over the side of the bed, as she placed my house shoes in front of me. I put them on, then my mom handed me my robe and again said.

"Come Malina. Come with me."

I did as my mommy told me.

There were no lights on in Matty's house, yet I could see my mother perfectly.

Mom held my hand as she walked with me to

Matty's front porch. Mom was smiling the entire time.

"Mommy, I miss you so much."

"I miss you too baby, come with me."

She walked down the porch steps, I held on to her hand and we walked down the sidewalk toward our old house. Before I knew it we were in front of our old house, all the lights off, no one living there anymore, no life in that old house, just darkness.

Seeing our old house made me so very sad.

"Don't cry baby." Mom whispered.

Then mom said again. "Come Malina."

Now we were in front of the church, the one her and dad had been married in, the same church that had her funeral service. I held my mom's hand so tight because I did not want to let her go.

Once at the church, she opened the door and we went in.

I was no longer crying, now I felt happy.

We walked through the church and directly to a back room. I followed my mom because this is all I ever wanted was to be with my mommy.

When we got to the back room, there was a stairway that led us up to a room.

Mom opened the door and the room was beautiful. So colorful, so absolutely beautiful. It was a small room with a bed, a dresser, a lamp, and on the night stand was a picture of each of her children.

She smiled and said, "All of you are with me always."

I cried again. My mom sat on the bed, I sat next to

her and cried. We both cried.. She comforted me and held me and told me she was ok, she wanted me to be ok.

"I can never be ok without you."

"Yes you can, I know you can." She spoke so softly.

"I don't want to live without you, mommy, why did you have to leave us?" I cried to her.

"But Malina I am here. I never left." She held my hand as she talked to me.

I looked up at her with my tear swollen eyes.

"You never died?"

She said nothing.

"Mommy you never died, you live here?"

What was I hearing? My mommy was never dead, she has been here all along. I was in shock. I was happy, I was excited.

But why would she do that? Why would she put her kids through all this, just to hide in a church?

Why would she want to do this? Just to get away from her husband?

No, my mom would never put her kids through this, she would rather die than intentionally abandon us.

What was I thinking?

I was creating a life in my mind, a life I wanted to force myself to believe was true.

"Mom"...I began to say.

She took my face in her hands, and said,

"Yes Malina I did die, but I never left you. I will

never leave you."

She placed her hand over my heart.

"I am here, I always have been, I always will be."

I looked at her beautiful soft hands, still wearing her wedding ring.

"It's not the same mommy, it's not the same." I was again crying.

"Yes Malina it is. I will never leave you, as long as you believe, I will be with you."

I was so confused, I understood, I didn't understand.

She kept her hand over my heart, my hand over her hand and we cried.

We sat together till almost day light, crying. She told me hundreds of times how much she loved me.

I begged her to let me stay with her forever.

"It's time Malina, we must go back now baby, but just remember, anytime you need me or want to visit me, just close your eyes and think of this room, think of me, think of the love I have for you, and you will be here, I will be here, I promise."

I did not want to leave my mommy.

I cried all the way back to Matty's.

Strange, there was not one car in sight, not one person anywhere, though the sun was just about to rise, it seemed me and my mom were the only two people on the earth.

I suppose the earth stood still for a few hours so I could be with my mom.

We went back to Matty's, back through the front door, and back to my room.

Mom sat next to me on my bed as I lay down.

She pulled the covers over me and kissed my forehead.

"Don't leave me mommy, please don't leave me."

"Malina I'm here baby." As she touched my heart one last time. She sat next to me and she begun to hum a song to me, holding my hand in hers. She kissed my cheek, I felt a tear on my face. Her tear.

I cried. My heart breaking so badly because it seemed again I was losing my mommy.

Every ounce of energy I had in my young body I used to stay awake, to spend as much time with my mom, fearing if I fell asleep, she would not be there when I woke.

I fell asleep, my mom and her love there with me.

I know she was there. I just know it.

Though I remembered nothing else for those months, I do remembered that dream, if it were in fact a dream..

Today, as I write my story, life began again for me right after that dream. I can remember waking that next morning, I could still smell my mommy's perfume, I just know I could.

I lay there in bed a few moments, when I got off the bed and stood up, something fell to the floor. I reached down to pick it up just as Matty walked through my room.

"Sher came by while you were asleep, she said she wanted you to have it." I picked it up, and it was a picture of my beautiful mother. A picture we had not seen since all her belongings were taken from us.

I began to cry.

I didn't say anything. I couldn't.

"Oh and Malina, do you know anything about the front door being left open. When I got up this morning it was open, did someone come in last night."

I ... could... not... speak!!!

Yes, I answered her in my mind only. My mom came and took me, she took me to a special place to save me, and in my heart, now I know, that is exactly what she did.

A dream? …. Perhaps.

Was it real?... To me!…. Absolutely

You have to wonder, so much of my life I do not, can not remember, except that one event, that one beautiful dream...

I've tried millions of times to recount my steps. It is impossible. But I do know one thing. Something happened to me.

An ohhh so real dream? Perhaps.

An actual visit from my mom? Possibly.

It is a fact, I do not believe my mom lives in a church, an escape from my dad.

But, I could convince myself of that, if I really wanted to.

And yes my friends, to tell you the truth, sometimes I lay awake and I take myself back to that room and there is my mom and we talk and we cry and we hug and she helps me when I'm unhappy, she helps me when I am happy also.
In my heart I believe it's okay to love someone and never let them go.
Anyone can do it. You really can if you want.

Do some think I'm crazy? ...Sure they do.
Do I? ...Not at all.
It's really about how much you want to believe.

A secret life for myself? You better believe it.
Does it help me to go on?
I could never have survived without my mom or that unbelievable dream.

A horrified, scared, lonely little girl, taken to a place to believe.
No one would have ever believed me if I told them what happened that night. No one.
But it did happen, and as long as my heart says it happened, then it really did..

And so to you, each of my readers, I pray that you have that special person in your life, that special kind of love. Cherish that love, cherish every second you have with them.

The love for my mother is a very special kind of love, one that will never die. Ever...

It was a dream, a subconscious dream, that brought me back to my conscious life.

Full memory restored after that day. I can tell you everything that has happened from that day forward. Some good, some not so good at all.

But it is a fact, all that has happened to me, everything I went through I could never have survived without my mother's love. She did from her "grave," what she always did in life. Once again she came to protect me and save me.

There is no way of knowing what might have happened to me had my mom not come to me that night, my mind was lost, completely traumatized. I pretty much feel I have to call it a dream, so as not to have to spend my life locked away. But whatever it was, it has me here today, telling you of the life of a scared lonely child.

My life began again the moment I saw the picture of my mom. So much had happened in six months, things I would never have guessed could happen, things I will never be able to recall, or explain, but I will try.

Life was about to change again for me....An innocent childhood, lost many times over. Perhaps waking from a dream was a good thing, perhaps not.

I'll let you decide.

www.ingramcontent.com/pod-product-compliance
Lightning Source LLC
Chambersburg PA
CBHW021136160426
43194CB00007B/611